THE GREAT FLOODGATES
OF THE WONDERWORLD

Also by JUSTIN HOCKING

Life and Limb: Skateboarders Write
from the Deep End *(editor)*

Beach 90th

The Great Floodgates of the Wonderworld

A Memoir

~

JUSTIN HOCKING

Graywolf Press

Some of the chapters in this memoir have appeared elsewhere, in slightly different form: "Beach 90th" in *Foulweather,* "Shipmates" in *Leaf Litter,* "All I Need Is This Thermos" in the *Normal School,* "The Midland Oiling Museum" in *Orion,* "The Mariner's Tale" in *Rattapallax,* "Ophelia Part I," "Moving," "The Duke," and "As We Begin our Final Descent into New York" in the *Rumpus,* and "The White Death" and "An Old Friend" in *Swap/Concessions.* "Beach 90th" was also published as a limited edition chapbook by Swift Season Press.

This is a work of creative nonfiction. The author re-created scenes and dialogue to the best of his ability, and with full knowledge of the fallible nature of memory. Many names were changed to protect the privacy of those involved; certain time sequences were altered to heighten the narrative.

This publication is made possible, in part, by the voters of Minnesota through a Minnesota State Arts Board Operating Support grant, thanks to a legislative appropriation from the arts and cultural heritage fund, and through grants from the National Endowment for the Arts and the Wells Fargo Foundation Minnesota. Significant support has also been provided by Target, the McKnight Foundation, Amazon.com, and other generous contributions from foundations, corporations, and individuals. To these organizations and individuals we offer our heartfelt thanks.

Published by Graywolf Press
250 Third Avenue North, Suite 600
Minneapolis, Minnesota 55401

All rights reserved.

www.graywolfpress.org

Published in the United States of America

ISBN 978-1-55597-669-9

2 4 6 8 9 7 5 3 1
First Graywolf Printing, 2014

Library of Congress Control Number: 2013946924

Cover design: Kapo Ng

For ANDY KESSLER, *the Godfather of 108*

Next to the wall of books is a painting of the seacoast
at High Island that your mother did in the early fifties
before you were born. Maybe it's no accident that you have
camped at that very spot a hundred nights, sleeping-bagged
under Meekham's pier, so you could be there when the
good waves rolled in with the main tide just before dawn.
Maybe that painting of Mother's kick-started this longing for
the sea that your readings of *Moby-Dick* only augmented.

~ MARY KARR, *Cherry*

Frightening as my dream of Cain was, it offered me hope
by offering me the shelter of a story. And stories are where
human meanings begin.

~ GREGORY ORR, *The Blessing*

ILLUSTRATION CREDITS

Thanks to Lucy Bellwood for her inkwash illustrations, which appear on pages 24 and 27, and to Gabriel Liston, whose scrimshaws on carved soap appear on pages 52, 57, 63, 111, 184, 253, and 254. The images were created specifically for *The Great Floodgates of the Wonderworld,* in response to the text.

THE GREAT FLOODGATES
OF THE WONDERWORLD

OPHELIA, PART I

L ate summer 2005 and everything's underwater. The news warns us that New York City could be the next New Orleans—flooded subways, ten thousand shattered windows. Lower Manhattan as the new American Venice, streets turned into canals, the seafloor studded with broken glass. The storms spin up from the Gulf in alphabetical order: Katrina, Lee, Maria, Nate. None make it very far north, not until mid-September, when Hurricane Ophelia ravages the Carolina coast, floods the Outer Banks with a foot of rain, and wreaks $70 million worth of damage.

On September 16, Ophelia arrives off the coast of New York. From far above she's your typical hurricane, a crown of cotton thorns. But down below, she thrashes the surface of the sea, capsizes ships in her self-destructive fury.

Like so many of us new to the city, she wants everyone to remember her name.

But even she can't handle the pressure, can't make it here in New York, and just days later Ophelia drowns herself in the North Sea. Her suicide's wake sends undulations of raw energy back toward Gotham. Smoothed out by hundreds of travel miles, this energy arrives in the form of perfectly shaped swells at Long Beach, Lido, Montauk, and the Rockaways.

Places that I watch obsessively, via satellite.

Curled over my computer at 6:00 a.m. in my Brooklyn apartment, I'm tracking the storm, reading the reports—*Chest-high to head-high swells with sixteen-second intervals, excellent conditions, go surf now!*—when an incoming text sparks my cell phone.

Waves look perfect, the message reads. *We're ditching work. U coming?*

It's from my friend Dawn, who despite working seventy-hour weeks in the fashion industry is a Texas-bred tomboy—she surfs any chance she gets, in any conditions, with a bad-ass exuberance that I admire. Having already called in sick, I step into surf trunks, load up my board, and swing by Dawn's apartment. She and Teagan are waiting on the curb in shorts, flip-flops, and hooded sweatshirts, their surfboards propped against a brick wall lashed with silver and blue torrents of graffiti.

We drive east, through Bushwick's drab cement grid, then arc over Maspeth Creek and English Kills—tributaries of Newtown Creek, a Superfund site spiked with ten million gallons of spilled oil—these ruined waterways like New York's trackmarked veins after a century-long overdose. Brooklyn spits us out into Queens, past cinder-block car washes and fast food joints and a cluster of graveyards: Linden Hill, Mount Olivet, Lutheran, and St. John—the only shards of green space for miles. Singing along with Teagan's collection of Smiths songs, we angle down into Woodhaven and Ozone Park, under crumbling subway trestles, past Indian restaurants and windowless strip clubs and cell phone stores, and on through Howard Beach's rows of seventies-era Italian banquet halls and seafood restaurants, all of it a blur in the borough's slow southward tilt to the coast.

We get the first tangy smack of salt water on the long bridge over Jamaica Bay; it's here that the pace of our conversation picks up, echoing our pulses as we approach the sea.

Teagan is sharp-witted, a fast-talker. Quick. So much so that she's been dating one of our mutual friends, Adam, without me knowing it.

"We've dated on and off for like *six months*," she says. "The problem with Adam is that, like most boys, he wants a girlfriend to take care of him, fix his problems, and deal with all his bullshit, but he also wants to sleep around with everyone else in the world. I'm telling you: men are all *lost*."

"I can vouch for that," I say. I'm suffering multiple variations on this *lost* theme at the present. For one: I'm in a failing long-distance relationship with a soft-spoken skater-girl named Karissa. I want her to still love and stay faithful to me, even though she lives two thousand miles away, in Colorado.

Then Dawn discusses her own chronic boy woes, and I follow up with my ex-girlfriend woes, until the conversation turns to work, another consistent letdown.

Like me, Dawn and Teagan are sick of working such long hours, cooped up in cubes. They envy our male friends, most of whom are professional skateboarders, artists, bohemians, underemployed construction workers, overemployed drinkers.

"Can you imagine any of our guy friends working in an office?" Teagan wonders out loud.

"Justin works in an office," Dawn reminds her.

"Oh, right," Teagan says. "How did that happen?"

I can't blame her for forgetting, for wondering. It's seriously incongruous with my career trajectory up to this point—backpacking guide in the San Juan Mountains; summer camp counselor on Mount Hood, Oregon; skatepark manager; creative writing instructor at a Colorado university. The fact that I work a corporate job on the sixteenth floor of a Midtown high rise both surprises and depresses me on pretty much a daily basis. A sad facsimile of my true self up there, wearing slacks, hunched in a cubicle, compulsively checking the internet surf report.

Finally: the toll bridge to the Rockaway peninsula, the long thin jawbone of Long Island.

I pay three dollars and fifty cents in exchange for a horizon that's lost to me back in the city.

We park and ferry our boards up cement stairs, across the wooden boardwalk, down to the beach. As we walk barefoot across morning-cold sand, the sky unfurls above us, reclaiming from the city all its stolen blue bandwidth.

This is what all the hype's about: perfect, sun-shimmering sets of head-high rollers coming in smooth, sixteen-second intervals, the ocean an endless stretch of blue-gray corduroy, the waves scrolling in silver and then peeling evenly into whiteness.

The best swells I've ever seen, anywhere.

But while Dawn and Teagan busy themselves with surf wax and

wetsuits, I stand shivering on the sand, heart racing, not sure if I'm ready for hurricane-grade surf, though by this point Ophelia has been downgraded to tropical storm status.

It's here, as I stare into the stirred-up maw of the Atlantic, tuned in to its relentless, percussive crush, that the association finally clicks: these waves are the aftermath of a storm named after English literature's most famous drowning victim. The fifteenth system in the worst hurricane season on record, the result of warming seas, a warming planet.

I've come a long way in getting over my fear of the ocean, but I'm still new to surfing, and on a day like this the gnawing apprehension persists. I moved to New York City with a naive sense of enthusiasm and hope, but now that I'm actually trying to get my life together in this place with so many social undercurrents and financial riptides— now I'm spooked.

"Come on, Justin," Dawn says after I express my Shakespearean anxieties. "These are the best waves of the year." She pulls up her wetsuit zipper, stretches into a deep forward bend. Armed with her surfboard, she charges down to the jetty, where the swell thunders in at its tallest, most powerful point. I hang back on the beach, where part of me wants to drop anchor, play it safe, surrender to paralysis. But there's a deeper pull at work, a stronger longing to get up and get moving—to hazard the risk and follow Dawn down into the churning sea.

MOVING

I'm obsessive.

Meaning I ruminate to excess about rip currents, sharks, heights, depths, failure, the future, death by drowning.

Or I latch on to something or someone I want and spend years in fervid pursuit.

My obsessiveness encompasses the word's Latin roots: *ob* (opposite) and *sedere* (to sit).

Meaning I can't sit still.

I crave motion, action, momentum. Skating, paddling, peddling: without these all-consuming physical activities I become easily bored, falling prey to darker obsessions, anxieties, self-destructive tendencies. I need an obsession to give my life a central organizing principle, to feel something like a sense of purpose. To keep from turning on myself.

In grade school, it was breakdancing. Some modern dancers from the local community college gave lessons in our school cafeteria, teaching us the moonwalk and the worm. When the film *Breakin'* came to town, the best breakers were invited to perform a floor show in the local movie theater. The most exciting event of my childhood: a bunch of us white Colorado kids rocking parachute pants, red bandannas, checkered muscle shirts, all of us dancing down on the syrupy theater floor, busting body locks, King Tuts, and backspins for a captive audience of a hundred or more. In return, we got to watch *Breakin'* from the front row, free of charge—something I did ten or twelve times, the characters Turbo and Ozone my new heroes, objects of my movement fetish, imaginary *homeboys*.

One of my best moves was the wave. It started in my fingertips: they reared up skyward like spindrift, then crash-curled downward, the energy rolling into my wrist—cresting up through my elbow and shoulder—before flowing out my other arm, dissipating into air. Sometimes the wave surged down my chest, through my hips, and into my knees, then rebounded back up and out my chin—the body wave. I did this for hours at a time, restless as the ocean, possessed by its rhythm.

I never stopped moving, popping and spinning, dancing, to the point that my parents grew concerned and eventually exasperated, suggesting that I sit still, slow down, take up other hobbies, or even just read a single book, *for Christ's sake.*

When I was eleven, my father—another craver of motion— moved us from Colorado to La Jolla, California, where I took up body boarding. I was just graduating to surfing when we moved again, this time to the arid inland hills of east San Diego. No waves in sight, I started skateboarding—a skateboard being the perfect on-land vessel to satisfy my motion-lust.

In this case, the obsession lasts twenty-five years and counting.

My first job out of college was part-time manager of a skatepark in Boulder, Colorado. In the summers I migrated north to Oregon, where I ran the skateboard program at a summer camp on Mount Hood. I eventually went to graduate school to study writing, but also because more school meant more summers off, which in turn meant road trips to almost every skatepark in the state of Colorado, mile-long drainage ditches in New Mexico, bone-dry swimming pools east of L.A., San Francisco's precipitous hills.

The constant need for motion and change made my romantic life difficult. When my long-term relationships ended—partly due to my skateboarding addiction—I spent months and sometimes even years obsessing over the women I'd lost.

After grad school, I sat still long enough to put together a book, albeit one about skateboarding. Called *Life and Limb: Skateboarders Write from the Deep End,* it included a short piece of mine titled "Whaling," which detailed my Ahab-like obsession with skateboarding and the novel *Moby-Dick.*

In late May 2003, I traveled from Colorado to New York to meet with a potential publisher for *Life and Limb;* it was during this trip that I spotted my first New York City surfer. Walking down Christopher Street on my way to pitch the book, I saw him ascend from a subway station, up between green Art Deco lampposts, a surfboard tucked under his arm. There was something astonishing about it, like an ice climber on the streets of Los Angeles.

Standing there staring, I felt a subtle shift in the Gulf Stream of my obsessions.

I'd been skateboarding for decades but had gotten only a small, teasing taste of surfing during my teenage years in East County, San Diego. Like the majority of actual New York residents, I had no idea surfing was even possible here. Could you really ride the subway to the beach? If so, could you surf in the morning and hit the Metropolitan Museum of Art that same afternoon? The surfer and the idea of this underground hypermobility—between the city and the ocean, between the natural world and New York's endless cultural universe—were both signal fires, drawing me eastward.

My meeting with the publisher went well and led to a modest book deal. Afterward I celebrated with my close friends Paul and Natalie in Brooklyn. They lived in a massive apartment in a former button factory, a quintessential artist's loft with a rope swing in the hallway and exposed-brick walls covered with Paul's enormous, photorealistic paintings of violet horses and polychromatic light bursts.

The kind of place that makes a tourist think living in New York is nothing but fun times, nonstop art-making, rainbows and rope swings.

And as it turned out, they were looking for a roommate.

A few months later, just after my thirtieth birthday—despite the serious misgivings of my friends and family, and especially my girlfriend Karissa, who still had a year of school left—I pulled up the moorings of my life, packed everything I owned into my little Toyota pickup, made the two-thousand-mile trip from Colorado to New York City.

New York, the place that Herman Melville scholar and biographer Andrew Delbanco calls "that peerless school for the study of literary careerism."

I was banking on the skateboard anthology's success and planned to follow it up with a novel, but other than that, I had zero job prospects. In an existence defined by motion, this was both the boldest and the most senseless move of my life.

THE AUTUMN BOWL

> Such dreary streets! blocks of blackness, not houses, on
> either hand. . . . At this hour of the night, of the last day of
> the week, that quarter of the town proved all but deserted.
>
> ~ HERMAN MELVILLE, *Moby-Dick*

From a skateboarding perspective, the timing of my arrival in
Brooklyn is fortunate. Some friends have just finished building
an epic wooden skate bowl inside a semiabandoned warehouse
on the East River in Greenpoint, a ten-minute ride from my new
apartment.

My first evening in the city, my old college friend Kyle Grodin
and I skate down Bedford, cut south at Kent, then roll through the
desolate, postindustrial border zone between Williamsburg and
Greenpoint. A blustery September night; blue and green lights crown
the Empire State Building, reflecting onto gray cloud cover like a dirty
halo. The distinct smell of petroleum; a lone guy in a fedora and checkered Vans playing the trumpet on an abandoned corner; elaborate
graffiti on every wall and water tower—*Neckface, SARS, LES,* multi-
valent wheat pastes by *Swoon.* The further north we skate the more
bombed-out and abandoned the neighborhood becomes, until a row
of massive, vacant warehouses rises up from the shadows. Smashed-
out windows and crumbling brick walls, rickety catwalks spanning
the upper floors, the entire complex tangled in razor wire.

Looming here on the banks of the Harlem River as it spills its
poisoned guts into the Atlantic, these warehouses comprise the defunct Greenpoint Terminal Markets, a once-vibrant center of naval
industry. Our destination was originally one of the largest nautical rope factories in the world.* Months later, after I get a job in

---

* In *Moby-Dick* Melville discusses a possible reason for the demise of the American rope industry: "Of late years the Manilla rope has in the American fishery
almost entirely superseded hemp as a material for whale-lines; for, though not so

Midtown, I sometimes ride my bike to work along the waterfront in east Manhattan, right below Bellevue Hospital, where, from the other side of the river, this whole area has a severely decayed, third world look to it, like Beirut in the 1980s or San Francisco in shambles after the Great Earthquake.

Grodin and I enter the building through a creaky metal door that we have to heave open with both hands. The passage leads into a dismal stairwell littered with broken beer bottles, bricks, piles of soot. Then down a couple uneven steps into a shadowy open-air corridor with rusty fire escapes spiraling up into the dark between sixty-foot brick walls. Above us, a thin slash of starless sky; straight ahead, a narrow porthole onto Manhattan's vertical sea of lights.

The muffled rush of urethane wheels circumnavigating the bowl reaches us from down the corridor, a sound like an old roller coaster coming off its rails. We enter another doorway, then find ourselves in a cavernous brick warehouse with fifty-foot-high ceilings. A stairway leads up to the deck, and there it is: an immaculate wooden bowl, sheeted with a fresh layer of Russian birch plywood, like the hull of a well-crafted ship. Amoeba-shaped, it fills up every square foot in the huge space, one section transitioning right up an extant concrete wall, which allows skaters to traverse the bowl's boundaries and actually ride the old building itself. And everyone's whipping around at supersonic velocities, carving and grinding to a sound track of eighties punk rock—Iggy Pop and the Stooges, the Dead Kennedys—so fast that it feels like they're generating some invisible form of energy, like frenzied atoms in a particle collider.

I take a few warm-up spins and then pop out onto the deep-end deck, where Grodin introduces me to his friend Andy Kessler. Andy's a compact guy with coal-black hair and a beak of a nose. Tan, weathered skin. As East Coast as they come. He looks to be in his forties,

---

durable as hemp, it is stronger, and far more soft and elastic; and I will add (since there is an aesthetic in all things), is much more handsome and becoming to the boat, than hemp." So to add to the Autumn Bowl's gritty mystique is the fact that the place was once used for producing not only rope, but an especially *ugly* rope.

but there's something youthful about him: he rocks a black sleeveless T-shirt, Levi's, and low-top Keds; his slick-backed hair has a little curl in the front, like Danny Zuko from *Grease*.

Grodin tells Andy that I just moved from Colorado.

Andy grins, shakes my hand. "Welcome to town," he says. "Now *get out of my town*." He breaks into a friendly cackle, then drops in and rolls around the bowl, riding an oversized skateboard with a sharp, surfboard-like nose. His back hunched slightly like a surfer in a barrel, he powers through corners with his elbow crooked in front of his face, shielding his eyes from invisible sea spray. He's pretty ancient by skateboarding standards, and doesn't really do any tricks beside deliberate frontside grinds, but he has this classic style, honestly one of the best I've seen in my twenty-plus years of skateboarding. I later learn that he's been skating since the early seventies, longer than anyone else in the city, longer than many of us in the room have been alive, and that in terms of skateboarding, New York City really is his town.

Grodin and I skate for hours, until just about everyone, including Kessler, clears out. After he's gone, Grodin tells me more about him, how he's a living legend in the skateboard world, a founding member of the Soul Artists of Zoo York, the seventies-era skate crew that was New York City's equivalent of Dogtown and the Z-Boys in Santa Monica. And how, during the late eighties and early nineties, Andy disappeared onto the New York streets, having traded skateboarding for heroin. But that's all history; he's been sober for over a decade and is completely religious about going to NA meetings and riding his skateboard.

Kyle Grodin is something of a junkie himself—but his drug of choice is sugar. Before we met at my house he'd picked up a two-liter bottle of soda and a couple Snickers bars from the local bodega. Between runs he chugs Coke straight from the bottle or forces down a candy bar. The more he gorges, the harder and more guerrilla-like his skateboarding becomes. To say he skates like a guerrilla is an understatement, considering the way he sweats out his T-shirts, how he has to double up on socks to keep them from turning to sweaty mush, or the way he sometimes blows a trick out midair, pitches his skateboard across the room, and howls like a primate. But the comparison isn't entirely fair. He looks more like a seminimble circus performer getting shot out of a cannon; he can do shit that no one else can do—like fully inverted handplants over four feet of sheer vertical on the concrete wall—and he does it all while going a million miles an hour, a crazed grin on his face.

The other thing about Grodin is that once he gets a session started, he never wants to quit. Whereas for me skateboarding is an obsession, for Kyle it's a borderline *mania*. If I had it in me to skate all night, he'd stay there with me, skating and sweating and grunting until dawn. But by one o'clock I'm ready to go home and get some sleep, at which Grodin voices his obvious disappointment.

"Home? Already?" he says, panting, dripping.

"Grodin, we've been skating *five hours straight.*"

"So? I'm just getting warmed up," he says, then mops his face with his already-soaked T-shirt.

"I can see that. And I'm afraid you might blow a fucking gasket."

"Are you kidding? I already blew all my gaskets back in the nineties."

"Look, you can stay all night if you want," I say, "but I'm going home."

Not one to skate by himself, Grodin helps me close down the warehouse, cut the lights. We shuffle our way out the murky corridor, then roll back home through half-lit Brooklyn streets.

THE WHITE DEATH

In the posthumous afterword to the poet Charles Olson's book *Call Me Ishmael,* the writer Merton Sealts describes visiting Olson in his tiny Greenwich Village office, where Olson was holed up, surrounded by old, heavily annotated copies of *Moby-Dick,* while he was finishing his doctoral dissertation on Melville. Sealts offered him a draft of one of his own essays on Melville. Olson—a great bear of a man—sat reading it, smoking his pipe, nodding in approval.

"Well," Olson said, "I see . . . that . . . THE WHITE DEATH . . . has descended . . . upon YOU . . . too."

THE WHITE DEATH. *n—*1: *Simo Häyhä, a Finnish sniper in the Winter War, nicknamed "White Death" by the Soviet Army* 2: *a slang term used to describe incurable diseases such as tuberculosis or AIDS* 3: *great white shark (vernacular)* 4: *an all-consuming obsession with the novel* Moby-Dick *and the life of Herman Melville*

I contracted my own White Death back in graduate school, when I was first assigned *Moby-Dick,* and had to wake up at five or six in the morning to swim its immense dark waters.

In a typically droll essay, David Sedaris details how he had to force himself to get through *Moby-Dick* by not taking a bath until he finished. I loved *Moby-Dick* from the beginning, but I can sympathize with Sedaris. Melville's language is often brilliant, pulse-quickening, Shakespearean—*the deeper midnight of the insatiable maw.* His intensity and worldly wisdom are apparent, but so is his insecurity about his lack of secondary education, a fact of his upbringing that he often tries to cloak with vainglorious prose or rampant alliteration: *mingling their mumblings with his own mastications.* You sometimes feel embarrassed for him, the way you do for historical interpreters or people in costume at a Renaissance fair. Or, like many *Moby-Dick* readers, you simply give up on him about halfway through, exasperated by long-winded tangents about the minutiae of whaling.

Not one to give up easily, though, I made it through *Moby-Dick*.

It's a book about constant movement—about the relentless pursuit of passions—to which I can seriously relate.

I became obsessed with a book about obsession.

Searching for critical work on Melville, a couple grad school friends and I ventured down to the fiction and literary criticism sections in the basement of the Colorado State University library. The library was flooded during a torrential rainstorm the previous year, copies of my favorites like *The Odyssey* and *To the Lighthouse* and *The Shipping News* tossed around and taking on muddy water, little paper vessels foundering in a storm. Though all the drowned books had been restored via irradiation, the basement still had a faint mineral smell of floodwater.

After browsing a few stodgy critical anthologies, I discovered a title called *Melville's Moby-Dick: An American Nekyia* by Jungian analyst Edward F. Edinger. I'd always been fascinated by Carl Jung's theories —with the fact that he accepted and honored spiritual experience whereas Freud denied it. In *An American Nekyia*, Edinger proposes the very Jungian interpretation that all the characters in *Moby-Dick* constitute one unified entity, that each individual crew member is actually a different splintered archetype within the psyche of the main character—a spiritual seeker named Ishmael.

As proof, Edinger quotes from passages like the following:

> They were one man, not thirty. For as the one ship that
> held them all, though it was put together of contrasting
> things—oak, and maple, and pine wood; iron, and pitch, and
> hemp—yet all these ran into each other in one concrete hull,
> which shot on its way, both balanced and directed by the
> long central keel; even so, all the individualities of the crew,
> this man's valor, that man's fear; guilt and guiltlessness, all
> varieties were welded into oneness.

The word *Nekyia* derives from the title of the eleventh book of *The Odyssey*, wherein Odysseus descends into the underworld to commune with the dead. According to Edinger, *Moby-Dick* is the quintessential *American* Nekyia—a metaphorical "night sea journey" through despair and meaninglessness, symbolizing the dark passages that we all embark on during our development as individuals and as a society. In Jungian theory, most spiritual journeys begin with a kind of universal descent into the underworld, where we come face to face with our own darkness, weaknesses, and fears—our shadow. So *Moby-Dick* can be read as Ishmael's confrontation with his dark side in the form of Ahab, just as most of us wrestle daily with our own dark moods and impulses, and our country reckons with its imperialistic shadow side. The clash turns bloody and violent, and Ahab's resentful pursuit of the white whale brings down the entire ship. Only Ishmael is reborn through the wreckage; having assimilated his shadow after this deep psychic battle, he floats upward through a spiraling whirlpool. In Jungian terms, this circular current is a mandala, an ancient symbol of wholeness and individuation.

I liked this spin on Melville's tale—especially because a more literal analysis of *Moby-Dick* tends toward the melodramatic and purely tragic. The Jungian interpretation allows for darkness and shadows and tragedy, but ultimately points toward the light.

This is where it began: my own White Death, a syndrome characterized by obsessive thoughts about *Moby-Dick* and Herman Melville, the collecting of old volumes of the novel and the schlepping around of one or more of these volumes at almost all times, and constant talk of *Moby-Dick*—its brilliance and relevance to contemporary life—to anyone who'll listen.

These early symptoms are mild compared to what manifests as the disease progresses.

GOING UNDER

In many ways, New York is perfect for someone with my peripatetic obsessions, my need to move. It's a city where everything and everyone are in constant motion, flux—via trains, helicopters, bicycles, skateboards, taxis, strollers, horses. Even in movie theaters you can feel the subway rumble and pitch beneath your feet. The weather's always changing; buildings are always rising up and coming down; everyone's trying to get somewhere else—from Brooklyn to Manhattan, from Manhattan back to Brooklyn, from entry level to management, understudy to lead, assistant to editor.

The problem for me is that, having grown up in the West, I've always been in control of my movement, the pilot of my own vehicle. But in New York, you're at the mercy of forces larger than yourself, both dark and light; you have to resign yourself to being a passenger.

My third night in the city, a friend invites me to an art opening near Union Square. I'd visited the city plenty of times as a tourist, but this is my first subway ride under the East River into Manhattan, and about halfway through it dawns on me that not only am I now living in New York City—*New York Fucking City*—but I'm also trapped three hundred feet below a polluted river—so deep that my eardrums pop—hurtling along at top speeds, with no way to stop what I've put into motion, to slam on the brakes and eject myself from this whole noisy, grimy, two-thousand-miles-from-home ride onto which I've willingly hitched myself. Suddenly my heart is a pipe bomb inside the suitcase of my chest, threatening to blow apart not just my body but also this entire train car and all the two hundred strangers who are about to witness me *completely blow apart*. I've been told that it will take me a few months to get used to the city, that these kinds of freak-outs are normal, but this does not feel normal, not at all.

The train ride mercifully takes only a few minutes, and then I'm released through sliding double doors, through silver turnstiles and dirty-tiled corridors and up a staircase back into open air. But "open air" is maybe not the right term for Union Square—not for someone from Colorado, who despite spending months in the woods, hiking without a compass or map through vast evergreen forests where people can and do become hopelessly disoriented—some of them even perishing in the cold, cold woods—now feels, perhaps for the first time in his adult life, utterly lost, abandoned by what he has heretofore considered a keen sense of direction.

TIMING

Just before I'd left for New York, Karissa's father lost his job at Hewlett-Packard, even though he'd been management-level for over twenty years. Her mother was having emotional problems, and then her grandmother passed away, and in the midst of all this chaos, Karissa had to move back home to finish her last year of college and try to save up enough money to follow me out East.

We talk for hours every night, cell phone pressed against my head for so long that I worry I might develop cauliflower ear.

Our conversations develop a predictable trajectory. First, I tell her all about whatever amazing New York City thing I witnessed that day: some new street art, the Brooklyn Bridge, the Autumn Bowl, the collection of medieval art at the Cloisters. Then, sensing her jealousy and longing, I apologize, try to downplay what I've seen, tell her how much the subway freaks me out.

"You're just saying that to make me feel better. You only hate the subway ride beneath the East River."

"I would say that in general, the subway makes me very nervous. It's growing into a problem, actually."

"You think you have problems? At least you don't have a boyfriend who moved to New York."

"You're moving out here soon, too."

"Right. Just as soon as I save up three thousand dollars. Working at a *sandwich shop*."

I remind her that she's flying in for Thanksgiving, that we'll talk then. That we'll work things out.

"All right then, *good times*," she says.

AN OLD FRIEND

> How it is I know not; but there is no place like a bed for
> confidential disclosures between friends. Man and wife, they
> say, there open the very bottom of their souls to each other;
> and some old couples often lie and chat over old times till
> nearly morning. Thus, then, in our hearts' honeymoon, lay
> I and Queequeg—a cosy, loving pair.
>
> ~ HERMAN MELVILLE, *Moby-Dick*

One night my roommates and I visit a bar just down the street from our apartment, a newish, comfortable place with wood-paneled walls that approximate a Swedish sauna—a quasi-Scandinavian aesthetic that's popular in Brooklyn and maybe has something to do with Ikea. We're standing around talking, drinking Pilsner Urquells, when someone taps me on the shoulder.

He's a tall guy with dark curly hair, and it takes a minute to place him, but then it all comes swimming back—it's Asa Ellis. The two of us worked together at a skateboarding/snowboarding camp on Mount Hood, Oregon, nearly six years ago. Before making the move out from Colorado, I'd heard from a mutual friend that Asa was in the city, doing well, writing for the *Village Voice,* so bumping into him isn't a complete surprise, but it's a nice coincidence that warms the part of my heart that's ambivalent about my move to New York. Like me, Asa grew up in the West—in his case Los Angeles, in a bohemian canyon enclave above Santa Monica. His parents were proto-hippies who gave Asa freedom to roam around the beach, surf all day, sleep in the sun, and hang out with budding pro surfers. He eventually moved to New York to study creative writing at the New School; he ended up writing for the *Voice* and occasionally the *New York Times,* and generally has the city dialed. But with his blue eyes and broad shoulders and beatific smile, there's something very laid back and West Coast about him.

Asa and I exchange numbers, and then a couple weeks later he invites me over for dinner at his studio apartment, in an ocean-blue building above a Park Slope hardware store. Just back from a surf trip to Ecuador, he's in well-worn huaraches, shorts, and an ancient T-shirt with tiny holes all over the shoulders, the look of someone stranded happily on a deserted island. Thick shoulders and ropy arms—it's apparent he's spent a hell of lot of time in the ocean. His place is cozy, with uneven hardwood floors, partially exposed brick walls, a couple cats lounging around on thrift store furniture, a record player and a substantial vinyl collection. And a stack of surfboards near his bed.

"Feel free to throw on a record," Asa says.

I'm on a Talking Heads kick, so I put on *Stop Making Sense*.

He makes gazpacho with cilantro and wedges of fresh avocado. We eat out on the fire escape, where his wetsuits are draped over the railing, and where a little arc of a moon curls over Brooklyn. We catch up on old times and mutual friends and chat about surfing. He tells me how he used to ride his bike to the subway station with his surfboard under his arm, then take the A train out to Rockaway Beach. One night he got home late, rode with his board through Crown Heights, where an old woman spotted him and said, "Now where you goin' *surfin'*?" Asa's imitation is spot-on, funny without condescension. We also talk books: it turns out he's really into *The Odyssey*, in the same way I'm obsessed with *Moby-Dick*.

I tell him about *An American Nekyia*, how it discusses similarities between these two classics.

"How so?" Asa asks.

Ishmael's voyage on the *Pequod* is a similar kind of plunge into oblivion to the section where Odysseus travels down into the underworld. Both characters have to descend into darkness as part of their journey home."

"What is it about the descent thing that's so intriguing for you?"

I look out at the multiplex of lighted windows in all the apartments of this cramped East Coast courtyard—feeling how little I know about life here, how completely foreign it all is for me, and maybe this has something to do with me telling Asa so much about my own life:

how in the past couple years I've been through some difficult times—
mainly the dissolution of a ten-year relationship, the one before
Karissa. And how tunneling blindly through that darkness led me to
a kind of gritty spiritual awakening.

"I've been coming to terms with some of my own darkness in the
past couple years," Asa tells me. "I grew up in a pretty severely alcoholic family. I think that's why I connect with *The Odyssey*—this
search for a true family, for home."

"Do you feel at home here in New York?" I ask.

"In a lot of ways, yes. This place is intense. You have to band together for warmth, you know? I feel like the friendships I've made
here are more real, more honest. There's a depth to people here that I
never found on the West Coast.

"What about you?" he asks.

"To be honest, tonight is the first time I've felt at home for months."

"The city can bring up a lot of loneliness," Asa says. "But the more
you get to know it, the more it opens up to you, the more it unfolds."
He reaches over and places his hand on my shoulder, squeezes. "I'm
glad you're here, man," he says.

Our eyes meet for a moment, then I glance at the open window,
through which I can see his bed and stack of surfboards, and part
of me wants to lean back over and kiss him. Earlier in the conversation Asa mentioned that his friends model for the famous young
photographer Ryan McGinley, who lives in the East Village and
cruises around on his bike, taking photos of skateboarders, angelic
twentysomethings, musicians, artists. I'd seen some of McGinley's
photos of beautiful young naked people in trees—like a congregation of lanky white birds—or naked couples in the woods, drenched
with rain, about to have sex or just having had sex, men and women,
men and men. And one I saw in the *New Yorker* was of two boys, possibly skateboarders, in bed together. Skaters in bed with each other
was definitely not a photographic tableau I'd ever seen in Colorado,
but coming out of the East Village, it seemed like no big deal, and I
realize that I sort of want to spend the night over at Asa's. I'm comfortable enough with my own sexuality and any ambiguity therein.

I'd done enough soul searching in my teens and twenties to know that while I prefer women, I'm also not 100 percent straight, and so I'm not totally against kissing someone like Asa, because what the hell? I'm in New York, after all—a place that despite all the grime, or maybe because of it, exudes a kind of rugged sensuality, exploration, pansexuality.

But eventually we crawl back in off the fire escape and hug each other good night—a strong, lingering embrace, during which the desire, but not the warmth, fades. Instead of kissing him, I make him promise to take me surfing.

THE BIRTHPLACE

A few days after my arrival in New York, I seek out a lesser-known Manhattan tourist destination: Melville's birthplace at 6 Pearl Street, right across from Battery Park on the southern tip of the island. The actual boardinghouse was demolished and replaced by a glass high-rise, but a plaque marks the spot (along with a sculptural bust of the prodigiously bearded author), and I'm surprised to find that Melville and I share very nearly the same birth date: he was born late on August 1, 1819; I was born early on August 2, 1973.

From this site it's a few blocks over to the South Street Seaport, where Melville reportedly spent time. The Seaport docks hold several large antique sailing vessels, all curated by the South Street Seaport Museum. The *Lettie G. Howard* is a sleek fishing schooner, 125 feet long, once used to supply the Fulton Fish Market and since restored for use in sailing instruction. And then there's the *Peking*: at 377 feet long, with a steel hull the length of a football field and four masts as tall as an eighteen-story building, it's one of the largest sailing vessels ever built.

Combined with salt air and pungent fish-market smells, the *Lettie G. Howard* and the *Peking* re-create a sense of the city during Melville's time—"*There is now your insular city of the Manhattoes, belted round by wharves as Indian isles by coral reefs*"—when Melville's contemporary Walt Whitman described it as "mast-hemm'd Manhattan."

In the first chapter of *Moby-Dick*, Melville paints a picture of this old, maritime Manhattan—something that, aside from these museum relics, no longer exists. What hasn't changed, though, are the "thousands upon thousands of mortal men fixed in ocean reveries." From Battery Park to the Seaport, hordes of people stand looking out into the bay; these "water gazers" are there every day of the year, regardless of the weather. Having grown up in the West, surrounded

by so many miles of open space, I find living in New York City aes-
thetically and emotionally overwhelming, and like the rest of the
water gazers, I gravitate toward the open space of the sea.

Later in the first chapter, Melville states that "meditation and
water are wedded for ever." In other words, we water gazers, beyond traversing the bounds of the city, are looking to transcend the
human condition, to plunge into the deeper mysteries of life and our
purpose therein.

Moby-Dick also braids the personal with the political:

And, doubtless, my going on this whaling voyage, formed
part of the grand programme of Providence that was
drawn up a long time ago. It came in as a sort of brief inter-
lude and solo between more extensive performances. I take it
that this part of the bill must have run something like this:
"Grand Contested Election for the Presidency
of the United States.
Whaling Voyage by One Ishmael.
BLOODY BATTLE IN AFGHANISTAN."

A lot is made of Melville's "part of the bill" after the events of
September 11, 2001—how uncanny and prophetic it was, coming
after the most "grandly contested" election of our generation—Bush
vs. Gore in 2000—and the beginning of our nation's own night sea
journey under the direction of Captain Bush. In post-9/11 America,
the label of Captain Ahab is bandied about constantly. In his quest
for vengeance against the West, Osama bin Laden is labeled an Ahab,
as is George Bush, especially after he steers the country away from
our own bloody battle in Afghanistan and into the dangerous waters
of Iraq.

As of my arrival in New York, we're only a few months into this
new war, and like the crew members of the *Pequod,* our country is in
for a long dark voyage.

DELIVERY

> It touches one's sense of honour . . . if just previous to putting
> your hand into the tar-pot, you have been lording it as a
> country schoolmaster.
>
> ～ HERMAN MELVILLE, *Moby-Dick*

After weeks of job searching, I finally land an interview with the president of a children's book company, a friend of a friend. The night before our meeting, I draft a proposal for a non-fiction children's book about skateboarding. It's a good move, because it turns out there isn't any freelance editing work available, but he likes the book idea. So much that he suggests I turn the one book into a series of six. He even offers me a small advance. The pay isn't great, but it's better than what I'm making for the skateboard anthology. And all combined, these writing gigs only scratch the surface of my rent, almost three times what I paid back in Colorado.

So I need another job, something menial that will provide some cash but also plenty of time to finish editing the anthology and write six new books. Walking back from the subway after my interview, I see a Delivery Driver Needed sign in the window of a tiny Indian restaurant, just a few blocks from my apartment. Since I have a car and a valid driver's license, they hire me on the spot.

Not lost on me is the fact that I'm over thirty and have a master's degree—and that I'd spent the last year as a university instructor—but now here I am delivering samosas and *saag,* the pungent smell of fried ghee seeping into my truck's upholstery. I remind myself that it's only temporary, plus I read and reread the section of *Moby-Dick* where Ishmael talks about making the transition from schoolmaster to sailor—"What does that indignity amount to, weighed, I mean, in the scales of the New Testament? Do you think the archangel Gabriel thinks anything the less of me, because I promptly and respectfully obey that old hunks in that particular instance? Who ain't a slave? Tell me that."

One major perk of the job is that it allows me to stay in Brooklyn and avoid the subway into Manhattan—a five-minute ride that increasingly strikes dread into my pickup truck–driving, country-boy heart. The other bright spot is that I love Indian food, and the couple who run the place feed me plenty of it. The husband is a Bangladeshi Muslim; his wife is a Brooklyn-bred Catholic. They raise two sweet girls, Amy and Sabiya, who seem overscheduled with visits to both mosque and church, and who have to hang around the restaurant until ten nearly every night. I feel bad for them, so I help them with their homework between delivery runs.

In October there's a full lunar eclipse. Before we all go outside to watch the moon flicker out, I sit with Amy and Sabiya at a glass-top table and slide little tea candles around in slow circles to illustrate how an eclipse works, how every so often the earth orbits in between the sun and the moon, casting the lunar glow in shadow.

"Does it go dark forever?" Sabiya, the younger sister, asks, holding her hand over the moon-candle flame—something for which her mother is always scolding her.

"Not at all," I say, taking the candle away, sliding it back into the sun-candle's light. I explain how the eclipse only lasts a few moments, that nothing and no one stays still for long.

Two weeks later, I find a *New York Times* classified ad for a freelance manuscript reader at a Midtown publishing company.

Still anxious about the subway, I ride my bike from Brooklyn up to Fifty-Third and Third for the interview. My future boss is a friendly man in a purple tie, *Simpsons* posters on his wall, and bookshelves full of trade paperbacks—thrillers, mysteries, romances, but also some interesting contemporary fiction.

I quit the delivery job and start my publishing career a few days later. It seems okay at first, a decent gig for a writer: I'm there three or four days a week, and I can show up at ten and leave early if I need to—all I have to do is read and comment on fiction manuscripts, basically the same thing I'd done in graduate school and as an adjunct writing instructor. With all my experience as a teacher, I know that what I should really be doing is applying for instructor positions here in the city. But I'm so intimidated by New York and its inhabitants that I can't imagine mustering the courage to teach here—not with my slow Colorado drawl, which I worry makes me sound like a plodder in a city of such fast, fluent speakers. So I content myself with sitting solo in my cubicle, quietly adrift on a small sea of other people's books.

THE L TRAIN

L TRAIN (Arrives at Bedford Street subway station.): *This is a Manhattan-bound L train.*

FEMALE PASSENGER (Boards train, takes seat.)

L TRAIN: *Stand clear of the closing doors, please. This is a Manhattan-bound L train. The next stop is First Avenue.*

FEMALE PASSENGER (Digs around in her handbag, looking for a cell phone.)

L TRAIN: Want to hear a story?

FEMALE PASSENGER (Ceases cell phone search. Looks around the empty train car, confused.): What kind of story?

L TRAIN: A blackout story. One that involves this guy Justin.

FEMALE PASSENGER: Blackout—you mean he passed out drunk on the train?

L TRAIN: People pass out by the hundreds on the train every day—there's no story there. I'm talking about an electrical blackout, a power outage.

FEMALE PASSENGER: Okay, sure. Tell me a story.

L TRAIN: So first of all, I run on electricity, understand, so when the power goes out, the trains cease to move. Even if they're full of passengers, three hundred feet below the East River.

FEMALE PASSENGER: So what happens to all those people?

L TRAIN: Sometimes backup generators power up the system. Other times, passengers have to wait until MTA rescue crews walk them out.

FEMALE PASSENGER: Walk them out *where*?

L TRAIN: Through the tunnels on the bench wall. Either to an emergency exit or back to the platform. In some cases, they have to walk directly on the track bed.

FEMALE PASSENGER: Oh wow.

L TRAIN: Yeah. It's not so pleasant. We get a lot of people who freak out. Some piss their pants, or puke all over the place. One lady stepped on a rat and had to be taken to Bellevue.

FEMALE PASSENGER: Bellevue?

L TRAIN: The mental hospital. *Please do not leave any unattended baggage or personal items on the train. If you see an unattended package, please report it to an MTA employee.*

FEMALE PASSENGER: So where does Justin come in?

L TRAIN: Before moving here from Colorado, he hears all these stories, about evacuations and trains getting stuck under the East River during the rolling blackouts of 2003—not to mention the threat of terrorist attacks—and it really freaks him out. I'm sorry to report that he develops a big problem with me.

FEMALE PASSENGER: What do you mean, *problem?* Like he's aggrieved with you? Annoyed?

L TRAIN: Hardly. More like he's terrified.

FEMALE PASSENGER: What, seriously?

L TRAIN: Seriously. I'm talking full-blown panic. He very nearly loses his shit every time he rides. Okay, well, not *every* time. He does fine on short rides through Manhattan, when there are plenty of opportunities to exit the train. But during the four-minute ride beneath the East River he comes close to losing it—or *blowing apart,* to use his words. Actually, it happens right about now, right *here,* in the very depths of this tunnel that's not only underground, but also underneath a river, the thought of which completely messes with his mind, triggers a serious claustrophobic drowning response. His heart races and he sweats and he has overwhelming feelings of dread, a full-on neurochemical train wreck in his head. Remember when the new prisoners arrive in that movie *The Shawshank Redemption,* and one chubby prisoner breaks down, starts blubbering *I'm not supposed to be here?* That's how Justin feels in the beginning, as if he's trapped—imprisoned even—so that when the train stops in the middle of the tunnel, as it does occasionally, it takes every ounce of self-control to keep himself from clutching at people and yelling *I'm not supposed to be here.*

FEMALE PASSENGER: Clutching at people? How would that help anything?

L TRAIN: Lord if I know. Between you and me, it turns out that he's had these *problems* before. He had a thing with airplanes, wouldn't fly for years. Aviophobia, they call it. Pathetic, right?

FEMALE PASSENGER: A little bit, yes. And ironic. I mean, he's all obsessed with motion and interested in this *Moby-Dick* "spiritual descent" stuff, but he's afraid go down and ride the subway?

L TRAIN: Tell me about it! *This is the First Avenue Station.*

FEMALE PASSENGER: So what ends up happening? I mean, I'm guessing he'll have to ride the subway regularly at some point.

L TRAIN: *Stand clear of the closing doors, please. The next stop is Third Avenue.* At first he tries to avoid me. Rides his bike everywhere, figures out the bus system. He avoids Manhattan, spends most of his time over in Brooklyn. But he ends up getting a job in Midtown and has to take the train every day. So eventually he has to man up and face his fears.

FEMALE PASSENGER: How does he do it?

L TRAIN: He brings a copy of Walt Whitman's poem "Crossing Brooklyn Ferry," where Whitman speaks of commuting across the Harlem River, with all the other anonymous passengers, having the same questions, doubts, hopes—the same periods of fear and darkness. He reads it over and over, holds it in his sweaty palms as if it were a close friend's hand. He likes the way Whitman reaches out across time to the reader, says, "I am with you." *I am with you*—he finds this comforting. He also memorizes a passage from the "Grand Armada" chapter of *Moby-Dick*:

> And thus, though surrounded by circle upon circle of consternations and affrights, did these inscrutable creatures at the centre freely and fearlessly indulge in all peaceful concernments; yea, serenely revelled in dalliance and delight. But even so, amid the tornadoed Atlantic of my being, do I myself still for ever centrally disport in mute calm; and while

ponderous planets of unwaning woe revolve round me, deep down and deep inland there I still bathe me in eternal mildness of joy.

This helps remind him that no matter how wired out the city makes him, or how much mental chaos his brain stirs up, deep down his soul is quiet and still and generally okay. And he meditates, uses breathing techniques. He throws in a yoga technique his stepmother taught him when he was a kid: *nadi shodhana,* alternate nostril breathing. But mostly he just forces himself to do something that scares him, over and over, until the fear finally eases up, little by little.

FEMALE PASSENGER: So he gets better? He's able to ride?

L TRAIN: Yes. Slowly he gets better. He calms down, surrenders himself to the whole experience. After a few months, he's not even conscious of it anymore; he can just sit back and relax and enjoy the ride like anyone else. That winter he reads *Anna Karenina,* almost entirely on the subway. *This is Third Avenue. The next stop is Fourteenth Street.*

FEMALE PASSENGER: So he gets over it. What about the other phobias?

L TRAIN: The subway is a watershed for him. Once he gets over me, it transfers to his other fears. He gets so he can fly again, no problem. Eventually he's flying back and forth to and from Colorado—he even starts to enjoy it, the way he did as a kid. *This is Fourteenth Street. Stand clear of the closing doors, please. The next stop is Sixth Avenue.*

FEMALE PASSENGER: That must feel good. To overcome that sort of thing.

L TRAIN: I don't want to be overly dramatic here, but when you're released from that kind of emotional bondage, it feels like a miracle.

FEMALE PASSENGER: So New York is good for him.

L TRAIN: In a lot of ways, yes. We toughen him up. *This is Sixth Avenue. The next and last stop is Eighth Avenue.*

FEMALE PASSENGER: You *heal* him.

L TRAIN: I'm not sure I'd go that far.

FEMALE PASSENGER: But it's such a happy ending. He literally goes down and faces all his darkness and fears, then emerges as a whole person. It's a spiritual thing, like Ishmael reborn from death into new life.

L TRAIN: The subway is just the beginning, a threshold. You have to remember that in and of itself, riding the subway is really no big deal. Five million people do it every day.

FEMALE PASSENGER: So you're saying he runs into other problems?

L TRAIN: I'm sorry to say that yes, yes he does. Problems much bigger than the subway. *This is Eighth Avenue. This is the last stop on this train.*

FEMALE PASSENGER: How's that even possible?

L TRAIN (Comes to a complete stop, opens doors.): Look, this has been a real picnic, but you need to step clear of the train now.

FEMALE PASSENGER: How about you tell me just one of the problems?

L TRAIN (Doors remain open.): *This is the last stop on this train. Please exit the train.*

FEMALE PASSENGER (Waits, expectantly, but is greeted only by silence. Exits train, disappears into a crowd moving up a stairwell.)

RED HAIRICKSON

One night after skating the Autumn Bowl, I give my new friend Ted a lift to the subway. Ted's a ginger whom I've never seen smile, and who skates the bowl like someone with a death wish. We have mutual acquaintances back out West—he shared a house in L.A. with an old college buddy of mine. His full name is Ted Erickson, although our mutual friends refer to him as Red Hairickson. But he seems like he has a bit of a chip on his shoulder, so I'm not about to call him that.

I drive him through Greenpoint toward the Lorimer stop, where he'll catch the train to his place in Bushwick.

"Bushwick? That's pretty far out there, right?"

"Thirty minutes by train. A long haul, but the rent's cheap."

"I hear you can still score pretty cheap rents here in Greenpoint."

"Yeah, but I'd never live in this neighborhood."

"Why's that?"

"There was a huge oil spill here back in the fifties. A total catastrophe. All the oil is still underground, trapped in the soil."

"No shit?"

"No shit. They say benzene vapors still leach up from the ground. Benzene causes leukemia, and this place has one of the highest rates in the country."

Ted seems, again, sort of permanently aggrieved, so I'm not sure I believe him. If this is true, then why haven't I heard about it before? Back at home it takes a couple Google searches to corroborate: I'm now living just a few minutes from the site of one of the worst environmental disasters in history.

Starting in the mid-nineteenth century, oil refineries and bulk storage facilities metastasized on the banks of Newtown Creek. Exxon Mobil or its predecessors own the majority. In 1950 a subterranean explosion rocked Greenpoint, blowing manhole covers thirty feet into the sky. The blast was mostly forgotten until 1978, when the Coast

Guard discovered a massive oil slick on the East River. The slick turned out to be just the tip of the iceberg for the *largest oil spill of the twentieth century:* further exploration revealed between eighteen and thirty million gallons of petroleum spread across one hundred acres of soil and waterways in northeast Greenpoint.

I find plenty of information in the *Village Voice* and the *New York Times*, but outside the city it never got much coverage, a fact I find baffling considering that the spill was so much bigger than the *Exxon Valdez* accident in the late eighties. Why had no one heard about this? The *Village Voice* reports anecdotal evidence that Polish and Puerto Rican residents of Greenpoint suffer a higher than normal incidence of bone cancer and leukemia, but thus far no major news outlets have flocked to Greenpoint the way they did to Alaska after the *Exxon Valdez* spill. The articles in the *Voice* and elsewhere have a likely explanation: leukemia's provenance is difficult to trace. There were no oiled otters in Newtown Creek, as there were in the *Exxon Valdez* debacle. Greenpoint's losing team had no mascot.

In fairness to Exxon, the spill didn't happen all at once—along with the 1950 explosion, it resulted from decades of seepage and leaky pipes from a number of different companies, including BP and Chevron. But in an era before oil industry hacks took over the government, the Environmental Protection Agency actually went after Exxon. Though Exxon pointed the finger at Paragon Oil, in 1990 the state ordered Exxon Mobil, BP, and Chevron to clean up the site. By 2006 the New York State Department of Environmental Conservation reported that about nine million gallons had been recovered—less than half the total amount spilled up to thirty years ago.

Articles about Newtown Creek link me to other environmental concerns in the neighborhood, including Radiac, a nuclear waste storage facility just a few blocks from my apartment. We're also three blocks up from a coal-burning electricity plant. But every day more and more people my age and younger are moving in, buying apartments, and getting married and raising children. In 2003 and 2004 everyone's talking about how much the neighborhood has blown out and gentrified since its late-nineties art-culture apex, but they haven't seen shit yet: in May 2005 the whole neighborhood is rezoned from commercial to residential, effectively clearing the way for scores of forty-story, Miami Beach–style luxury condominiums all along the waterfront, from the site of the old Domino Sugar factory all the way to the oil-plumed shores of Greenpoint.

HAPPY THANKSGIVING

As planned, Karissa flies in to visit over the holiday weekend. When I pick her up at LaGuardia, I see immediately how much stress she's been under the past two months, her face broken out in angry blemishes, some of which look like they've been worried over in the airplane bathroom.

She buries her face in my chest when I hug her.

"I look horrible," she says.

"Sweetie, you know I think acne's sexy on a girl." It's true—on certain women a splash of acne across the cheeks is a total turn-on.

"You're seriously weird, you know that?" she says, looking up at me with overcast eyes.

Back in Brooklyn, we walk around on Bedford, people-watching and checking out all the new boutique stores cropping up in former hardware shops and defunct Polish delis.

"Everyone's so stylish," Karissa says, spotting a guy in a slim-fitting gray suit over a pair of chunky vintage high-tops, his hair done in the typical shag: long bangs that flip up on one side, hair down over the ears, collar-length in the back.

"Tell me about it," I say. "After a while you start to feel assaulted by fashion."

We stop at Brooklyn Industries, where Karissa admires an army-green winter coat with a faux fur hood. She really loves it, but her credit card is maxed—as is mine—and she's trying to save everything for the big move.

She wants to spend the rest of the night in my apartment, where no one can see her face, but I convince her to meet up with some friends at Pete's Candy Store, a bar located in a former confectionary shop.

We have some beers and listen to a folksinger from Ohio until about eight thirty, when my friend Jocko shows up. He's a big part of the reason I'm in New York; he helped me get the book contract with Soft Skull Press. He'd grown up in Colorado too, near Rocky

Mountain National Park. Learning to skate up in the mountains features prominently in his memoir *The Answer Is Never*. He also makes an aptly titled zine called *Elk*.

When I introduce him to Karissa, he asks what part of the state she's from.

"I live in the thrilling metropolis that is Fort Collins," she says.

"Fort Collins? I used to skate a vert ramp there back in the eighties," Jocko says.

"I skate in Fort Collins right now, in the—what is it that we're calling this era? The zeros?"

"A Colorado girl who skates. I could totally hug you right now."

"Well, why don't you?" Karissa says.

Jocko gives her a big bear hug, which genuinely thrills Karissa. It's something I love about her, the way she truly appreciates people, her authentic warmth. There's absolutely no pretense to her, a rare thing in this neck of Brooklyn.

The next day Karissa and I drive up to the Berkshires for Thanksgiving dinner with my mother's best friend and her family. We have a big kosher meal, and it's a little awkward, spending the holidays with someone else's family. Karissa hardly says a word.

After dinner, we finally get out for a walk, alone.

We slump around in the November drizzle, shuffling through fallen leaves, our hoods pulled up. I reach over to hold her hand, but she pulls away.

"I don't think I belong here," she says.

"They're old family friends," I say. "They're happy to have us."

"I'm talking about *here*. New York. That city; this whole coast."

"You can belong wherever you want."

"Maybe. The problem is *you* don't think I belong here, either."

There's a long pause. I look down at the sodden earth beneath my feet, unable to lift my eyes out of the mud and dead leaves to face Karissa.

"You don't want me to move here, do you?"

"Of course I do."

"Don't lie. You don't want me to come. I can feel it."

I finally look up. Her face seems hollowed out beneath her hood, two Rorschach semicircles of mascara beneath her eyes. I'm just as lost in these dark woods as she is; the only thing I know now is how to step on a city-bound train, regardless of how truly awful and alone it feels.

"I love you, but it doesn't seem like you're ready to move anytime soon, and I don't know how to make this work long distance. It just seems like we're at different places—"

"No," she says, cutting me off. "We're not *at different places in our lives*. You're in this fucking place, and I'm nowhere."

It's silent on our drive back to the city, save for the sound of rain lashing the windshield. The next two days are equally silent and awkward, until it's time for her to fly home. She goes on a shopping spree a couple hours before I take her to the airport.

She returns wearing the Brooklyn Industries army-green coat, the hood pulled up to cover her face.

I put my arms around her and she hugs me back weakly.

"I figured screw it," she says. "I might as well spend the money on something."

We get in my truck and she shows me the cookie she'd bought for herself at a bagel shop—a big sugar cookie with a smiley face made from yellow icing. It's quite possibly the saddest thing I've ever seen considering that she is, at the moment, weeping. Just before I drop her off at LaGuardia, she looks at me one last time.

"You know, you talk about loving everyone all the time like you're some sort of enlightened being," she says. "But the only reason you love anyone is to make yourself feel better."

SAMSARA

The next few weeks I spend as much time as possible skating the Autumn Bowl, trying to numb out the pain and guilt over Karissa. Sometimes I skate well and the sessions are transcendent, and I feel like I'm exactly where I need to be. Other times we're just a bunch of dudes carving circles inside a big brick cave on a Saturday night—moving really fast, straining ourselves, risking serious bodily harm from moment to moment, but never really getting anywhere.

ON THE PERILS OF THE ATLANTIC OCEAN AND ADULT-ONSET DIABETES

My breakup with Karissa is theoretical at first; we continue talking on the phone almost daily, even after five or six months, when the weather finally warms up. This makes it difficult for either of us to move forward, but the one bright spot of summer is that I finally have time to learn how to surf.

It starts out on Long Island, where I spend Memorial Day weekend at Kyle Grodin's beach house. Career-free and on the back side of thirty, Grodin spends his days surfing, skateboarding, and rock climbing; he's independently wealthy* and has what seems to me like the perfect life. His place is a rustic and comfortable Cape Cod with split cedar shingles, but it has a spooky, *Great Expectations* vibe to it. His father passed away when Kyle was still young, and then his mom died before he turned thirty. He was adopted, so losing his parents was doubly traumatic. He keeps up the house like a dusty museum, the living room lined in loud, seventies-era orange wallpaper with the words *peace* and *love* spelled out in silver foil. An old piano sits near the front entrance, covered with unused sheet music and knickknacks; the built-in bookshelves in the hallway are still filled with all his parents' old books.

That first night at his house, Grodin leads me into a spare bedroom off the kitchen, a place cluttered with more books belonging to his father, who was also a writer.

"This is the room where my dad died," Kyle says. "I thought since you're a writer, you might like to sleep in here," he says, his macabre sense of humor cranked all the way up.

---

* I once followed Kyle into a heavily air-conditioned ATM booth, where he withdrew a tall stack of twenties, then tossed them all around like confetti—a hilarious, giddy moment, like being inside one of those state-lottery globes where it snows money.

While I'm getting ready for bed, I realize I forgot my contact lens solution. Kyle takes me upstairs, to his bathroom, where he still keeps some of his parents' personal effects, including several boxes of saline. "Here," Kyle says, handing me a bottle of Opti-Free with a 1995 price tag, "use all you want."

Fortunately, Kyle doesn't live alone. He shares the house with his fiancée, Anka, and a couple roommates, including a self-admitted boozehound named Scott Dio. I bump into Scott down in the kitchen, just before he heads out to the bars.

"Do you like my vest?" he asks, pointing both index fingers at the khaki, multi-mesh-pocketed affair.

"It's great," I say. "What is it, a fishing vest?"

"No sir. This here is a *beer* vest." Without further explanation, he invites me out for drinks, then calls me a pussy when I decline.

"What are you going to do, hang around here with my tubby roommate?" Scott says, motioning upstairs, toward Kyle's room.

"Actually, I'm just going to bed."

"Okay, good night, sleep tight. You *pussy*."

Later, when Kyle comes down for a nighttime snack—half a box of Honey Nut Cheerios—I bring up my conversation with Scott.

"Pay no attention to that fat ass," Kyle says, mouth full of cereal. "He still owes me two months' rent. I'm about to kick him out of this dirty flophouse."

On our way to the skatepark the next afternoon, we battle the notorious Hamptons traffic. Fueled by refined sugar and caffeine, Grodin explodes into constant fits of road rage; they abate only during moments when he ogles young, well-heeled Manhattanite tourists, like the Uggs boot–wearing teenager who jaywalks in front of us on her way to the East Hampton Häagen-Dazs.

"You know what I'd do with that girl right there?" he says.

"Oh Jesus, Grodin. She's like *fifteen*."

"Yeah, she is a little old for my tastes. But I'd still like to buy her a nice big chocolate ice cream cake," he says, checking out her ass in the rearview.

"Let me guess what you'd do with it." In Kyle's favorite fantasy tableau, he violates the object of his affections with various dessert items—cherry cobblers, upside-down pineapple cakes, all manner of fresh fruit, entire tubs of cake frosting, Hostess Ding Dongs.

"Oh yeah," he says, "I'd cram that whole cake right up her crack."

I bury my face in my hands, a little nauseated even though I've been hearing about his perverted dessert fantasies for years. It's all just talk, of course, except for his love of sweets. He could easily devour an entire ice cream cake in a couple sittings, just like I've witnessed him eat a whole pumpkin pie, or a half dozen doughnuts, or two packages of jelly-filled Dutch cookies dipped in dark chocolate. The next morning, at a Kiwanis club community pancake feed in Amagansett, he eats seventeen flapjacks.

"I think I could do five more," he says, relishing his last pancake. "But I want to skate later."

"What this place needs is a vomitorium," I say, feeling bloated even after my relatively meager seven pancakes.

"I feel great," he says, rubbing and slapping his distended, deeply suntanned belly. It looks like a twenty-pound Thanksgiving turkey, lavishly basted and oven-browned. "This is actually an improvement on the breakfast I ate yesterday. Half a box of Fruity Pebbles, half a pound of peanut M&M's, and a two-liter bottle of Pepsi."

Kyle is the very definition of an emotional eater. A mutual friend remembers how, feeling terribly sad for him just after his mother's death, she'd asked if there was anything in the world he needed. *Pizza,* he'd replied, grinning impishly. She thought there was something childlike and innocent about it, until the delivery pizza arrived and Kyle began gorging himself—folding two slices together and shoveling them down—clearly his way of dealing with grief. On more than one occasion I've heard Kyle make off-the-cuff remarks about killing himself with food.

"Grodin, have you ever heard of adult-onset diabetes?" I ask.

"Why, you think I'm gonna get it?"

"You're like the ultimate candidate," I say. "In one day you dump more refined sugar into your bloodstream than most people do in a month. Keep it up and you'll have to inject yourself with insulin every day."

He shrugs. Licks some maple syrup off his finger. "Ah, fuck it. Let's go surfing."

Grodin takes me out to a beach break called Wiborgs, where he outfits me with a full wetsuit and his yellow nine-foot-five longboard. I follow him reluctantly into the cold, churning Atlantic, remembering my days as a skinny twelve-year-old in San Diego, before I had the sense to duck under the waves, when I got constantly worked over, held under, tossed around, and washed up onto the beach, choking for breath and swearing never again. On my thirteenth birthday, my dad bought me a six-foot fluorescent green surfboard and a wetsuit, then sent me out by myself on a stormy day at La Jolla Shores. I hadn't even made it out into the lineup when I got nailed by a big guy on a ten-foot longboard. His massive single-fin slashed the top of my thigh, knifing through neoprene into my flesh, the blow so severe it temporarily paralyzed my entire left leg, leaving a permanent dent in my thigh. The apologetic longboarder picked me up and carried me out of the water, dripping and limp, like a reverse baptism. Shortly afterward we moved inland, where I took up skateboarding, and despite the constant road rash and sprained ankles, found it much safer than surfing.

"Get out here in the lineup," Grodin yells, beckoning with his left hand. I flop my way through the shallows, trying to heft the huge board up and over neck-high ramparts of whitewater while staying clear of incoming surfers. Farther out in the bigger swells, I duck backward under a few breakers and pull the board over my head as Kyle had instructed.

"Why you paddling like that?" Grodin says when I finally reach him, panting and sputtering, my arm muscles cramping after ten minutes in the water. "Don't let your legs hang off the side of the board. You look like a little girl on a pony."

By the time I manage the proper position, Grodin has already caught a wave in, leaving me bobbing around by myself out in the open ocean, clueless and scared. I watch from behind as he drops into the peak and throws his arms up in the air like a referee signaling a touchdown, the same thing he does sometimes after landing a difficult trick on a skate ramp. He catches five or six waves while I flail around, paddling my heart out with zero results. Fortunately, he comes back out and explains what I'm doing wrong.

"You'll never catch anything this far out," he says, a hint of genuine patience in his voice now. "You have to come farther inside where the waves are actually walling up. And you have to paddle at the same speed as the wave or you'll never—" Spotting another promising wave, he breaks off midsentence and rides it all the way in to the shore, where he bellies up on the beach to sleep off the pancakes.

Determined to catch at least one ride, I stay out in the water, reluctantly coming closer in to the shore where they're breaking at their heaviest, most dynamic point. What Kyle makes look easy and sometimes even graceful is actually one of the most difficult things in the world, even for a lifelong skateboarder. Imagine crossing a deep, swollen river on the back of an unbroken horse. Now imagine trying to stand up in the saddle. The muscles in my arms are completely spent, feeling almost as sore and paralyzed as my thigh after getting bashed by the longboarder back when I was thirteen.

Finally, after twenty minutes of flailing, I catch a small wave, wobble my way to my feet, and ride it for a solid six seconds or more, licking salt spray off my lips and totally enjoying the feeling of skimming across the surface. I jump off in the shallows, splash in to shore, and sit down next to Kyle, feeling triumphant as I peel off the wetsuit.

"Broseph," he says. "You finally caught one."

"Yeah, it felt awesome."

"Huh," he says, smirking.

"What?"

"Your stance was so wide, I thought you were about to take a shit or something."

"Oh," I say, deflated by the realization that my stance had been about equal to a snowboarder's circa 1993—a wide-legged, butt-out style commonly known in surfing and skateboarding as *stinkbug*.

"But other than that," Kyle says, "you looked pretty good."

"Yeah?"

"Sure. But if I were you, I'd stick to skateboarding."

That afternoon we barbecue with Kyle's future in-laws, an amiable older couple who'd grown up on neighboring farms in rural Poland. They cook us traditional Polish food, grilled kielbasa and mashed potatoes and sautéed spinach, and we all eat together on the back porch in the late-day light, watching Kyle's little dog chase rosy-headed finches around in the big backyard, the smell of citronella candles mingling with the salt tang of the ocean. Ravenous after hours of physical exertion in the sea, I put down two or three kielbasas, a giant helping of mashed potatoes, and a couple imported Polish beers. For dessert Kyle and I polish off an entire apple strudel. It's the most relaxed I've felt since moving to the city a year earlier, and I'm discovering it's not just the surfing I love—regardless of what a hopeless kook I am—but also the blissed-out feeling it gives me, this slow, quiet-minded serenity that eludes me in Brooklyn. I don't know what to name it at the time, but I'm in the early stages of what my roommates will soon come to refer to, ironically, as "stoke stroke," a nearly insatiable obsession with surfing and the ocean.

SURMISES ON THE ORIGINS OF SURFING

> The author has not given his effort here the benefit of knowing
> whether it is history, autobiography, gazetteer, or fantasy.
>
> ～ FROM A *New York Globe* REVIEW OF *Moby-Dick*, 1851

As with any noble pursuit, debate exists over the true historical origins of surfing. Most claim that the earliest form of surf riding—most likely bodysurfing, or riding in primitive canoes—originated in Polynesia, thousands of years ago. Some Peruvians claim that ancient South American fishermen recreated on "surf planks" as far back as 2000 BCE. The theory is that these planks originally served as transport between the shore and fishing boats and vice versa, and one day some sure-footed fisherman stood up on his plank, thus transforming his commute into sport. My personal theory is that surfing, like the erection of pyramids in places as disparate as ancient Egypt and pre-Columbian South America, may have originated simultaneously and synchronistically in different parts of the world. But there's something disingenuous about even this idea, very similar to the notion—still popular in pockets of Brooklyn—that Italian-born Christopher Columbus discovered America. The true originators of surfing are creatures like the dolphin, known by surfers around the world to actually catch waves and ride them with what can only be described as bliss, and that have been doing so for millions of years, since well before the dawn of humankind.

Still, the topic at hand is human surfing, meaning surfing on boards, and the most common theory claims that the pursuit developed in the South Seas. Surfing migrated from Polynesia to Indonesia, the Marquesas, Tahiti, and eventually Hawaii. Hawaii is the undisputed wellspring of modern surfing, the place where it became known as the Sport of Kings. Hawaiians learned to ride standing up well over a thousand years ago. Hawaiian kings surfed to display their physical prowess; they rode special boards called *olo*. Since *olo* boards were fashioned from solid balsa or a tree called the *williwilli*, and often reached eighteen to twenty-five feet in length, it took three or more underlings to launch from shore. While the kings postured on their giant logs, the commoners rode much shorter boards, known as *alaia*. As Nat Young says in his *History of Surfing,* the commoners often know best, as anything above ten feet is unwieldy, while the *alaia* boards were much more maneuverable.

In Hawaii, the sea was and is believed to have its own persona, its own distinct emotions. The ancient Hawaiians used kahunas to pray for good surf. The kahunas performed ritual dances and chants, hoping to please the sea and conjure up good waves. Surfing was an integral part of Hawaiian spiritual life; the act of surfing was imbued with an ecstatic, even supernatural quality. When the waves were up, female surfers stripped off their clothes and ran into the ocean; for them surfing was a form of baptism—a way to wash away ills, to be renewed and connected to life through the infinite sea. With so many naked bodies in the undulating ocean, surfing was also integral to the act of courtship, which often took place right out in the lineup.

But like any human activity, surfing wasn't free from politics. Only royalty had access to certain beaches and better-crafted surfboards. Members of the elite class also used surfing as a form of gambling, in which reputations, money, and even marriages were at stake.

The arrival of the British explorer Captain Cook in Hawaii in 1778 bore ill portents for the culture of surfing. Cook himself was impressed with surfing and wrote eloquently about it in his journals. But his written descriptions of naked "heathens" frolicking in the surf caught the attention of European missionaries, who subsequently flocked to Hawaii to "redeem" the natives. These missionaries were deeply offended by Hawaiians' placement of spiritual significance on an activity involving nudity. Countless hours of unfettered enjoyment in the ocean was also an affront to the Protestant work ethic. As a result, surfing was actually banned in Hawaii for nearly a century. On the heels of maltreatment and heavy taxation by their native rulers, the dismantling of native culture was a devastating blow for the Hawaiians, and these life-sustaining activities went almost completely dormant. Fortunately, even as the native population dwindled, a few dissidents kept surfing alive, a fact proven by documentarians like Mark Twain, who wrote about the act in the late 1860s.

Melville also has a place in the written history of surfing and the culture of the South Seas and Hawaii. In his book *Typee,* he narrates his desertion of a whaling ship and the months he spent in hiding with the Polynesian Typee tribe. Melville was always an anticolonialist at heart; he despised Christian missionaries and their desire to "snivilize" native peoples. He revered the Typees' laid-back lifestyle, their constant napping, their lack of taboos, the way they lived in balance with nature, free from modern life's preoccupations and traps. But he never completely shed certain Western biases: he eventually fled the Typees for fear of being cannibalized. On his way back to the States in 1843, he stopped off in Hawaii. If Melville witnessed any surfing in Hawaii he fails to mention it in *Typee,* as he does in his 1849 book *Mardi,* where he gives an impassioned account of surf-riding in Tahiti: "An expert swimmer shifts his position on his plank; now half striding it; and anon, like a rider in the ring, poising himself upright in the scud, coming on like a man in the air. At last, all is lost in scud and vapor, as the overgrown billow bursts like a bomb."

It makes sense that Melville witnessed no surfing in Hawaii, as he arrived just three years after the first missionaries' arrival, on the heels of Captain Cook. The influence of the Western traders and their booze and firearms had already weakened traditional religion and customs; the missionaries capitalized on this. They were apparently enabled by Kamehameha III, who ruled from 1825 to 1854, and whom Melville criticized for handing over his kingdom to his American adviser and minister G. P. Judd, in what many consider America's first conquest in a long line of imperial actions.

Melville was very much on the side of the natives—making him pro-surfing by default; his open defiance of the missionaries apparently raised Judd's hackles. Fearing he might be discovered as a deserter from whaling ships like the *Acushnet* and the *Lucy-Ann,* Melville left his job as a bookkeeper and fled the islands.

BEACH 90TH

Why did the poor poet of Tennessee, upon suddenly
receiving two handfuls of silver, deliberate whether to buy
him a coat, which he sadly needed, or invest his money in a
pedestrian trip to Rockaway Beach?

~ HERMAN MELVILLE, *Moby-Dick*

In August, my roommates and I throw a small party at Rockaway Beach, in Queens, to celebrate my birthday. Asa brings a couple surfboards; some other partygoers invite their friend Dawn, whom I meet for the first time. Three solid weekends of paddling out on Long Island pay off, as I catch ride after ride on Asa's nine-six longboard. Totally hooked, I join Dawn on a walk to the local surf shop to buy some wax and end up leaving with a brand-new board and a $600 hole in my wallet. Later that evening, Asa, Dawn, and I all catch a wave together, ride it in toward shore, where the sun's setting over the city instead of the sea—a fact of East Coast life that always leaves me disoriented. But the skies are beautiful nonetheless, all tagged up with looping swirls of chemical pastels. From that moment on, Rockaway becomes my new stomping ground, Asa and Dawn my constant surfing companions.

Whereas Wiborgs and other Long Island beaches are semipristine retreats from the world, Rockaway is arguably the most urbanized beach in the country. Originally a playground for Manhattan's elite, it had a private train line, lavish amusement parks, and opulent mansions.

But the cruel economic tides of the late 1960s and the 1970s swept the poor into the city's increasingly brackish outer boroughs. Several dozen blocky, utilitarian housing projects sprung up on Rockaway's shores, like a bulky, crumbling seawall spanning sixty city blocks. To this day, parts of Rockaway are considered among New York's worst neighborhoods. Among those willing to surf Rockaway, rumors persist of burglarized cars, muggings, surfers who tape knives to the bottom of their boards.

Yet, like so many areas of Brooklyn and Queens, Rockaway is a neighborhood in flux. Like the classic Ramones song and the Rockaway reference in *Moby-Dick,* the Rockaway I discover is a destination worthy of hitchhiking or the squandering of a day's wages. Fronted by a big plaster and tile sculpture of a cartoonish gray whale, a wide, wood-planked boardwalk skirts the coastline. The beach itself is fairly narrow even at low tide, but covered in warm, inviting sand, of a grain similar to that found in Florida or California, though more likely littered with chunks of concrete and brick, used syringes, spent .22 shell casings.

Off on the glimmering, gun-metal horizon sit ubiquitous cargo ships and oil tankers; closer to shore the sea is partitioned by a series of rocky human-made jetties—the space in between bulwarks on Ninetieth Street having just two years before been designated by the city of New York as an official surfing beach. On any given summer day, this narrow break teems with surfers of all stripes: Puerto Rican guys on shortboards, crusty and toothless old-school rippers in crash helmets, Wall Street players on $3,000 custom Takayama longboards, other tattooed skateboarders like me seeking shelter from the heat, NYU coeds on rented soft-tops, talented local kids with Afros, Japanese scenesters with expensive haircuts, and local thirtysomethings who look like edgier, scarred-up versions of Patagonia surf catalog models. There are too many people battling for limited resources, as there are everywhere else in the city, but even so the Rockaway vibe is generally mellow and accommodating to beginners. Everyone's just happy to be out of the city, floating in cool salt water that's balm after a week of sultry, concrete heat. The only reminders that we live in New York City are the housing projects and the clanking of the elevated A train in the distance.

THE STROKE

I increasingly gravitate to the beach, spending long afternoons out at Rockaway, or weekends camping in Kyle's backyard, rising at dawn to check the waves. In the city I'm plagued by worry and regrets, credit card bills, loneliness, but these all fall away out in the water at Rockaway, where, at dusk, schools of tiny fish flash beneath the surface, then make what seem to me miraculous leaps above the water, tens of hundreds of them, arcing over the rippled gray glaze of the Atlantic before splashing back in like silver rain. Out here in the ocean, on my surfboard, I'm totally in the moment, out of my head and in my body—*meditation and water are wedded for ever.*

My new aquaphiliac addiction spreads around my household. Not long after I buy my surfboard, Natalie and Paul pick up their own. They even buy a used Volvo wagon, purchased from an ex-Californian and dubbed the Surfmobile, with room for boards in the back and a little plastic hula girl on a surfboard mounted to the dash.

During the warmer months in the city I have a Saturday ritual: wake up early, step into flip-flops, and ride my bike over to Atlas coffee shop, where I spend four or five hours drinking tea and working on my novel. Because this novel is, to my increasing distress, basically going nowhere, I do my best not to zone out on the watery parts of the world atlas hanging on the café wall. During frequent breaks I check the surf report on my laptop, and maybe call Asa to see if he's down for a beach run. In the afternoon I head back and visit with Paul in his studio while he works on a painting. As Paul finishes up, I visit our next-door neighbors, Jill and Luke, an Australian couple who work as photographers for *Teen Vogue*. Luke grew up surfing, and will only go out when the waves are overhead, but he's always up for checking the surf report or watching YouTube surfing clips on his giant Mac monitor.

Once Paul cleans his brushes, we pack the boards in my truck or the Surfmobile and drive out to Rockaway for a late-afternoon session. Like me, Paul grew up skateboarding, so he's a quick study. During the height of summer, he surfs hard for several weekends straight, until he has a bout of sharp chest pain that keeps him out of the water. When the pain doesn't subside after a couple days, he worries that maybe he's having heart or lung trouble, possibly a result of his daily pack of Parliaments. One morning it's so bad he thinks he might be having a heart attack, so Natalie and I rush him to the hospital.

The ER doc gives him a thorough exam, runs an EKG. "Have you been swimming a lot lately?" he asks.

"Not really," Paul says. "I've been surfing every weekend, though."

"That would do it," the doctor says. "There's nothing wrong with you internally; it looks like you just overexerted your chest muscles."

"Stoke stroke strikes again," Natalie says.

Then, on the way home from the hospital, she begs Paul to take her to the beach that evening.

"Who's the one with stoke stroke now?" he says, but agrees on a beach run, even though the doctor suggested staying off his board for two weeks.

That evening Natalie stays out even longer than I do. She struggles to get her long legs beneath her, but she seems perfectly content— thrilled even—to ride waves in on her stomach. Determined to get her upright, Paul and I stand shirtless and barefoot in the shallows, the glassy sand reflecting a brick-red sunset. We cheer her on, over and over, until she finally stands up and rides one in, dripping wet and beaming.

THE DUKE

Fortunately for Hawaii and the world, there was a great re-surgence of surfing in the early 1900s, led largely by Duke P. Kahanamoku, the undisputed Father of Surfing. The Duke grew up beachside at Waikiki and was the essence of a waterman—an excellent swimmer, fisherman, sailor, and lifeguard. According to surfer Tom Blake, "His exceptionally fine massive leg development does not come from riding in autos, but plowing through the sand barefooted, in his youth. His well-muscled shoulders and arms came from the surfboard work. . . . Duke religiously avoids arousing any-one's ill will towards him; he is kind, tolerant with all and is well thought of by his fellows." Early in his career, Duke rode sixteen-foot-long, 116-pound finless surfboards made from redwood or Hawaiian koa (the same type of wood used in the manufacture of authentic Hawaiian ukuleles). In 1912 he traveled to the Olympics in Stockholm, Sweden. Accustomed to swim-ming in the open ocean, he learned to flip turn off the walls of a pool just weeks be-fore the competition. Even so, he hand-ily won the gold medal in the 100-meter freestyle.

In the summer of 1912, on the way back from winning the Olympic gold, Duke Kahanamoku gave a swimming demonstration at Far Rockaway. Dis-agreement persists over whether or not he also surfed Rockaway. According to surf/skate historian C. R. Stecyk, when someone asked him what he thought of the waves on Long Island, the Duke said

What waves? I like to think he did surf, making Rockaway one of the very first mainland American spots to be ridden, nearly a hundred years ago, decades before the development of California breaks like Malibu or Rincon. What we know for certain is that he imbued the place with the aloha spirit, a spirit that's still very much alive at Rockaway today. In 1990 a street near Rockaway Boulevard was rechristened in his honor: Duke Kahanamoku Way. And in a 2007 edition of the *Surfer's Journal,* writer Andrew Kid documents his midwinter visit to Rockaway, where he discovers surprisingly nice waves and deserted lineups, and describes the feeling he gets there as *very Duke.*

THE PIT

Along with the stoke stroke, I'm plagued by another ailment more common to New Yorkers: lack of cash flow. As rent payments devour my savings and increase my credit card debt, I become a little desperate, in the way only freelance writers can. So when my boss offers to make me his full-time assistant, I jump at the opportunity for steady income and benefits.

Plus, he's one of the most authentically nice bosses imaginable—a rare find in Manhattan's business district.

But my first morning of full-time work, a fortysomething co-worker from New Jersey walks past my cubicle toward her own windowless office, where she spends her days editing romance and thrillers.

"Congrats on the new job," she says. "And welcome to wage slavery."

That weekend, out at the beach with an old friend from Colorado, he tells me what I increasingly know to be true, especially for a motion-obsessed person like myself: that New York is filled with many traps.

And then a few weeks later, the same coworker who gave me such a hearty welcome mentions something about me being in *the Pit*.

"What do you mean, 'the Pit'?" I ask.

"Oh no," she says. "You're in the Pit and you don't even know it."

She goes on to explain that the Pit is the configuration of low-walled cubicles at the center of the editorial department, the collection of shabby desks and PCs where all the freelancers and editorial assistants toil.

"It's called the Pit because there are no windows," she says. "No privacy. Nothing but the stench of rotting careers. I hope you make it out alive."

THE MIDLAND OILING MUSEUM

> For God's sake, be economical with your lamps and candles!
> not a gallon you burn, but at least one drop of man's blood
> was spilled for it.
>
> ~ HERMAN MELVILLE, *Moby-Dick*

The more time I spend in the Pit, the more my preoccupation with the ocean deepens, as does my obsession with *Moby-Dick*—the story of Ishmael, another disgruntled young New Yorker with a deep spiritual longing for the sea. One weekend when the waves are bad, I make a trip north to Arrowhead, the Melville family estate in the Berkshires, the place where Herman relocated his family from New York City and wrote *Moby-Dick,* partly on the encouragement of his new country neighbor and spiritual mentor, Nathaniel Hawthorne.

From the window of Melville's second-floor study, you can see a flat, white, whale-shaped rock bluff to the north, the fabled Mount Greylock from which he drew inspiration for his literary leviathan. It was at Arrowhead that Melville completed his masterwork and, free from the confinements of the city, lived thirteen years in relative contentment. In a letter to a friend, Melville expressed his disdain for Manhattan life: "What are you doing there, My Beloved, among the bricks and cobblestone *boulders?* . . . For heaven's sake, come out from among those Hittites and Hodites—give up mortar for ever."

But financial struggle plagued Melville's writing career—*Moby-Dick* earned the author less than $600 in his lifetime. On the knife-edge of insolvency, he sold Arrowhead to his brother, moved his family back to the city, and took a job as a customs clerk. Confined to a desk near the docks for the next twenty years, the same man who sailed the world and produced one of the greatest novels ever written now toiled six days a week at four dollars a day, with only two weeks off a year—the exact amount of vacation time I'm allotted by my publishing company 150 years later. Battling traffic on the way back to the city on a Sunday before a long, dull workweek in the Pit, I can almost feel him in the car with me, riding shotgun, silent and sullen—sick with his own failure—especially in the urban waste- land that is the eastbound turnpike through Yonkers and the South Bronx.

Weeks later, on a solo surfing trip up to Cape Cod, I make a similar pilgrimage to the New Bedford Whaling Museum, a fascinating repository of nineteenth-century maritime artwork, scrimshaw, har- poons, and various whaling implements, plus a half-scale re-creation of a successful whaling ship, the *Lagoda*. The museum makes con- crete much of what I've gleaned about the historic whaling industry from reading and rereading *Moby-Dick*. What most intrigues me— but is given somewhat short shrift by the museum—is the indus- try's gross unsustainability. In two or three hundred years, U.S. whaling corporations fished out entire oceans and severely depleted the global whale population, cutting a critical lifeline for many in- digenous peoples, who had harvested whales sustainably for two thousand years or more. Whereas native peoples in Asia and the Americas had a deep reverence for the whale, nineteenth-century Americans had a more entrepreneurial attitude toward whaling. After being tapped for spermaceti oil and ambergris and stripped of blub- ber, immense sperm whale carcasses were dumped unceremoni- ously back into the sea. Baleen from right whales was used to make hoop skirts and corsets (also known as "whalebone prisons"); am- bergris was a key ingredient in the production of perfume, the same substance that Melville's contemporary Walt Whitman "knew and loved," but ultimately considered a useless vanity.

Aside from indulging American superficiality, by and large the most profitable aspect of the whale was oil—whaling was, in fact, the original "Big Oil" industry. In 1853, just two years after the publica- tion of *Moby-Dick,* the industry had its most successful season: eight thousand kills rendered hundreds of thousands of barrels of oil and netted $11 million. Spermaceti was used as a clean, clear-burning, Benjamin Franklin–endorsed lamp oil and illuminant, providing light for the developed world. And like its dirty, crude oil descendant, whale oil lubricated the furious machinery of the industrial revolution. In *Call Me Ishmael,* Charles Olson writes, "So if you want to know why Melville nailed us in *Moby-Dick,* consider whaling. Consider whaling as FRONTIER, and INDUSTRY. A product wanted, men got it: big business. The Pacific as sweatshop . . . the whaleship as factory, the whaleboat the precision instrument."

As America grew, so did the demand for whale oil, but soon demand outpaced supply. As whale populations dwindled—as we reached a kind of nineteenth-century Peak Whale—voyages to distant seas like the South Pacific and even the Arctic became necessary. The New Bedford museum evokes this era with a series of haunting, sublime paintings of whaling ships dwarfed by icebergs. Two-year voyages became the norm, as did the increasingly dehumanizing and dangerous aspects of life aboard a whaler. In the mid-1800s close to one-third of all American whaling hands deserted their ships—just as Melville abandoned the *Acushnet.* Another death knell for the industry was the discovery of petroleum near Titusville, Pennsylvania, during the late 1850s. Originally developed as a cheaper replacement for whale oil, petroleum soon inundated the modern world, its omnipresence fueling the rise of the automobile, petrochemicals, and plastics.*

My next stop at the Whaling Museum is the auditorium, where an educational film called "The City That Lit the World" plays on a constant loop. Though it occasionally references *Moby-Dick,* the film is narrated in an unironic tone of nostalgia and patriotism, as if ridding the ocean of whales was a national pastime of which every red-blooded American should be proud. And while largely attributing the demise of whaling to the discovery of petroleum, without men-

---

* Through his cold-blooded exploitation of the petroleum industry, monopolist John D. Rockefeller became the nation's first billionaire. His company Standard Oil was often portrayed in the popular media not as a whale but as a giant octopus, with its tentacles wrapped around every aspect of American life and labor. Standard Oil still exists today, largely in the form of subsidiaries such as Exxon and Chevron—the main culprits behind the Greenpoint oil spill.

tioning overfishing, the film fails to make any spiritual links between the two unsustainable industries—to point out what seems obvious to me: that history is repeating itself.

As I wander the small deck of the *Lagoda,* wondering how it compared in size and shape to Melville's *Pequod,* I can't help but imagine our current national leader and his vice president as a pair of deranged Ahabs, forcefully steering the American military into the dangerous waters of Iraq—an ill-conceived detour from our original mission. It's a depressing vision, until I remember that in the end, Ahab's own madness is the source of his undoing, in a watery demise that makes Ophelia's seem painless—a grim allegory of the way nature roots out hubris.

Maybe someday, I hope, I might bring my own children to a Texas attraction called the Midland Oiling Museum, where visitors will marvel at display cases lined with hundreds of old dipsticks, dirty oil filters, cans of Pennzoil and Valvoline. The larger rooms will contain antiquated oil derricks, photos of defunct refineries, well-preserved gas station pumps, lovingly restored Cadillac Escalades, and a half scale model of the *Exxon Valdez.* All of this will be presided over by large painted portraits of the long-deposed Bush dynasty, Dick Cheney, and members of the Saudi oil cartel, edged with gilded frames and tastefully illuminated by recessed lighting. We will all stand around smiling, pointing, feigning interest while patronizing curators wax nostalgic about the relatively short lifespan of such a wasteful, violent, environmentally toxic, yet wholeheartedly American enterprise.

THE SERMON (ALL SOULS)

> I say, we good Presbyterian Christians should be charitable
> in these things, and not fancy ourselves so vastly superior to
> other mortals. . . . Heaven have mercy on us all—Presbyterians
> and Pagans alike—for we are all somehow dreadfully cracked
> about the head, and sadly need mending.
>
> ~ HERMAN MELVILLE, *Moby-Dick*

I read somewhere that if you mention God at a Manhattan dinner
party you'll silence the room; mention God twice and you'll never
be invited back.

It's for this reason—plus the fact that my roommates are non-
religious and suspicious of anyone they think might be in a cult—that
I sneak quietly out of my apartment on a Sunday morning. Walking
past Neckface graffiti, children's clothing stores stocked with infant-
sized AC/DC T-shirts, record shops, and trendy pan-Asian restaurants, it's a safe bet that of all my fashionable Brooklyn brethren, I'm
the only one headed for church. The streets are mostly deserted, save
for a few wasted-looking souls in tight jeans and leather jackets, just
now heading home from strangers' beds or coked-out afterparties on
the Lower East Side.

My secret morning sojourn is partly research-based: I'm headed
for All Souls Unitarian, where Melville and his family were members. Exiting the number 4 train at Eighty-Second after a long ride, I
walk a few blocks north and find the old stone church, adorned with
a regal purple banner above a wide staircase. As I pass through the
corner entrance, a cordial volunteer offers me a service pamphlet.
The main chapel's vaulted white ceiling soars high above me, the
whole room spartan and clean and bright. I take a seat and read the
pamphlet, which explains that Unitarian tradition calls for transparent windows rather than stained glass, to "let the Light in."

From my solitary back-row seat, I check out the artwork hanging
above the altar. A large, three-dimensional piece made from hun-

dreds of intertwining strings, it apparently represents the unity and interconnectedness of all things, like a more elaborate version of the cross-shaped "God eye" I made from popsicle sticks and orange yarn back in Sunday school. The shape of this Unitarian "God eye" is vaguely reminiscent of a Christian cross, but the overall effect is ambiguous—an apt symbol for the Unitarians' ambivalence about Jesus and the Christian faith.

I feel a little awkward about being here—I'm one of the few single, youngish people in the room—but flipping through a Unitarian hymnal gives me some encouragement. Many of the hymns are adaptations of writings from the Tao Te Ching and the Bhagavad Gita, Buddhist chants, Native American stories, and two of my favorite transcendental writers, Ralph Waldo Emerson and Henry David Thoreau, both famous Unitarians. I like the idea of this inclusive, literary brand of worship, especially since it involved Melville, who isn't easily classified as a Unitarian or Transcendentalist, but nonetheless was concerned with the history and future of Christianity.

Though Melville's connection to Unitarianism is questionable (Melville scholar Herschel Walker claims that Melville "hated Unitarianism" and only attended to appease his wife), his hope for a more universal, inclusive approach to religion is written all over *Moby-Dick*. It's evident in Ishmael's embracing of the tattooed pagan Queequeg, and also in his knowledge of Eastern ideas like meditation. It's likely that Melville, like his Berkshire neighbors Henry Wadsworth Longfellow and Dr. Oliver Wendell Holmes, drew from his knowledge of mystical Asian texts like the Tao Te Ching and the Bhagavad Gita, and was moved by the description and actual practice of meditation. And like Emerson and Thoreau, Melville cited the fourteenth-century Sufi poet Hafiz as an influence. Like other famous ecstatics—Rumi, Ramakrishna, and Saint Francis—Hafiz believed that all individuals contain a spark of the divine: "You are a divine elephant with amnesia / Trying to live in an ant / Hole. / Sweetheart, O sweetheart / You are God in / Drag!" In letters to Nathaniel Hawthorne, after reading the older writer's positive response to *Moby-Dick*, Melville evokes similar feelings of mystic union: "I felt pantheistic then—your heart beat in my ribs and mine in yours, and both in God's. A sense of unspeakable security is in me this moment, on account of your having understood the book . . . I feel that the Godhead is broken up like the bread at the Supper, and that we are the pieces."

A young minister named Galen Guengerich leads the Sunday service at All Souls Unitarian. Dressed in a billowy maroon robe that seems straight out of a Harvard commencement ceremony, he looks handsome, pedigreed, slightly reserved but altogether kind, like a pious member of the Kennedy family. Given his appearance, it comes as a surprise that his service centers around the lyrics from a recent Green Day hit, a melodramatic ballad of urban alienation conveyed via the familiar trope of a solitary, defeated soul walking down Hollywood's broken-dream boulevards. I first heard it playing at the deli counter of the Midtown skyscraper where I work, and it's annoying in the way most Green Day songs are, but now that I'm living a somewhat isolated life in a shadowy leviathan of a city, I can relate to the sense of loneliness the song evokes. The point of Guengerich's talk is that in a community like All Souls, you don't have to go it alone, that you can instead walk together with others on a spiritual journey, connected and supported, with life's dark paths illuminated by collective grace. The lecture is polished and sincere, and I appreciate his attempt to reach out to a younger crowd, however transparent the effort. I've never much liked Green Day, especially compared to my favorite hardcore punk bands like Minor Threat, Fugazi, or Hot Snakes. But looking around the room at mostly gray heads, I have to give Guengerich props for risking this pop-culture reference. Of the few young people in attendance, I imagine most are probably more familiar with Coldplay or even Vivaldi than with Green Day. It's a safe bet that I'm the only one in the room with remotely punk rock roots: the only one with multiple tattoos, or who's seen Fugazi live from the front row of a Wyoming cowboy bar, or who's skated Burnside solo on a rainy Christmas Eve.

And although it doesn't match up with my current situation in

New York, I have in the past experienced the kind of spiritual community and connection Guengerich spoke about. In college I was fortunate to have close friends, but I always felt like something was missing, that endless conversations about Sonic Youth, the Pixies, and *Twin Peaks* reruns were stimulating and fun, but that some essential part of myself wasn't getting the sustenance it needed. During my early twenties, while my friends were starting indie bands and taking summer internships at Sony records, I went off for weeks and sometimes months at a time into the Colorado wilderness, where I experimented with meditation, read *Siddhartha, Man and His Symbols* by Carl Jung, the Tao Te Ching, *Leaves of Grass*. In my mid-twenties, I turned back to skateboarding, making pilgrimages to empty swimming pools and Burnside skatepark with a clearly religious devotion.

From age nineteen to twenty-nine, I had a tumultuous, on-again off-again relationship with a woman named Nicole. Lying in bed one night the summer before our final breakup, she stated nonchalantly that she didn't believe in God. No big shock there—I certainly didn't believe in the kind of God that many Christians do: a gray-bearded curmudgeon imposing judgment on some and doling out favors to others. That all seemed like a fairy tale, and yet I wasn't ready to say with ultimate finality that I didn't believe. I'd spent too much time reading Joseph Campbell, who quoted Meister Eckhart: "The ultimate and highest leave-taking is leaving God for God, leaving your notion of God for an experience of that which transcends all notions." I wasn't ready to give up on Albert Einstein's concept of a universal, mysterious God, or Martin Luther King's kindhearted, forgiving God, or on the prayers of the famous religious ecologist, Saint Francis: "Lord, make me an instrument of thy peace." Maybe I was a little like Melville, who, according to Hawthorne, could "neither believe, nor be comfortable in his unbelief."

After the final dissolution of my ten-year relationship with Nicole—which had serious flaws other than the religious kind—I went through a terribly difficult emotional period. I originally thought I'd spend my carefree bachelor days doing nothing but skateboarding and dating

women, savoring the last scraps of my late-twenties marrow. I could
never have predicted that I would instead find myself sitting in *church,*
meditating and praying for release from a crippling pattern of attachment that had caused me and Nicole so many years of pain and soul
sickness. This was all definitely a little strange considering that one of
my all-time-favorite bands is Black Sabbath, or that I'd learned most
of what I knew about the Exodus story not from Sunday school, but
from the old Metallica song "Creeping Death." But unlike a couple
of my former skateboarding friends who'd gone the "born-again"
route and joined conservative evangelical congregations, I attended a
Unity church, the same progressive denomination that my prochoice
mother and recovering-Catholic stepfather had been active in for
years. And yet, despite Unity's progressive politics, I kept my church-
going mostly a secret, worrying that my friends would think I'd converted to the dark side. Mention to a crowd of twentysomethings,
skateboarders, graduate school intellectuals, and writers that you're
headed to a yoga class or a Buddhist meditation circle and no one
blinks, but tell them you're going to *church* and you'll be considered
the worst kind of crazy. Even my lifelong best friend, Gabriel—who
came from a Lutheran family of five siblings, all with biblical names
like his—automatically assumed I'd joined some sort of cult.

The truth was that I went to Unity for myself—in hope of healing my guilt and loneliness, but also because I felt there was something fundamentally wrong with what the right wingers were doing
to this country—condemning homosexuals and denouncing all other
religions and supporting the invasion of Iraq and other essentially
non-Christian acts. The ecumenical, all-accepting attitude at Unity
seemed like the perfect antidote. There were gay couples in the congregation, warmly accepted and integrated—a relatively rare thing in
rural Colorado. And the minister, Lynn Kendall, was like a cross between a wise sage, a chipper diner waitress, and a stand-up comedian.
The first time I heard her speak she related a story about how, just
after being dumped, she dove on the hood of her ex-boyfriend's car,
pounded on his windshield, and said, "Why won't you love me?"

"I was trying to get him to do for me what I couldn't do for myself," Lynn said, and I knew immediately she had something to teach me.

Without a formal degree or ministerial training, she'd honed her spiritual chops in the real world, through surviving abuse as a child and a marriage gone bad, then finding eventual salvation in twelve-step programs. She never quoted from the Bible or spoke much about Jesus's life; even on Easter Sunday she avoided the story of the crucifixion. She was more interested in helping us forge our own direct connection with spirit. Rather than telling us that we were all sinners or that Jesus had died for our transgressions, she assured us that we all contained within us a spark of the divine, like Ishmael's serenely calm soul even in the midst of chaos. I met other seekers at Unity, all of them tremendously kind and supportive. They loaned me books about Buddhism and Gnosticism and mystical Christianity, including the now-classic *Course in Miracles*. I found some major resonance between the *Course,* which teaches that we're more than just bodies, and soaring passages in *Moby-Dick:* "My body is but the lees of my better being. . . . Take my body who will, take it I say, it is not me."

Six months after our breakup, I called Nicole and invited her to lunch. I had a cracked notion that maybe we'd get back together, just like we had seven or eight times before, but that things would be different now that I'd started down a path of spiritual healing.

The day before the lunch I made an appointment to see Lynn Kendall, who offered counseling sessions by donation, a foreign concept for someone who's spent thousands of dollars in therapy. The little Unity library where we met was well lit and warm and smelled faintly of cigarette smoke. Smoking generally turns me off, but the fact that Lynn did it made me appreciate her even more—she was human and flawed just like the rest of us.

"I'm nervous about this lunch," I said. "I feel like I have a big decision to make."

"I thought all your decisions were made six months ago," Lynn said. "When you *broke up.*"

"We've broken up and gotten back together so many times."

"So you're thinking it's a good idea to do *that* again?"

"I don't know," I said. "Maybe. I miss her. This might be my last chance to work things out. I want to have a plan."

Lynn thought about it for a while. "Do you really have to decide about this today? Or tomorrow? What if you just allowed yourself not to make any decisions? Hell, you don't even have to decide what to order from the menu. You can just ask for the sampler plate."

For some reason this struck me as tremendously funny. I left Unity smiling, trying to hold on to this sense of levity, but it left me the moment I sat down across from Nicole at the Rio, a Mexican place we used to go for margaritas and combo plates on warm summer nights. I could barely look her in the eye, much less speak. She was and is one of the most beautiful women I've ever known: sea-green eyes and impossibly long lashes, olive complexion, an aquiline nose and thick dark hair. And she's such an essentially good person—an accomplished grade school teacher who gives thoughtful gifts and loves animals, and who is well loved by everyone who knows her. Sitting there across from her, I couldn't for the life of me figure out why we couldn't make it work, how I'd transformed her love into what seemed now like barely contained spite.

"Please don't just sit there and look at me," Nicole said. "You have to at least attempt a normal conversation."

After a long, uncomfortable silence, I finally managed to speak. "I've changed a lot in the past six months," I said.

"So have I," she said.

"I've actually been going to church. I think it's helping."

"Church, huh? I'm not surprised."

"It's not like you think. It's a different kind of church, with progressive politics."

"Okay, cool, I'm happy for you. But why are you telling me this?"

"I don't know," I said. "I guess I've just . . . changed."

"You *change* every time we break up. But nothing about *us* ever changes, not really."

"But this time it's different. I can be different."

She turned and looked out the window. "I knew you'd try this again," she said. "But the thing is: I'm happy. Things are working out for me. And I can't spend the rest of my life thinking about tattoos and rock shows and skateboarding. Or *church*."

I sat there nodding, the brick walls and bright Mexican murals and cute waitresses with trays of margaritas going all blurry as Nicole collected her things and walked out.

I drove myself home in a state of semishock. I wanted to scream. I wanted to sleep with three women at the same time, smoke cigarettes, beat the shit out of someone twice my size, put my fist through a plate glass window, pour whiskey on the wounds. I wanted to tear free from my skin and bury my bones in another state, as far from my own heart as I could get.

I wanted to sleep but I couldn't.

Dawn came and I was still wide-awake. I felt shaky and hollow and sick, as if I hadn't eaten for days. I tried standing up but my vision erupted with sparks. Something dark was descending upon me—*God help thee, old man, thy thoughts have created a creature in thee.* I thought about calling my mother. I thought about calling Nicole, or 911, or the psychic hotline, or every woman in the phone book until someone came to help me. I fell to my hands and knees and crawled to the bathroom, where it all came spilling out.

Please help me, I said, over and over again. Please help me. *God, please help me.*

I thought of that scene in *Boogie Nights,* when Mark Wahlberg's character, after taking too much coke and then getting chased by a half-naked maniac drug dealer with a shotgun, and subsequently having hit absolute rock-fucking-bottom, comes begging Burt Reynolds's character for help. Who knew Burt Reynolds could be so godlike? But that's what he is, a white-bearded, divine pornographer who takes his blubbering prodigal son in his arms and welcomes him home. Prostrate, my face in my hands, I wept harder than I'd ever wept, begging for help, saying it over and over again, my Mark Wahlberg mantra.

Something cracked apart down in my core—a slow tectonic shift finally reaching its apotheosis, and then up from this raw, superheated fissure rose a tiny seed of a voice, small and still and warm.

It was my own voice, of course, but also something larger, transcendent. The Sufis refer to God as the Friend, and that's how it felt, like an ancient friend who'd always been there, since the beginning of time—the atman, my true self. What it said: *You're going to be just fine.* How it said it: with the deepest tenderness I'd ever experienced from my own self-condemning heart. And in repetition, the same way I'd repeatedly pleaded, so that I was sure to hear and know this was the answer. So that I'd know for certain.

I stayed there in child's pose, listening. I could've stayed there forever, but eventually I got myself up into a hot shower. The water felt like a million tiny, sparkling hands reaching out to hold me, like liquid grace, like the rain that follows in the path of a hurricane.

I dried off and called Lynn, saying that it was important, I needed to talk to her right away. I could tell that I was imposing on her schedule—she'd just seen me the day before, and she had a whole church to run.

She gave me fifteen minutes.

I rushed over to Unity, driving like a maniac, like the Blues Brothers on their divine mission. When I told her I thought maybe I'd had an encounter with God, she smiled, like it was no big deal.

"You mean the *holy spirit*," she said.

"Like 'father, son, and holy ghost'?" I asked.

"No," she said, smiling, "that makes it sound so supernatural. What I'm talking about is special but also mundane. It's the spirit of holiness and love that lives in all of us, that saves us when we ask it to. That's what you experienced. Plus you really needed a goddamned good cry. So congratulations," she said, collecting her things for her next meeting.

"Congratulations? That's it?"

"Yes," she said. "You're back in the world of the living. And don't forget what the Zen masters say."

"What's that?"

"First enlightenment, then the dishes. Now if you'll excuse me," she said, "you're not the only one in spiritual crisis."

CATHEDRAL

Lynn was right about the dishes. I was still the same person with mostly the same feelings and fears and hopes. And yet, after a white-light moment, I'd been transformed in subtle ways. That summer I went back to work as the head skateboard coach at my old summer camp on Mount Hood, Oregon—a place that I'd worked for many years beforehand and that was like paradise to me, with nothing to do but skate, swim in mountain lakes, hang out with the campers, and host breakdancing contests on the miniramp flatbottom. For some reason, camp was staffed that year by a large contingency of young, fashionable snowboarders who happened also to be evangelical Christians. During a trip to deliver an injured camper to the hospital, one of them explained to me that the Bible was the "absolute truth," and that since the "absolute truth" was that all non-Christians were going to hell—courtesy of that oft-quoted and widely misunderstood Bible phrase "No one comes to the Father except through me"—he felt it was his God-given duty to convert as many nonbelievers as he could. I pointed out that this was a form of spiritual imperialism, one that assumed the logistical improbability that of the six and a half billion people on the planet, only a fraction would make it to heaven, if a "place" called heaven even exists. He avoided me the rest of the summer, and certainly never invited me to Thursday-night Bible study, which was just fine with me.

A few nights later, I was standing on the deck of the skate bowl, just about to drop in, when a girl named Karissa Vasquez walked up and invited me to Taco Night at a bar down the hill. I'd met Karissa a few times in Colorado and then bumped into her randomly at a Fourth of July party at an indoor skatepark in Portland, where we climbed up on the domed roof and watched fireworks bloom over the Willamette River.

It just so happened we were both working on Mount Hood for the summer, both skateboarders, both single. At Taco Night, we drank beer and played Putt-Putt golf out on the large patio, trading quotes from the film *Office Space*. Her chestnut hair fell halfway down her back in two thick braids; she had dark eyes and a sweet, shy smile. Before driving home a couple hours later, we shared a stray can of PBR I found in the backseat of her Honda Accord.

"You might not know it from looking at me, but I'm full-blooded Mexican," she said. She told me all about her big family, her favorite *abuela* in Arizona—the one who belts out traditional Mexican songs at weddings—and her darker-skinned brother and all her crazy cousins. I asked what her grandmother thought of her tattoos.

"She told me that if she was young again, she'd get a Virgin of Guadalupe tattooed on her chest. When she passes away, I'll get *La Virgen* in her honor." Using our PBR like a microphone, Karissa then broke into an animated lip-synch to an Ugly Casanova song about dressed-up alligators and cum-stained pianos.

Back at camp we met up with some friends at her summer rental, a canary-yellow Swiss chalet with a beer bong hanging off the balcony that Karissa swore belonged to her younger roommates. Up in her loft bedroom she showed us her black hardcover journals, filled with Polaroids of her and her friends skateboarding, a trip to Pacific Beach in San Diego, cool line drawings of trees and birds interspersed with poetic journal entries and a few Bible quotes—*In all my prayers for all of you, I always pray with joy*. Something lit up inside me when I flipped through her journals, but I was also worried at first she might be one of the evangelicals, especially when she explained that she'd attended a megachurch service with a friend on their trip out from Colorado to Oregon.

"There was nothing church-like about it," she said. "It was a bunch of people sitting around talking about how they're right and everyone else is going to hell. There's no soul in that." It turned out that Karissa was an occasional Unity-goer; that she and her closest friends sometimes attended the Unity in Boulder, a place I'd been a few times with my parents. It was a revelation—a sort of miracle.

What were the odds of finding this kind of soul connection at a skateboard camp, of all places?

After she hugged me good night, I floated back to my cabin, chanting *thank you thank you thank you* in my head.

Karissa and I drove down to the Oregon coast the next weekend. During the ride, she complained about one of her roommates, a twenty-year-old snowboarder named Richie.

"He's just an all around filthy person," she said.

"You mean he doesn't clean up after himself?"

"None of my roommates do. But it's more than that with Richie. There's something not right with him. He never showers. He spends his evenings reading dirty magazines and making lewd comments about women. I think he actually has dirt *in his heart*."

We laughed about this for the rest of the ride, until we reached the parking lot at Short Sands and took the long path through a rain forest down to the beach, holding hands. Lying in the sun, Karissa snapped Polaroids of our friends surfing, then drew a series of hearts with the letters DLH on the inside.

It stood for Dirty Little Hearts, the name of our new two-person crew. We spent the rest of the summer skateboarding, making art, making out. We tagged DLH everywhere—in huge letters on the sand, on our skateboards, on a cinder-block wall in a Portland alleyway.

Our first night together, Karissa woke me up before dawn. "I feel perfect when I'm with you," she said.

At the end of August we carpooled home, heading back to our new life together in Colorado. During the journey I prepared the reading list for the college literature class I was signed up to teach in the fall. On a foggy stretch of Utah desert, I read Karissa the short story "Cathedral" by Raymond Carver, a piece that somehow I'd never encountered, though I'd just finished my MFA in creative writing. Reading the story's epiphanic climax—a skeptical, broken man has a spiritual awakening while he's helping a blind man draw a cathedral—it felt like the top of my head blew off, because what Carver described felt so close to what I'd experienced in my own bathroom several months earlier, and because my awakening had all come to fruition with this person sitting next to me who understood, and because there was a chapel full of people back home who also knew. Like the narrator in "Cathedral," I'd found a way out of the isolation chamber of my own ego. It was a deep feeling of homecoming, like falling into your own bed after one too many nights on the road.

THE BASEMENT

B
ack at All Souls Unitarian in New York, I feel a little melancholy after Galen Guengerich's service about the importance of community. After all, I had a spiritual community and deep connection with Karissa back in Colorado, but I gave it all up to move to New York and try to make it as a writer. I'm fortunate to have such a large group of friends in the city and roommates who share my new surfing obsession, but I still suffer from a constant, low-level homesickness and insecurity around my fellow New Yorkers. So I accept when, at the end of his talk and apropos its theme, Guengerich invites everyone downstairs to mingle with the All Souls congregation.

Feeling shy as usual, I hover around the literature table, drinking tea and checking out pamphlets about Unitarianism and compelling books by the All Souls head minister, Forrest Church. I strike up a conversation with an older gentlemen who explains how he originally came to All Souls not from any sense of need or trouble— which he clearly feels are inferior motivations—but because he "wanted to be challenged." Before I can ask what that means, he introduces me to a clean-cut Asian guy named Steven who looks to be in his midtwenties, and who gives me a tepid handshake and a quasicrystalline smile. In typical East Coast fashion, the first thing Steven asks is what I do for a living. When I tell him I'm a writer working in publishing, he asks if I've read David Rakoff's "Lush Life," an essay about the particular indignities of working as an editorial assistant in New York.

"No," I say, "but I'll get right on it."

"You really should," he says. "All those manuscripts he had to read and reject—the hordes of good writers who go unpublished— the way he describes it is devastating."

"Yeah," I say, "devastating. I know all about it."

Steven perks up at my little self-deprecating admission. He's already decided I work in a shabby industry, and now here's another way for him to feel superior. "So you've never been published?"

"I've been published," I say, feeling defensive. "It's the manuscript part I'm talking about. I spend a lot of time reading and rejecting them. It gets old."

"I can only imagine," Steven says.

I scan the room, searching for some conversational escape route.

"I'm a corporate lawyer," Steven volunteers, "with Goldman Sachs." There's a patronizing tone to his voice, indicating not only his perceived sense of occupational superiority, but also my lack of social grace for failing to inquire.

Now that he's said it, I hope maybe he'll take my silence as a hint that I want to put him in a firm headlock and stuff his face in the coffee cake.

Fortunately, a girl in cardigan sweater walks up and says hello.

Forgoing any pleasantries, Goldman Sachs says, "Hey, Lillian, did you hear? I just bought an apartment."

She squeals and gives him a warm congratulatory hug, then holds him at arm's distance and speaks earnestly, one eyebrow raised. "You have to go tell Brady. We've been looking for the past three months and he's starting to lose heart." Before excusing himself, Goldman Sachs introduces me to Lillian, who's genuinely charming. Unfortunately, I'm too rattled by the first conversation to pay much attention to the second.

This is when I spot him in the corner of the All Souls basement—an old man with winter in his coarse, chest-length beard. He sits alone, straight-backed, legs crossed, regarding the congregation with his deep-set Spanish eyes. Eyes that reveal a sense of pride verging on arrogance. But also a brokenness with the gravitational pull of a black hole.

Melville spent most of his childhood living a privileged life in New York City. His social-climbing father, Allan, moved the family into a series of increasingly opulent homes, staffed by servants. Allan was a vain man—an importer of French fineries—who severely overleveraged himself to attain all the trappings of success. When young

Herman was only eleven, his father's business went bankrupt. The family fled to Albany, where, without money for a carriage, and in the midst of a nervous breakdown, Allan contracted pneumonia after crossing a frozen river in his thin-soled French boots.

For several days before his death, he lapsed into a state of raving psychosis.

Witness to this unspeakable trauma, Herman then had to drop out of school and find work to support his demanding mother. He never went to college. A whaling vessel was his—like Ishmael's—"Yale college and [his] Harvard." He later settled in the Berkshires, where he found a creative and spiritual community with neighbors like Sophia and Nathaniel Hawthorne. But after the collapse of his writing career, Melville had to move his family from Arrowhead back to New York City—a reverse version of his father's descent. Like many New York churches, All Souls for a time actually charged rent for pew space. Rumor has it that Melville often couldn't pay for his family's pew, so heavy were his financial burdens.

He turns his head, observes me with his sunken eyes, and it's clear from his expression that he's not comfortable surrounded by such a wealthy lot of seekers. That there's no connection here, not for us.

Feeling uneasy, I get out of All Souls and walk to Central Park, where I have the uncanny sense of being followed.

I try calling Karissa from the Belvedere Castle observation deck, but I'm sent straight to voicemail. I walk around aimlessly, nowhere in particular to go and no one to see on a Sunday afternoon. I walk past picnickers, couples holding hands, families of Eastern European tourists in their uncomfortable shoes. I wander down through the Ramble, where I spot three cardinals bunkering up for the winter. He hangs back in the shadows, just out of sight, but close enough that I can sense a similar heaviness in the heart, the same aching isolation. I walk over a wooden bridge where couples float around in paddleboats and spot, off in the distance, the Dakota building where John Lennon and Yoko Ono lived. I walk through the zoo and past the park bench where Karissa and I ate hot dogs during a weekend trip, in the more carefree days before I lived here. I walk for hours, not even stopping for lunch, covering nearly the entire perimeter of the park before he finally leaves me. I keep walking, alone now as late-afternoon shadows lurk slowly toward the Upper East Side.

GOOD NEWS FOR PEOPLE WHO LOVE BAD NEWS

On a Monday, I get a phone call from an old college roommate, Drew, whom I haven't spoken with for maybe ten years. He tells me that another of our friends, James, has taken his own life. Like me, James aspired to be an English professor. Drew explains that he was instead working as a bartender in San Francisco, where he struggled with alcoholism, so severe that it developed into Korsakoff's syndrome.

Drew relates the details of this disease: the hallucinations, memory loss, confabulation, borderline psychosis.

Drew tells me that James used a shotgun.

After hanging up, I mourn for my friend, whom I last remember at twenty-one, dancing and shadowboxing on a bed in Boulder, Colorado, completely wasted, a Charlatans UK song on full blast—*everyone's been down before, everybody knows the pain.*

Later, I call another friend to see if he's heard. At the end of our conversation, this friend gives me an additional piece of unwelcome news.

Nicole's engaged to be married, the wedding just a few months away.

Ragged genomes from these two pathogenic messages splice together and begin replicating, attacking my already-weakened defenses. Back in school, James and Drew were deep into drugs and this second-wave British invasion music that I mostly hated. Even more than James, Drew seemed like he was on a bad path. Once, at a party, he approached Nicole and me, almost in tears, told us how solid he thought we were together, how someday he hoped for that kind of relationship. A year after graduation, Nicole saw him wandering the streets at nine or ten in the morning, wearing only one shoe, so whacked out he even didn't recognize her.

Now, in our thirties, it feels like things have somehow flipped. I'm not into substances, but I'm clinging to an undergraduate lifestyle, living with roommates still in their twenties, in an apartment that my friend—the same one who gave me the news about Nicole—sarcastically calls the "adult dorms." On the other hand, Drew completely pulled himself together. He's a doctor now, married to a woman he met back in college; they own a house and have a baby on the way.

And two years after the dissolution of our ten-year relationship, I'm still not over Nicole. Or maybe I'm not over the idea of what I could've had with her—*safety, comfort, hearthstone.* Maybe this is why I came to New York, why I left Karissa—*to get over it.* But now I'm hung up on Karissa, too. *Multiple pathogens:* I had a job as a university English instructor but gave it up to write children's books, deliver Indian food, send rejection letters from the Pit.

Though it was mostly my fault, some dark side of me wants revenge against Nicole for those ten years—the whole of my twenties—and for where I've ended up now. Which is to say I want revenge on myself: *beware of thyself, old man.*

That night I drive to the ocean. There are no waves, so I put on my wetsuit, walk out into the water, swim alone at dusk at a beach known for strong rip currents.

FIRST LOWERING

My first full-time job out of college was at a residential treatment center for teenage criminals and addicts. On Friday nights, we drove them in unmarked white vans to an AA meeting at a local church—a calming activity in what was otherwise a very stressful position. When I was growing up, some of my stepsiblings had addiction issues, and then as an adult I'd read *Infinite Jest,* so I had some secondhand knowledge of twelve-step programs, both the light and the dark, the profound and the inane aspects of the recovery movement. These particular Friday-night gatherings were "speaker meetings," meaning that one person would stand up and tell their story: the depths to which they'd previously sank, how they got better, where they are now. I sometimes felt embarrassed for them, or bored, but as an aspiring writer I was mostly riveted. In my undergraduate creative writing classes there was a lot of abstract discussion of "character development," but rarely do you see this concept play out so dramatically as in twelve-step programs.

I didn't really have a problem with alcohol or drugs; I enjoyed the occasional beer or two, and had my share of youthful benders, but anything more than a couple drinks just puts me to sleep. Still, the more I went to AA meetings, the more I felt that I somehow belonged there. One night a gentleman told a story about fixing his kitchen sink. He detached the drainpipe, put a bucket beneath to catch the leaking water. After a few minutes the bucket began overflowing; out of habit he dumped it into the sink—forgetting the detached drainpipe, sending a dirty tide of water across the floor. When the bucket filled up again, he emptied it back into the sink—and being half-cocked on whiskey, he did this not once or twice but *five* times.

"It was the very definition of insanity," he said, "doing the same thing over and over, but expecting different results."

This story in particular stuck with me. Nicole and I were living together at the time, and both being basically decent, caring people, we were doing okay and taking pretty good care of one another, though in our hearts we knew we weren't right for each other. It was the togetherness phase of a pattern we acted and reenacted for the better part of a decade.

Knowing it wasn't right between us, we'd break up. But being codependent, I couldn't handle life without her. It felt exactly the way I imagined coming down off drugs must feel like—*the blackness of darkness*—which for me meant intense obsession coupled with depression, panic attacks, phobias, even a kind of agoraphobia where I began to fear the world outside my apartment. It probably had a lot to do with the fact that I'd been through three divorces by the age of fifteen, or that my father's third marriage had some very similar on-again, off-again patterns. And that, partly as a result of my vulnerable, latchkey-kid status after my original parents' divorce, I suffered a particularly traumatic form of abuse at the hands of a seventeen-year-old neighbor, after which, at age seven or eight, I had my first series of shame-induced anxiety attacks.

After my breakups with Nicole, I remember typing "Relationships Anonymous" and "relationship addiction" into a search engine, but nothing came up. Not wanting to face all the overwhelming feelings alone—or more accurately, not thinking myself capable without some kind of lightning-strike miracle—I'd come crawling back to Nicole, beg her to take me back. And for whatever reason, she would, and we'd swallow and inject one another back into our bloodstreams with the most intense, though always ephemeral, sense of relief and elation. It sounds like a prosaic soap opera plot, but for us it was debilitating, isolating, soul-suffocating. This is not to say that we didn't love each other on a basic level—we spent a lot of good years together—but the pattern's end result never changed. We were always just pouring more water down a disconnected drain.

Three years later, in Brooklyn, Asa Ellis calls me up, tells me he's having some problems, feeling depressed, and would it be okay if he talks it out with me? He tells me about his mother and her heavy drinking, and about his last relationship, which had gone sour, and how he's having a terrible time getting over it—something to which I can definitely relate.

"I'm scared this shit's getting the upper hand on me," he says. "To be honest, I think I might be suicidal."

I give him as much support as I can, check to make sure he's seeing a therapist, then share some of my own issues. We talk for a solid hour, until we both feel a little better. I'm worried for him, but also glad for the conversation, for the way it briefly erases my own isolation.

A month or two later, he calls back, invites me to a twelve-step meeting he found out about through Al-Anon. But this is not Al-Anon, he explains; it's a meeting for men struggling with relationships and codependency.

The following Wednesday I take the subway up north, to 116th Street, where I meet Asa in front of a Catholic church, and together we descend into the basement, to a room with low ceilings and bad fluorescent lighting. That the meeting is held below ground—requiring a literal descent—is not lost on me. Sitting in concentric rings of folding chairs are men, forty or fifty of them, enough to crew a large ship. This is a speaker meeting, and the speaker, David, seems like a decent, middle-aged man. He relates an honest story about a shameful sexual experience he had as a kid; he tells us how his entire adult life has been categorized by longing for unattainable women, how it consumes him.

I connect with David's story, but then the meeting chair says, "Let's give it up," and suddenly everyone's standing up, hugging each other, crowding the room with loud conversation, laughter. Once everyone settles in again, the chair opens up the room for sharing, and twenty or thirty hands shoot up all at once. And then they come, one after another—three-minute tales centering mostly around sex: casual sex with women, casual sex with men, anonymous sex with women and men at the same time.

One gentleman mentions how, in addition to this one, he's working four other programs: AA, OA, DA, and MA. That's a total of *five* programs, I think to myself. I wonder where he finds the time. And

I don't know what OA, DA, or MA stand for, though I think maybe the latter should be Meta Anonymous, for people hooked on twelve-step programs.

Then a short Puerto Rican man stands up and starts shouting, telling everyone how furious he is that he never gets called on to share.

"Fuck all you guys," he yells, tears streaming down his face.

There's not much talk about relationships—about being hooked on someone emotionally—which is what I'm there for. I have some issues around sex, sure. But I've mostly been in monogamous relationships my whole life; I can count the total number of people I've slept with on both hands. So I'm not sure I'm in the right place, and I'm feeling unsettled.

More so when I look over and see him—Melville—in the corner, sitting in a folding chair with his arms crossed, looking defeated and ashamed.

And when, by surprise, I get called on to speak, it's all I can think to say. That I'm deeply *unsettled.*

OPHELIA, PART II

After watching Dawn charge out into Ophelia waves, my nerves fail me. It's only been a few months since I started surfing on the East Coast; I'm not sure if I'm ready for waves taller than I am, that are surging in off the horizon, one after another, lashing the beach with such unrelenting rhythm.

I sit down on the sand, chest and stomach muscles clenched, heart pumping arrhythmically.

Teagan, who has also just started surfing, stretches into a borrowed wetsuit.

"Come on," she says, "we'll go out together. We've totally got this."

Shoulder to shoulder with Teagan, things seem less perilous. With glassy conditions and just a slight offshore breeze, paddling out is easier than I thought, and to my surprise, so is catching waves.

My first is a perfectly shaped, head-high wall of water—)))))))))))))))))))))))))—the concave lip breaking from left to right, from Queens toward Brooklyn.

I paddle into it at a slight angle. Just like Kyle Grodin showed me the weekend before. Arching my back and popping up to my feet, I cut frontside down the stained-glass face, my back knee cocked in slightly.

Dropping right into the pocket—the power source—the wave folds into itself just behind me, while the silver-blue, sun-flecked lip keeps welling up in front of me, feathering white at the upper edge, the wind hollowing it out, holding it up like a crystal cavern wall— and I skim across it faster than I've ever surfed, my left fingers combing the surface, a long frothy wake tailing my board—until it curls and tumbles all over itself, rolls itself up like a long, bleached bale of hay, then collapses.

It only lasts a few seconds, but still it's a kind of peak flow experience, something I've experienced many times on a skateboard, where all sense of time drops away, inducing a sense of euphoria combined with intense focus. In this case, the experience is heightened by the ocean, by the fact that I'm in physical conversation with a reverberation of energy from a distant storm system.

After cheering on Dawn as she rips a right-breaking peak, I catch a few more perfect lefts, riding the last one all the way back to shore, where Teagan's already out of the water, waiting for us. Emerging from the brisk sea into warm, hazy sunlight, I feel like I'm being reborn into the world as a different person—I just surfed my first storm swell without flailing or even falling once.

Back on the beach, we peel off our wetsuits, spread a Mexican blanket across the sand, and lie down, Teagan's tan, sun-warmed leg touching mine. I watch as she rubs some sunscreen between her hands, then finger-combs it through her thick brown hair.

"Hair can get sunburned?" I ask.

"Not so much burned as damaged. Here, you want me to give you a little condition?"

She squeezes a tiny white pearl into her palm, rubs her hands together, then massages it into my hair and scalp. I haven't been touched by another human for weeks. Combined with my lingering surf buzz, it feels phenomenal.

"All right, angel-face," she says, "you're all set."

"So what's the plan for tonight?" I ask.

"Dawn's got a hot date. Me, not so much. But I'm meeting up with her for drinks at midnight."

"You want to grab some dinner after the beach?"

"Deal," she says, leaning her shoulder into mine.

Dawn stays out in the ocean for another half hour, while Teagan and I nap and flirt on the beach. It's late afternoon by the time we make it back to Brooklyn. I shower and put on a T-shirt and jeans and cowboy boots. Before heading out I do a quick double take in the mirror, a little surprised at how surfing has transformed my upper body.

Teagan and I meet up at Bonita, an upscale Mexican place just around the corner from my apartment.

"Hi hi," she says—it's always double *hi*'s with Teagan—and returns my kiss on the cheek. We score a coveted sidewalk table, right on Bedford, and drink Pacificos with lime while waiting for our orders. We talk about her birds: she makes little stuffed pigeons, knits and sews them by hand, sells them from her website.

She also tells me about a friend who showed up at her apartment the previous weekend ripped on cocaine. He basically hung around all night, tweaking out, eating her food, throwing her pigeons around, and trying but failing to sit through a movie.

"Finally at about four in the morning he comes up with this *brilliant* idea that we should make out. But by that time I was way past bored and ready for bed. I was like really, dude, *really?*"

"So what'd you do?"

"I figured what the hell. We're not a couple or anything. I mostly just did it to shut him up. So yeah, I let him French me for a minute, then pushed him out the door."

Her use of *French* as a verb kills me. And also the way she used actual *Frenching* so strategically. I consider my own strategy, wondering if I'll plant a first kiss on her, but at the same time starting to doubt if I can even keep up with her.

After dinner, Teagan wants me to hit the bars with her, then meet up with Dawn at midnight. But it's already past eleven, and I have a strict rule about waking up early on Saturdays to write. Plus I had two whole Pacificos—about all my lightweight constitution can handle. The fact is, I'm just not that into drinking. In this way I've maybe set myself up for some major isolation—drinking is what New York women in their thirties do on the weekends. At least the ones I've met so far.

Teagan and I say our good-byes and then I head home, still ecstatic about surfing but at the same time completely lonely. Teagan's intelligent and beyond attractive, but we're totally incompatible. It's the same story with all the women I've dated in the city.

Then it hits me—what feels like an epiphany: I want to be with Karissa. After my Ophelia ride I'm feeling better than ever. I've gotten over my subway fear, my ocean fear, and now that I'm stronger, more independent, I'm ready to leave New York on a high note. And I want to be with Karissa again, share this feeling with one person who will understand, and who won't just want to go partying all night. Who will instead let me take her to bed early, so we can take our time folding into each other's bodies, and then wake up early for a service at Unity.

I picture the two of us standing hand in hand at a church altar in Portland, Oregon—where Karissa lives now, and where I've always wanted to live—in front of all our friends and family.

She picks up when I call, sounds happy to hear from me.

"I want to talk to you about something," she says.

My stomach goes all fluttery, hoping maybe she's been thinking the same thing, that we can work it out and get back together, that this is all going according to the two-Pacifico plan I formulated five minutes ago.

"You know that black party dress I told you about, the one I sewed by hand?" she says.

Though I've never actually seen it, I can so vividly picture her in it, the way it must curve around her hips and chest, expose her smooth skin and tattoos.

"I wore it the other night, when a bunch of my new friends and I went out and sang karaoke. And something clicked with me—I got up on stage and sang song after song. Everyone was cheering for me because they were glad to finally see me happy, you know? Then my new friend Alex got up and sang with me, and everyone was cheering for us even more. And then it dawned on me—I almost couldn't believe it was happening—but it dawned on me that Alex and I are *together* now."

After a long silence, Karissa asks if I'm still there.

I finally manage to speak. "I guess I don't know why you're telling me this."

"I'm telling you because I don't think we should talk so much anymore. It's not really fair to the person I'm dating."

Though I was the one who'd gone and left her for my ostensibly awesome new life in New York, the news hits me hard, sucker punches me right off my blissful little surfing peak.

Feeling panicked and desperate, I tell her how I've dated some people too, but that I realize now how *special* what we had was, that *no one else makes me feel like she does*—trying not to, but still heaping on the clichés, because I so desperately need to get this out, to get her back. I tell her about surfing and my epiphany—that I want to move to Portland. That I'm *ready* to move to Portland, to *be with her*.

Now the silence emanates from her end.

When she finds her voice, it quavers on the edge of anger and hurt. "I thought you'd be happy for me. You were the one who left me, remember? But instead you dump all this shit on me."

"I'm sorry," I say. "It's how I feel. I'm just being honest."

"Well, as usual, your timing sucks. Because I'm *with* someone now. And this conversation is over."

I hardly sleep that night; instead I lie awake obsessing over her, over what might have been, doubting that I'll ever find another soul connection like I had with Karissa, especially here in New York City. This marks the beginning of a long, treacherous tide of obsession and regret; it runs strong and deep, and I try to channel it, like my chronic dissatisfaction with my work, all back into the ocean, spending more and more solo time out at Rockaway, attempting to surf my mind and body into a state of numbness, to recapture those ephemeral few minutes of Ophelia bliss.

THE REJECTION

August 15, 2005

Mr. Jerry Clark
2580 S. Wilcox Lane
Orlando, Florida 23756

Dear Mr. Clark,

Thank you for your recent submission of WET GODDESS. After having read it, I'm afraid this is going to be a pass for us. Although the manuscript is well written and has some nice details, I'm afraid that we do not see a large enough market for a story about an amorous relationship between a man and a porpoise.

Thanks again for the look, and best of luck with your writing.

Sincerely,

The Editors
_____ Publishing

DARKNESS AND THE LIVING WATER

Afte my first Wednesday-night men's meeting, I'm not sure I ever want to go back. I grew up partly with a single mother and multiple stepsisters, so I'm most comfortable around women. I've always had plenty of male friends, but aside from skateboarding road trips, given a choice between a group of women or a group of men, I'll choose women any day. It just seems logical; who—besides members of the Promise Keepers or the Elks club—honestly wants to sit in a poorly lit room full of forty or fifty *dudes?* And this room in particular is full of so much testosterone, like the womanless *Pequod*—a ship ruined by unbridled masculine force.

But after the phone call with Karissa, I realize that though our relationship was categorically different from Nicole's and mine, in the end I've elicited the exact same baffling, crippling pattern. Through my anti-Midas alchemy, I've turned another available, lovely woman into an unavailable object of obsession and misery. I'm haunted by what she said at the airport that Thanksgiving—*the only reason you ever love anyone is to make yourself feel better.* No one had ever nailed me like that before. It was a fairly polite way of bringing me face to face with my own darkness—with the fact that, relationship-wise, I was kind of an imperialistic asshole. I'd bounced in and out of relationships my entire adult life, using them to narcotize myself and hurting people in the process. I know I need help—*God, please help me*—no matter how many lurid stories I have to endure.

I know that Asa will be there, so I go back the following Wednesday. I tell myself that if nothing else, the two of us can talk about surfing.

That evening, a small, quiet man with wire-rimmed glasses tells his story. His name is Attiq; he describes how growing up in a half-Iraqi, half-Iranian Jewish household, he always felt at war with himself. At the beginning of his share, he says he'll spare us all the graphic details of his history with women.

"Because the thing that really got me—brought me to my knees, over and over," he says, "is love addiction." He describes how he dated a woman for several years, but it fell apart, and then by some twist of fate they ended up working together in the same office. Worse yet, she started dating some six-foot-tall, athletic blond guy, prominently displaying pictures of him on her desk.

"Even two years after we broke up, I'd wake up in the middle of the night, in a cold sweat, imagining them sleeping together. And thinking about how the guy probably had a much bigger dick than me." This last line is totally unexpected from someone with the looks and mannerisms of a Buddhist monk; it sends the group into hysterics. But not me. Instead of humor I feel a jolt of anxiety—what if *Karissa's* new boyfriend has a bigger dick than *me?*

He goes on to talk about how he got better—through prayer and meditation, constant contact with a power higher than himself—and, in his case, writing poetry and reading the work of Rumi.

"For me, Rumi gleaned the essence of this program, but he did it back in the thirteenth century, in my homeland. So much of his poetry centers around an ecstatic connection to *the lover.* What he's really talking about is entering a relationship with the divine, a part of which resides in our own hearts," Attiq says, looking out across the room.

Then he reads from a Rumi piece, tells us that if we're not comfortable with its use of the word *God,* we can substitute *higher power:* "Loving God is / the only pleasure. Other delights turn bitter. What hurts / the soul? To live / without tasting the water of its own essence. People / focus on death and this / material earth. They have doubts about soul water. / Those doubts can be / reduced! Use night to wake your clarity. Darkness / and the living water are / lovers."

The last line—*Let jealousy end*—feels like it was written for me.

He puts the book aside, says a few more words.

"Most of my life I clung to women, hoping they could fix me. It makes me sad to think of it, how imprisoned I was—how I turned other people into my higher power, because I didn't have my own. But once I went through withdrawal and worked this program, I rediscovered it, recovered my own Self. That's the miracle of these rooms. And it's the reason I'm in a good, equitable relationship with a woman who is now my fiancée."

After we hold hands for the closing prayer, a crowd gathers around him, two or three guys thick, like a guru with his acolytes. Asa wants me to ride the subway back to Brooklyn, but I tell him to go on without me, that there's someone I need to see.

After half an hour, I finally get to speak with Attiq. Up close, he has heavy brown lids, not the kind that make some New Yorkers look pretentious, but that make him look wise and kind and maybe a bit fragile.

I tell him how much I related to what he said, how I'm right in the throes of it with Karissa. Though I can tell he's worn out from speaking and all the attention, he listens patiently to my whole litany of woes.

A large Kenyan man, a former crack addict, interrupts us briefly so he can bend down and give Attiq a bear hug.

Attiq turns his attention back to me, places his hand on my arm. "Listen, you might not comprehend this yet, but what Karissa has done for you—letting you go, helping you see your own destructive patterns—is a gift. As far as what you do with it, that's for you to decide."

WATER MEETINGS

After connecting with Attiq, I keep going back to Wednesday-night meetings, where I find myself feeling increasingly at home. The more I put myself out there and talk to people, the more I realize we have in common. And the more I discover that what we have is a kind of underground, twelve-step surf club. Along with Asa and me, at least half a dozen other guys are into surfing, in the same obsessive way I am. There's a lot of talk about how easy it is to swap one addiction for another; in our case, surfing seems like a healthy substitute.

There's Mick, a former Californian whom I end up seeing at Rockaway almost every time I go. He has a waterproof housing for his homemade pinhole camera; he shoots black-and-white photos of Asa and me surrounded by darkness, standing on water in small round apertures of light. And Benny, a guy with whom I develop a really tight bond. Originally from a small village in Northern Ireland, Benny survived a long period of heavy drinking and drugging. He got sober in the nineties but, like the rest of us, still struggles with relationships. A private contractor, he remodels apartments most of the year, but always spends a month or two in the tropics, surfing in remote parts of Ecuador or Brazil.

Asa and I start referring to our surf sessions as *water meetings*. While waiting for waves, we sit on our boards and talk about what's going on with us, listening, offering support. Sometimes Mick and Benny are there, or any number of friends in one form of recovery or another, all of us out in the ocean together, trying to heal. In this way I'm able to do what I never thought myself capable of doing: actually surviving outside a romantic relationship, and doing it in perhaps the most difficult city in the world in which to be single.

It's what, in program language, we call *withdrawal*—it's like giving up drugs, but in our case it means resisting the urge to rebound back into yet another relationship.

And my own painful, imperfect withdrawal—during which the ocean becomes my surrogate girlfriend—lasts not just for weeks or months, but, with the exception of a few slips, for well over two years.

THE ACCIDENT

As of the 1990s, there wasn't a single skatepark in New York City. By the time I move there in the early 2000s, several good parks spring up, thanks in part to Andy Kessler. He showed up at hundreds of parks department meetings; he raised enough hell that in the late nineties the city finally agreed to set aside a large space in Riverside Park, on 108th Street, very near the same spot that he and his Zoo York crew used to skate back in the seventies. Two decades later, Kessler led the work crew that built a small vert ramp, street course, and a miniramp in Riverside Park; this was how he earned his nickname: *the Godfather of 108.*

Around the time I meet Andy in late 2003, a high-end sunglasses retailer hires him to build a small wooden bowl inside their Soho storefront. Known as the Blind Bowl, it's capsule-shaped and only four feet deep, but one side shoots straight up the wall, giving it over six feet of pure vertical, like an asymmetrical bathtub.

I skate the Blind Bowl a few times with Grodin and Andy; one night the legendary pro skater Mark Gonzales shows up and blows my mind. He doesn't do any tricks per se, just rocks these stylish frontside turns all the way up the vert wall. Rumor has it that when Gonzales first moved to New York back in the nineties, he signed up for ballet lessons. And after thirty-plus years of skating—similar to Andy Kessler—there is something simultaneously raw and balletic about the way he handles a skateboard.

A few weeks later, during a party at the Blind Bowl, Kessler trips up on the vert wall and takes a disastrous nine-foot slam, landing straight on his knee. The impact shatters his kneecap and jams his femur bone so violently upward that it cracks his pelvis nearly in half. He's laid up in the hospital for several weeks, and with no health insurance he racks up a $51,000 medical bill. After a few months' recovery, he gets back on his feet and along with some friends puts together a benefit art show/skate jam at the Blind Bowl. Artists like

Julian Schnabel, Wes Humpton, and many others donate work, enough to raise $20,000. It's rare for guys to skate well into their forties, and after that kind of slam most would hang up their Vans, but Andy gets right back on the horse. He actually *skates* at his own benefit show—in the same bowl that nearly crippled him—even though he's just graduated from crutches to cane.

So while the accident doesn't keep him off a skateboard, it's a turning point for Kessler. As a form of rehab for his hip, he spends more time in water, and especially the ocean, where, at age forty-five, he gets seriously into surfing. He falls in love with Montauk around the same time I do. We've skated together many times, but it's while hanging out on the beach and in the clean water at Ditch Plains that I really get to know him.

His first full summer in Montauk is 2005, when he lives for three months aboard an ancient little sailboat belonging to his friend Casual Chuck. The exterior isn't much to speak of—it doesn't even have a mast—but Chuck refinished the interior cabin with reclaimed hard wood flooring. Andy keeps all his belongings down in the hold, his clothes folded and stacked, his skateboard decks and a surfboard leaning against the wall next to a hammock, old hardcover editions of the Narcotics Anonymous and AA "big books" propped up by his pillow, the way a monk keeps a copy of the Bible at his bedside. There's something monastic and pure about the way he lives aboard this small vessel, recovering from his injury, waking at dawn to meditate and pray before surfing.

I visit him out on the docks one Saturday evening in July. After showing me around down in the cabin, he gives me a pocket-sized package containing something called a Mighty Kite. As we climb back up on deck, he tells me he buys them by the case in Chinatown.

"I freaking love these things," he says, launching a diamond-shaped Mighty Kite off the edge of the boat. Midnight blue with pink paper tails, it's about the size of a playing card. "I brought a case with me on a surf trip to the Dominican Republic last winter. Paid a bunch of local kids to help me sell them to tourists. Made about two hundred bucks; doubled my investment." He lets out some slack on his Mighty Kite. Just a few feet above his head, it shivers in the wind, occasionally diving down toward the bay before darting up again into a series of playful McTwists.

"I guess I wouldn't have pegged you for a salesman," I say.

Andy cracks up. "Oh yeah, I have a long history in sales. *Drug* sales, that is."

I knew he'd been a junkie, but I'd never heard anything about him dealing drugs. It's hard to reconcile with the Andy I know, the guy who helps out so many people, who builds skateparks and encourages kids to skate and live healthy lives.

"You wouldn't have recognized me," Andy says. "I was out there on the streets delivering that shit every day. Selling it, or just pretending to sell it and straight up stealing people's money. There are probably some junkies over on the East Side still waiting for me to deliver drugs." He breaks into a cackle. "I bet they're out there right now, fucking standing around on the block, just *waiting*."

As the sun pearls below the horizon, he reels in his Mighty Kite and walks me back to my truck, past rows of fishing skiffs and sailboats.

"This seems like the way to go," I say. "I don't think I can ever afford a house out here at Montauk. But a boat's like the perfect little surf shack."

"Seriously, man. I love every minute I spend out here."

We pass a sailboat with a For Sale sign. It's moderately sized, but they're asking over three hundred grand.

"Okay, so maybe I won't be able to afford that either."

"Hey, you really never know. When you make room for a dream like that in your head, that's when things start to happen."

Kessler and I meet up the next day out at Ditch Plains; I follow his lead when he suggests we walk south a ways to a spot called Poles. We paddle out together and I get a couple good waves, bigger than what I'm used to at Rockaway. A teenager heckles me because I ride one with my knee cocked in, like I'm on a much larger wave, but I'm too stoked to care.

I watch Andy catch a good left-hander and cruise frontside with his characteristic laid-back style, until another guy on a longboard drops right in on him, bashes into his board, leaving a sand dollar–sized hole in his rail. I follow him back to the shore, where we assess the damage and decide it requires some patch work to keep water from seeping in and ruining the core. It's a special board, given to Andy by his friend Joel Tudor, a pro surfer and shaper who sometimes lays over in Montauk for the summer between stints in California and Hawaii.

"Fucking guy," I say. "He dropped right in on you."

"Whatever. He meant no harm; these things happen."

We walk on the sand back toward the parking lot, checking out girls in bikinis along the way, the sun on our backs.

"Looks like you're getting around pretty good these days," I say, noticing that his limp has subsided.

"I'm feeling a lot better. My doctor's amazed at my recovery. He didn't know if I'd ever walk again. Surfing has definitely helped. Plus the way everyone showed up for me after the accident," he says. "I felt a real healing, you know, coming from all those people."

"That's the thing about you, Andy. You help out a lot of people. That all comes back around."

"Yeah, I guess I help some people every now and again . . . when I'm not busy *heckling* them," he says, then breaks into another cackle.

It turns out that Casual Chuck's the caretaker for the artist Julian Schnabel, who owns an estate just above Ditch Plains. Chuck lives in a cottage on Schnabel's property; I drive Andy up there to fetch some sun-cure resin to fix the ding. Back at Ditch Plains, we buy tacos at the Ditch Witch—a food and coffee cart that sets up shop in the summertime, and that always has a mile-long line. Andy and I grab a picnic table, where we hang out and talk, taking our time while the patch job dries.

The moment finally feels right to tell him about the twelve-step program.

"That's great, man. Congratulations. What, are you in the beverage program?"

I explain that no, for me it's about relationship and codependence issues.

"I know what you mean. My ex-wife and I had some serious codependency shit going on for years. My opinion is that humans can turn just about anything into an addiction. Good for you for taking care of yourself."

"How long have you been in NA?" I ask.

"Eleven years as of January. What can I say? That program saved my life."

I tell him I'm reading a book called *The Spirituality of Imperfection*, how it claims that the twelve-step program is one of the most significant spiritual movements of the century, that the original founders of AA had consulted with Carl Jung—a man who believed that some alcoholics were so far beyond traditional medical help that only a spiritual awakening could save them.

"Look at me—I'm living proof," Andy says. "If it wasn't for NA, I'd probably be dead. As far as spirituality goes, I think it's the best thing going."

Later that afternoon, Kessler asks if he can catch a ride back to Amagansett for a Saturday-night AA meeting. He invites me to come along. "An addict's an addict," he says, "and a meeting's a meeting."

On the way, we stop by Grodin's house, where I'm spending the weekend. We shoot a few games of pool with him while he chides Andy about his deep suntan.

"Jesus, Kessler, you think you got enough sun today? Your face looks like a stewed tomato."

After Grodin slaughters us both at pool, he invites us to barbecue with him down at the beach later that night. I'm embarrassed to tell Grodin that I'll meet up with him later, that first I'm going to an AA meeting with Andy.

"You're going to meetings now too? I've never even seen you drunk."

"I don't really have a drinking problem," I say. "I'm just going for the spiritual part."

Grodin looks at me like I've lost my mind, then heads for the refrigerator.

The meeting takes place in a cinder-block church house just down the road from Grodin's. It's an odd mixture of working-class residents and wealthy Hamptons vacationers, including one Zsa Zsa Gabor type who goes on an indulgent, weepy rant about how she caught her little lapdog eating its own shit—*doo doo,* she calls it— and how this ruined her entire day.

After things wrap up and we all hold hands for the Serenity Prayer, Andy introduces me to his friends Collette and Nadia, good-looking city women who are out for the weekend, staying in a Montauk beach rental for sober folks.

Nadia and I walk outside together, stand around talking in the dirt parking lot.

We hit it off—that is, until she asks is how long I've been sober.

"I'm not really an alcoholic" is the best I can manage. Nadia looks puzzled, but fortunately Andy walks up and invites her to our beach barbecue. She and Collette follow us to the grocery store, where we pick up three pounds of fresh clams for the grill, plus a couple six packs of soda.

Nadia and I converge on the checkout line.

"Hi! How *are* you?" she says, playfully, as if we hadn't just seen each other in the frozen seafood section.

"Well," I sigh, "I *was* doing great, until my dog ate its own shit and totally ruined my day."

Nadia grasps my forearm, doubles over with laughter.

It's dark by the time we meet Grodin and Anka out on the beach, a bonfire illuminating their faces. Nadia pulls up a chair beside me, hangs out while I strum the ukulele.

"You know, you'd be a lot better on that thing if you could figure out more than three chords," Andy says.

"Ah, don't listen to him," Nadia says. While everyone else hovers over the grill, she asks me again about my sobriety.

"So if you're not an alcoholic, then why come to AA?"

"I don't usually. I'm in another twelve-step program, though, so I just came for the support."

"So you're in NA, right? You don't have to be embarrassed about it."

But I'm not in NA, and I *am* embarrassed. How do you tell someone you're hooked on a destructive relationship pattern? And I'm not and probably never will be comfortable with the term "love addiction." I'm tempted to tell her I'm in Al-Anon, which is partly true since I've been to a few of their meetings, too. But I want to be honest—honesty being the bedrock of recovery—so I go ahead and tell her about the men's meetings.

"Wow," she says. "That's not at all what I expected. Considering you were with Andy, I thought you must've been a total junkie. But I was confused because you don't look like the average heroin addict."

She goes on to ask me about the group, about my issues. I explain it the best I can—that I have a really, really hard time getting over ex-girlfriends.

"That just seems like human nature," she says. "Everyone has trouble getting over relationships."

Without going too deep, I try to explain how it's different for me—that I have a codependent pattern of losing myself in relationships that has basically ruined my life, over and over. But I can tell she's not fully convinced. It's a reaction that I'll find increasingly common and troubling—to struggle with an affliction that people don't even believe in. Even my own therapist, a kind of old-school Freudian, seems to think that I really just need to get laid. And oddly enough, after I tell Nadia all this, she seems even more interested in me.

"What about you?" I ask, hoping to change the subject. "How long have you been sober?"

"Not long," she says. "About ten months." She tells me about her life; I'm surprised to learn she grew up in Alaska. She assures me that she didn't have the typical Alaskan upbringing—"There sure as hell weren't any family camping trips," she says. There was no camping at all, not until she got sent away to a wilderness program for wayward youth.

"Suffice it to say I was a *bad girl*," she tells me. "Although not compared to some of the others. Once I had to share a canoe with this guy who ended up in prison for murder. As if being thrown together with people like that was going to help me."

She explains how, after finishing high school, she escaped to L.A., and then New York—as far from Alaska as possible. And how she's getting healthy now for the first time, and feeling pretty good about things. She definitely *looks* healthy. She has the flawless, pale skin of someone who grew up in a northern place, away from the sun. Pretty blue eyes and a stunning figure. But in the light of the bonfire, I think I detect something a little off in her gaze—a wound that hasn't quite healed, a deep need that's yet to be satisfied.

We all feast on clams and shish kebabs and a big loaf of crusty French bread. Then Collette and Nadia invite Andy and me back to Montauk, to meet up with the rest of their sober crew. As we clean up, Grodin douses the bonfire with seawater, then pulls me aside and says, "Okay, *now* I understand why you went to an AA meeting." But it's after midnight and I'm worn out, ready for bed. Asa is also taking the train out the next morning, and I'm looking forward to an early surf session.

It's painful watching Nadia walk away, looking over her shoulder at me—her eyebrow raised in one final, seductive invitation. Maybe I'm just squandering a chance for a good time, a harmless little post-Karissa rebound? Attiq has warned me about getting involved with program people, at least in the beginning. And with only ten months' sobriety, Nadia seems hungry in a way I imagine might swallow us both up—making her even more of a dizzying temptation. Although this is probably just a projection, because history proves that *I'm* the dangerous party in these situations. Attiq has also suggested I refrain from any relationships, even just a harmless fling, at least for a solid few months. He said this will cause me to suffer, but that more than anything I need to sit with this suffering, that it's precisely what

I've been running from for so many years. At any other point in my life, I would've chased after Nadia, guided by my dick and my slobbering ego, losing myself for something that might last one night or ten years, just a couple people crashing into each other by accident, ripping our tenuous mends.

Even after Grodin and Anka pack up, I linger by the smoldering ashes, alone with the waves as they churn themselves into foam.

DIAMOND BUCKSHOT

I meet Asa at the train station the next morning, and then we head straight for Ditch Plains. I tell him about Nadia during the drive.

"Sounds like you made the right choice," he says.

"Yeah?"

"Definitely. You stayed true to yourself and your recovery."

"It brought up so much shit for me. I wanted her so bad, and then when I let it go, I started thinking about Karissa. I woke up feeling completely obsessed."

"I hear you, man," Asa says, "and I think you just need to sit with the feelings." This is a mantra I hear repeated over and over in the program, in one form or another, including my favorite, *don't just do something, sit there.*

We're two of the first people in the water, and floating around with Asa in glittering sunlight, I start to feel better. We surf all day, taking breaks for food and water, or to nap on the beach. It's my ideal day, when I feel fully present in a place and in my own body—enough that my mind shuts off for a while. Someone else in recovery once told me that the ego is like a dog on a leash, that to get anywhere we have to train it—teach it not to bark or shit on the neighbors' lawn or hump a stranger's leg. For me, surfing's like letting the dog run wild on the beach all day, chucking a stick for it to fetch out in the break, again and again, until it wears itself out. I once heard that it's impossible to experience anxiety during the act of intercourse—directly before and after, sure, but not during the actual deed. I have a similar theory about surfing: it's impossible to feel depressed during the actual riding of a wave.

Along with feelings, my problem's also with language, the way I'm plagued by certain words, words that are like the *whale lines* that Melville says all men live entangled in, words that trigger the feelings in the first place: *should've, would've, Karissa, never, failure, regret, future.* The way the water out beyond the break at Montauk reflects symphonic patterns of sunlight—now like static snow on a TV screen, now like diamond buckshot up from below, now like a conflagration of tiny lightning birds, now concentrating into a single shimmering portal, yet all of these descriptions so completely failing the signified—helps me move past language's breakwater, to drift out farther, beyond words toward the ineffable, toward silence. Toward something like serenity as Asa and I skim across the wind-woven surface of the Atlantic.

A GREAT DESIRE

Next to Duke Kahanamoku, Tom Blake was the most important figure in the history of early twentieth-century surfing. A native Wisconsinite who grew up skiing, he moved in the 1920s to Oahu, where he befriended the Duke and was eventually inducted into native-only groups like the Hui Nalu (translation: United in Surfing). Blake spent time at the famous Bishop Museum, where he helped restore ancient Hawaiian surfboards in their collection. Blake then transformed surf technology by incorporating these ancient board designs into a modern hollow-core construction. At the time, Duke was riding ten-foot boards that weighed about seventy pounds. Blake's new boards were more streamlined, with a hollow core and a pintail, and though they were two feet longer than the Duke's board, they weighed only forty-four pounds. Known as cigar boards, they revolutionized not only surfboard design but the art of surfing itself. Blake himself used a hollow-core board during a twenty-six-mile race from Catalina to the California mainland, which he completed in five hours, fifty-three minutes, shattering previous records. Blake also built sixteen-foot hollow-core boards, called *okohola,* that were more exclusively designed for surfing waves. Duke followed in his footsteps, building a sixteen-foot redwood board, allowing him to do some of the best surfing of his life: "In one instance, at zero break, he caught a twenty-five-foot wave and rode across the face of it, through first break, clear into Queen's surf at a speed of about thirty miles an hour."

Along with his contributions to surfboard design, Blake helped promote the laid-back surfing life with his book *Hawaiian Surfriders, 1935.* His love for the easy life by the sea, which he contrasts with the social obligations and superficialities of city life—as well as his description of a kind of Universalist, multicultural existence in Hawaii—all have echoes of Melville:

Acquaintances in the States have asked me why I bury myself in the Hawaiian Islands. The reason is because I like it. It fits my nature, it is life's compensation for such a nature as mine. I like it because I can live simple and quiet here. I can live well, without the social life. . . . I like the opportunity of studying and seeing the great mixture of races gathered here, each one retaining many of their old customs of eating, dress and living. I pick a custom or two from each race to use at my convenience. Perhaps it is the Buddhist religion of the Chinese—the poi eating and surfriding of the Hawaiians— the raw peanut eating of the Filipinos—the happiness, enthusiasm and appreciation with which the Japanese meet their daily duties.

In *Hawaiian Surfriders,* Blake also relates a number of ancient Hawaiian surf legends he encountered during research at the Bishop Museum. In one, a ruling chief named Aikanaka stole the wife of his younger brother, Kawelo. Betrayed and despondent, Kawelo spent his days plotting revenge against his brother. But his quest for vengeance was interrupted when a large swell arrived at the local break. According to the story, "a great desire came over Kawelo."

Instead of seeking revenge, he went surfing.

THE MARINER'S TALE

> If they but knew it, almost all men in their degree, some
> time or other, cherish very nearly the same feelings towards
> the ocean with me.
>
> ~ HERMAN MELVILLE, *Moby-Dick*

Despite my ancestors' Midwestern roots—five or six genera-
tions in Missouri, Illinois, and Colorado—I'm not the first
ocean-obsessed member of my family. On my mother's side,
my uncle John Lawrence spent the better part of his late twenties and
early thirties living and cruising on a sailboat—much like Herman
Melville, who spent his young adulthood bouncing from
whaling vessels to merchant marine ships to tropical islands. "This is my substitute for pistol and
ball. With a philosophical flourish Cato throws
himself upon his sword; I quietly take to the
ship," Melville wrote in the first chapter of
Moby-Dick. In my uncle's case, going to
sea may also have been a matter of life or
death, but unlike me and Ishmael during
our New York years, he didn't ship out to
quell his own self-destructive thoughts or
his urge to go about the streets *"knock-
ing people's hats off."*

In John Lawrence's case, the threats
came from the outside.

My uncle's first taste of nautical life
was in England, aboard a 149-foot
trawler, the *Avon River.* He'd grown up
in a Missouri hamlet called Arrow Rock,
population eighty-one, where his domi-
neering father encouraged him to follow in

his footsteps and become a doctor. When John quit his premed studies at the University of Missouri, my grandfather disowned him, at least in the emotional sense. Exiled and aimless, John was eventually lured to Saint Hill Manor in England, where a man named L. Ron Hubbard was launching a new religion.

John worked his way up the ranks, and eventually became director of accounts worldwide. His main responsibility was transferring Hubbard's book royalties into Swiss bank accounts. For his full-time work and dedication to Scientology, he was paid ten pounds a week, or about $1,300 a year. He also labored as darkroom assistant to Hubbard—with whom he spent hours in the pitch black, listening to the leader's private thoughts and ruminations. John earned enough trust that Hubbard hired him as a special Scientology tutor for his own children—none of whom, curiously, had yet been taught much about the religion. My uncle was eventually bestowed with the rare ordination of "doctorate of Scientology," as well as a doctorate of divinity. After graduation, Hubbard asked him to join an elite group that came to be called the Sea Org, the official name for the Scientology Navy. Having been hounded by government officials in the United States, Africa, and now England, Hubbard hoped to move much of his organization to international waters, where they could live tax-free and plunder the seas for sunken treasure. He created Sea Org to expedite this Ahab-like undertaking.

Driving a fellow Scientologist's Land Rover, John executed a Sea Org mission in Scotland to purchase the *Avon River,* a vessel that was to become one of Hubbard's main exploration crafts. John and a small crew sailed her to Hull, England, where they spent a winter refitting the *Avon*'s hold; much of the old fishing ship's interior was coated in rancid cod liver oil. Enduring the stench and lack of heat, they followed Hubbard's orders and installed a blacksmith's forge for the purpose of melting gold ingots into ballast, so that any recovered treasure could be transported in secret. They also supplied the ship with a hundred cases of soda for Hubbard, who seemed to live off Coke and cigarettes.

With encouragement from Hubbard, John took up the danger-

ous trade of "hardhat" commercial diving. Wearing a copper hel-
met the size of a dollhouse, a canvas dry suit, and lead boots, my
uncle submerged himself in frigid waters to repair the *Avon*'s hull.
He was so natural in the ocean that he began teaching others the
trade. Hubbard had high hopes that his skills would easily transfer to
undersea treasure hunting.

John and his fiancée, Ann, eventually married and lived together
at Saint Hill Manor. Ann studied Scientology, but with much less zeal
than her new husband. Over time she grew alarmed by the increasingly covert and dangerous nature of his missions. She was encouraged, though, by his nascent fascination with ships and the ocean
after his winter on the *Avon River*. Using part of a loan from her stepmother, she and John purchased a used twenty-seven-foot sailboat,
the *Tio Pepe*, for $5,000. After a winter on a stinking, frozen vessel,
John needed some time off, and though they'd gotten engaged several
months earlier, they'd yet to have a proper wedding ceremony. But
word of their relatively "extravagant" purchase spread through Saint
Hill Manor, quickly reaching the ears of Hubbard's wife. Deciding
there was no way John could afford a sailboat on his meager salary,
and not bothering to ask for bank statements confirming Ann's family
loan, she accused my uncle of embezzling from the church. Equally
quick to judgment—even of his most trusted inner circle—Hubbard
himself declared my uncle a "suppressive person" and banished him
from Saint Hill Manor and its carefully cultivated gardens.

John's exile from Scientology was absolute and infinitely more
severe than his emotional banishment from his father. Like the biblical figure Ishmael—the illegitimate son of Abraham who was exiled
into the wilderness—my young uncle was deeply in touch with the
orphan archetype, even if subconsciously.

Herman Melville, having lost his own father and been repeatedly
rejected by his mother (in favor of his older brother Gansevoort),
also clearly identified with Ishmael, so much so that he named his
main character in his honor. According to Edinger, "What makes
the image of exile in the wilderness so important today is that it
expresses a state of mind that is currently widespread." In another

passage, he states that "*[Moby-Dick]* speaks so deeply to us today because this state of alienated meaninglessness is so prevalent in twentieth-century man. In the story of Ishmael's voyage we recognize dimly the state of our own souls."

John was barred from the Saint Hill grounds; none of his closest friends and coworkers were allowed to speak with him or even acknowledge his existence, for fear of being declared "suppressive persons" themselves. Concerned that these fascist tactics might lead to a lawsuit or even physical reprisal, John and Ann decided to leave England the day after their wedding. They later learned from friends that Sea Org had labeled them "fair game," a term akin to an open hunting license on "suppressive persons." John had come to England seeking the acceptance and connection he'd never had with his father. Now he was cast out, banned from the garden, fleeing for his own and his wife's safety.

My grandmother Mariana loved the ocean. She was a graceful swimmer and a Red Cross–certified lifeguard; on trips to visit my great-aunt Trudy and uncle Art in California, they ferried her across the channel to Catalina Island, to her and Trudy's favorite swim spot, Love Cove. In her white one-piece bathing costume and mint-green swim cap, she spent hours in the glimmering ocean, floating like an angel from the deep in her perfect backstroke.

Trudy and Mariana's love for the ocean also manifested in their musical choices. They both played the ukulele, an instrument that evokes a tropical, beach-barbecue dreaminess like no other. The ukulele became popular on the mainland after World War II, when GIs returned from the Pacific Islands and launched the tiki craze. My grandmother and Trudy picked up their first set, a beautiful pair of Martins made from real Hawaiian koa wood, after visiting the home of some Hawaiian transplants living in L.A. My grandmother and aunt were mesmerized with the ukulele's exotic, chimey sound. They played constantly, singing traditional hymns like "Amazing Grace," classics like "Shenandoah," and bright Hawaiian tunes about the sea. But Mariana's festiveness always faded once she left the West Coast.

Back in Missouri, she confined her musical practice to the bathroom, behind a locked door. She'd often sit in a bubble bath for an hour or more, the faucet gushing to drown out her singing and the tinkling of her uke.

It's a little sad that Mariana stayed in Missouri, her creative connection to the ocean relegated to an old-fashioned bathtub, when she might have moved to California with her progressive sister and led a more unencumbered and adventurous life, where she could have slipped into the ocean at dawn and gone out dancing at night, the way she'd danced almost every night during her college years. My guess is that her suppressed sense of adventure contributed to Johnny's own wanderlust and his great love for the sea. Perhaps she was secretly supportive of his wanderings, of his eventual escape to the ocean. This was in stark contrast to the relationship between Melville and his mother. After their father's early demise, Melville and his brother Gansevoort were expected to provide for the family, and especially for the demanding Mrs. Melville, who was known to harp on Herman for his lack of focus and direction. After holding down a series of odd jobs—teaching, importing, sales—and finding success in none of them, Melville embarked on a life at sea.

On my uncle John's twenty-eighth birthday, and despite their minimal sailing experience, he and Ann set off across the English Channel. There was a definite sense of freedom for Herman Melville in escaping familial pressures and heading out to sea; my uncle John must have felt some of the same exhilaration as he sailed east from Dover. I imagine him and Ann aboard the *Tio Pepe* on a warm July day, seabirds hovering overhead, salt tang on their lips, watching the White Cliffs of Dover recede behind them. That incredible sense of liberation that only the sea can elicit, mixed with a healthy dose of apprehension, the same way I feel each time I escape the pressurized heat of Midtown Manhattan and paddle out into the brisk blue at Rockaway or Montauk.

John and Ann sailed up the Seine to celebrate Bastille Day in Paris—apropos their escape from Scientology's psychic shackles and the beginning of their revolutionary new life at sea. Together they watched fireworks erupt over the river and wash the darkened silhouette of Notre Dame with waves of crimson, electric green, pink, and gold. After several days in Paris they cruised down the canals to Marseille, then on to the Mediterranean, where they spent three years adventuring around Greece, Corsica, Morocco, and Turkey, the watery paradise west of Palestine, the holy waters of the Holy Land. John became a self-taught master seaman, learning from books and observation the arts of rigging, piloting with a sextant and compass, and celestial navigation. In the mornings he and Ann swam in the gray-green sea, embracing underwater, no one to witness their nakedness but spiraling gulls and the abundant silvery life teeming underwater—monk seals and hundred-year-old sea turtles called *Caretta caretta*. They lived on a tight budget; John dove for most of their food with a speargun—disappearing underwater, then surfacing with fresh-caught silversides, golden gray mullets, mackerel, albacore, cuttlefish, and squid. When funds ran out completely, he earned money with his diving skills, recovering lost anchors and repairing boats, or even salvaging small treasures—strands of copper, gold, lapis lazuli—from ancient Roman and Phoenician vessels, German warships, British minesweepers.

They eventually sold the *Tio Pepe* and put the money toward a larger craft, the *Aquarius*. Departing the Canary Islands, they made a full-sail, downwind Atlantic crossing in twenty-eight days. Most mornings they found flying fish marooned on deck, pan-fried them in butter, and ate them with toast and coffee. They made landfall in the Caribbean port of Bequia, where they set up their headquarters for the next few years. John became a certified commercial diver and started his own diving and engineering operation. He was still haunted by what had transpired with his father and the Scientologists, and like Melville always considered himself a bit of an Ishmael figure, but he loved the sea and found great solace in mastering these new skills on his own.

The ocean was for him—as it was for me during my New York years—the one place that felt like home, a lush wave garden free from all the thorns and thistles of the broken world.

THE PINK GHETTO

There are certain queer times and occasions in this strange
mixed affair we call life when a man takes this whole universe
for a vast practical joke, though the wit thereof he but dimly
discerns, and more than suspects that the joke is at nobody's
expense but his own.

~ Herman Melville, *Moby-Dick*

One afternoon my boss calls me into his office.

"Go ahead and sit down," he says. "And close the door."
Whenever he says this I know something's up, that I've either
done something wrong or I'm getting a raise, so I feel an attendant
spike of anxiety.

"As you probably know, the publishing industry is changing," he
says. "People are reading less, fewer books are moving, and the kind
of avant-garde fiction you've been working on isn't selling as well as
it used to."

"Okay," I say, picking at a ragged cuticle.

"I know you might not want to hear it," he says, glancing out the
window, off toward the Chrysler Building and then back at me, "but
right now romance novels are the only thing selling very well for us.
And that's what Sharon wants us to focus on. So I need you to step up
and start editing more romance."

I leave his office feeling a sense of defeat, disbelief, and complete
absurdity. Theoretically I don't have anything against the genre, although, back in graduate school, even mentioning the word *romance*
was the equivalent of standing up and yelling *pigfucker* during
church. I'd read a few contemporary romances since I started out in
publishing, mixed in with everything else I worked on. And some of
it I actually liked. The dark romantic stuff, the gothic stuff, reminded
me a little bit of Melville, whose work is often labeled "dark romanticism." But romanticism and romance really have little in common.
As a genre, romance traces back to masters of the novel like Jane

Austen and Charlotte Brontë. I have nothing but respect for both writers; I'd read and loved *Jane Eyre*. And a century later, their brand of spooky romance is back in vogue, and I think it's sort of cool.

At the same time, a new brand of hypermasculine "frat lit" is building steam—in fact, my company publishes one of the genre's poster boys. Some female coworkers told me what an asshole he was, how he'd deeply insulted them over drinks one night, as a kind of transparent, douchebag ploy to make them feel so bad about themselves that they'd sleep with him. So given the choice between frat lit and romance, I'll take romance any day.

But despite my hating frat lit and clinging to a progressive, postfeminist ideology, having to work on romance feels emasculating, mainly because I'm in a twelve-step program to deal with codependence—with my obsessive romantic entanglements. Compounding the emasculation is my own stalled writing career: the skateboard anthology isn't selling well—partly due to the publishing company, Soft Skull Press, being on the verge of bankruptcy—plus my novel project's going nowhere. It feels like a cosmic joke, then, to have to sit in the Pit and read romance all day, with its overuse of euphemisms like *her swollen bounty* and *the juncture of her thighs*— like a recovering alcoholic at a cheap wine tasting. The problem is that, while the writing is often better than you might expect, the relationships in these novels are characterized by idealization, obsession, heavy intensity—all hallmarks of my past relationships. Even worse, there's a new emphasis on Latina romance, stuff that gets really steamy, and that reminds me, page after agonizing page, of Karissa.

When I bring this up in my men's meetings, how it feels like this sick joke being played on me, the guys break into laughter, but they're also mostly compassionate about it. My new Puerto Rican friend Carlos tries to help me be more lighthearted.

"So you have to edit some romance novels, so what? Is reading a book going to kill you?"

"No. But it might drive me completely fucking nuts."

"Look," he says, "you're a surfer, right? You have to just let this wash over you, like a wave. You can't let it bring you down. Pretend you're out there in the water, in some tough conditions. You just have to flow with it."

And Attiq reminds me how he had to work in the same office for years with his ex-girlfriend, his "qualifier," to use program language, and how miserable it made him, but he recognizes it now as a necessary condition for his recovery. He also suggests that I avoid any major life decisions during my first year in recovery.

"Rather than trying to change anything in your outer environment," he says, "you need to transform your own inner patterns."

Ignoring all this good advice, I decide to quit anyway. I line up a freelance gig proofreading scholastic exam-prep materials for the Princeton Review. The work itself doesn't sound particularly engaging, but the pay is decent, enough that I can work just three or four days a week, giving me more time to write and surf. And SAT prep books, while tedious, are the least romantic genre I can imagine— not a single *pale mound of fragrant flesh* to be found amid all the geometry sets and synonyms. My therapist seems skeptical—I'll be giving up a full-time job with benefits—but I decide to go ahead and give my two weeks' notice. It's not easy, as my boss has been really good to me, and I can tell he's disappointed.

"Well, I understand your choice," he says. "But you'll be hard to replace."

The next day, he calls me back into his office.

"I've been talking with Sharon," he says. "We think you're a good editor and employee. So we want to know what it would take to have you stay."

This catches me off guard, but he gives me a couple days to think it over.

I talk with my therapist, who suggests I ask for a very significant raise, with the stipulation that I won't work on romance.

"I doubt they'll go for that," I say.

"If they don't, then you move on. To get anywhere in this world, you have to ask for what you want."

So I meet with my boss, tell him my terms. He looks surprised by the amount of money I ask for, but says he'll run it by Sharon. As opposed to our last romance conversation, I feel like I have the upper hand here, because I'm so close to just walking anyway.

He calls me in again the next day.

"Sharon almost choked when I told her your terms," he says. "That's nearly the amount we pay senior editors. So I'm sad to say it, but I'm really going to miss you."

I walk out feeling mostly at peace with it, ready to escape the Pit, but also a little hurt that they didn't meet me in the middle with the salary offer. It's a matter of a few thousand dollars a year, a fraction of the amount I see Sharon throw weekly at half-assed bloggers turned novelists and midlist romance writers.

But as my impending last day approaches, I start to seriously doubt my decision. I'm giving up my health insurance. A caring, supportive boss. And along with the romance, some interesting editing projects.

At night, alone, my doubt turns into panic. I'm single in New York, and work has become a major source of security in my somewhat rootless life—my current partner in yet another love/hate relationship.

My final week on the job I have two nearly sleepless nights in a row. I wake in the middle of the night feeling adrift, a castaway like Melville's character Pip, a cabin boy who despite being told not to, jumps from a whaleboat, only to find himself left behind in the ocean's immensity.

The next day, I call my therapist, schedule an emergency appointment. I end up in his office, literally shaking.

I tell him that I don't think I can go through with this, that I'm in no shape to start a new job.

"*Justin*," he says, trying to snap me out of it. "You can't go back now. You already made your decision; you're doing this because you want more time to write, remember? Take some deep breaths, get yourself some lunch, and go finish packing up your things."

"I think I'm having a nervous breakdown," I say.

He doesn't respond immediately, not wanting to confirm what for me feels self-evident.

"There's no medical diagnosis of 'nervous breakdown'—it's an antiquated term. You're having some generalized anxiety now, but that's to be expected during a career change."

On my last day of work, a Friday, I can't stand it anymore. I go back to my boss's office, sit down, and ask if he's found anyone to take my job.

"Like I said, you're hard to replace. I've done a couple interviews, but nothing too promising."

"So you haven't found anyone you really want?"

"Why do you ask?" he says, tilting his head. "Am I getting the sense you want to stay?"

I lean forward in my chair, clasp my hands together. "I've been thinking about it, and yes, I really do. I'll do whatever it takes—I'll work on romance. If you'll have me, I want to stay."

"Well *of course* you can stay," he says, breaking into a wide smile and leaning back in his chair. "Now I can put all these résumés aside and get back to work."

Sitting there across from him, being welcomed back so warmly, I feel myself lifted completely from all the stress and anxiety, as if he's reached a hand down and pulled me back into the life raft. I thank him, over and over, tell him what a great job I'll do from here on out, and then I float back to my cubicle, feeling such relief, such *elation*, like I'm back in the arms of my lover, home again in her warm, romantic embrace.

It feels so wonderful, so intoxicating that I barely notice how pathetic my coworkers think I am, the same way my friends thought it was pathetic when Nicole and I got back together after the sixth or seventh breakup.

A woman in the office known as the Romance Maven tells me that she's glad I'm staying.

"But Jesus, kid," she says, "don't ever do *that* again."

Another coworker, a kind, graying man in his late forties, who started off his career in theater but is now stuck in the Pit, welcomes me back.

"I just hope you don't regret it," he says.

SHARKY

One sweltering afternoon in July, just after my quitting fiasco, Natalie and Paul and I all escape down to Rockaway. While we're circling the parking lot, we spot a cute, tan woman walking barefoot across the blacktop, a tank of a longboard tucked under her arm. It's my friend Sadie, a friend of Andy Kessler's whom I'd met at a book release party.

I roll down my window and say hello.

"Oh my God, I have to tell you the craziest thing," she says, rushing right up to the car. "I got out here just after dawn. I was the only one out in the water—and I saw a *shark!* A shark, right here at Rockaway!" She turns around and points to the spot where she'd seen it, just beyond the jetty, the exact place we're about to surf. That the shark could have eaten her leg off apparently hasn't crossed her mind. And the story freaks Natalie out so much that she won't go near the water that day. She thinks Sadie is completely nuts and from then on refers to her as "your friend *Sharky*."

Sadie is far from nuts, though. She's an instructor at the Harbor School, where she teaches inner-city youth about ocean biology and ecology, the curriculum centered on the relationship between humans and water. She's a shark fanatic; for her, Animal Planet's Shark Week is more exciting than the Super Bowl. During a future trip to Portland, my friend Dan will tattoo a great white shark, surrounded by roses, on the inside of Sadie's bicep. Sharks don't faze her at all; the only aquatic life at Rockaway that causes Sadie serious consternation are the jellyfish. Another day on the beach she explains the problem: jellyfish are like cockroaches of the sea. As the ocean becomes less and less biodiverse—as humans kill off large predators like sharks and swordfish, and as global warming heats up the entire planet—jellyfish populations continue to explode. During the four or five years I've known Sadie, at any given point she's always reading one book or another about the ocean; this particular summer she's reading one about the devolution of the sea.

"If we don't change our habits," she tells me, "the ocean will become more and more acidified and swamp-like, filled with nothing but algae and jellyfish and trash. Did you know there's a massive island of discarded plastic swirling around the Pacific? And giant jellyfish swarms all over the world. They had to shut down the beach at Waikiki for a while because of them. Waikiki! That's where surfing was practically invented."

As Sadie explains, certain jellyfish are like barometers of the sea—they go where it's warm. During dog-day summer afternoons at Rockaway, the water warms up to bathtub temperatures, drawing in swarms of jellyfish. The Rockaway specimens aren't the stinging kind, fortunately, but they are annoying and sort of disgusting. Oval shaped and hollowed out on the top, they look like translucent ashtrays or discarded diaphragms. When it gets really bad, you can feel several brushing against your arms with every paddle stroke; it's like surfing in a warm bowl of tapioca. Combined with all the plastic bags and assorted detritus in the water—including "Coney Island white fish," a.k.a. used condoms—it's enough to make you reconsider ever surfing again at Rockaway.

But Sadie is undeterred. She has summers off from teaching—a fact that causes me no small amount of jealousy—and takes the A train to Rockaway almost every morning. She's like a punk-rock, street-smart Gidget, except in her case she catches the surf bug and then never returns to conventional life, not really. And she's seriously heartened by her shark sighting; she talks about it all summer. Whereas it scares the hell out of Natalie, for Sadie a dorsal fin just off the beach in New York City is a little sign of hope in an otherwise damaged environment.

One of the few perks of my job is that we get alternating Fridays off during the summer months. We work longer hours other days of the week, but it's definitely worth it. On a Friday a couple weeks after her shark sighting, I pick Sadie up at her place and then drive down to Rockaway.

Arriving just after nine, we score a parking spot and a fun swell, mostly just the two of us, trading wave after sun-silvered wave, cheering each other on, splash-fighting between sets, trying to identify different seabirds and keeping our eyes out for dorsal fins on the horizon. Afterward we hang out on the beach, eating deli sandwiches before Sadie gets immersed in her ocean ecology book and I read a few *Moby-Dick* chapters, all of this followed by a long, totally satisfying nap. Nothing really happens—and that's just it. Back in the city, the stress of commuting and working full time in Midtown, along with my recovery, are taking a toll. And my coworker was right—my post-breakup honeymoon with work lasts all of two weeks.

On the drive home that evening, I can already feel the weekend slipping away. I tell Sadie how I've been struggling with work, how I tried to leave but couldn't. How I'm considering just up and quitting until I can find a teaching job.

"Maybe you just need a girlfriend," she says. "I mean, look at you. Why the hell don't you have a girlfriend?"

"That's kind of a long story," I say. "But I'm serious about the job thing. I really miss teaching."

"You can't just quit your job," she says, sounding alarmed.

"I know. But it's making me depressed. Surfing's the only thing that seems to help."

"I can relate," she says. "Not sure if you knew, but my dad passed away last year." I had heard this from someone—Dawn or Teagan. But I didn't know all the details.

"He actually took his own life," she says.

"Oh my God," I say. "I had no idea, I'm—"

"It's okay," she says. "You don't have to say anything."

But I feel ridiculous now, having gone on so long about my petty career woes.

"I've dealt with it. I mean, I'm dealing with it. The way I do that is by coming down here to Rockaway, every day I can. Especially at first, it was one of the only things that kept me going. Being in the ocean—communing with something so vast—definitely does something. So whatever you need to do, I'm with you, you know? I understand. Just promise me you'll get something lined up before you quit. Because while surfing is great, being unemployed is not."

CIRCLES

Most evenings after work and a long subway commute, I don't have time to hit the beach or even the Autumn Bowl. But being an intensely physical person, I need daily exercise, especially here in New York, where, without serious cardiovascular exertion, I'll cross over from neurosis to complete incapacitation. So along with swimming laps, I start running on the McCarren Park track. Sprinting ten or twenty laps on the spongy surface, while Mexican and Dominican guys play soccer in the center field, sufficiently wears me out. But running around in circles by myself—*circumambulating the city*—tends to stir up my ruminative mental processes, my spiraling obsession with Karissa.

So during my cool-down laps, I typically make some calls on my cell phone, most often to Asa or Attiq. *Program calls* is how everyone refers to them, and in those first white-knuckle months of my withdrawal period, I make hundreds.

Not long after starting the program, I call Attiq, tell him what I'm thinking—that I'm in a codependent relationship with my work, and I think I need to leave New York entirely, that I definitely don't want to spend the rest of my life here. And how I want to move to Portland, where life will be easier, and where I can maybe make things right with Karissa before she gets serious about this guy.

Attiq listens patiently as always.

"Look," he says, "it's fine that you recognize New York isn't right for you in the long term. But the fact is, you're here right now. You might not realize it, but this work you're doing in the program is important— much more so than your regular, moneymaking work. This doesn't mean you can't leave New York eventually. Think of Brooklyn as a temporary apartment, where you reside while you rebuild the entire foundation of your house. You're down in the mud and ashes right now, and I know it's uncomfortable, but it's exactly where you need to be. It's a holy place, a sacred place; the lotus grows up from that mud."

THE TOOTH

Dawn and I drive to Rockaway on a warm September evening, taking the freeway route past the Verrazano-Narrows Bridge and down near Coney Island. During the trip she tells me she was on the diving team in high school and college, then worked summers as a lifeguard at Barton Springs in Austin. After college she moved to San Francisco, where she lived with her boyfriend, a BMW-driving yuppie. Along with working in finance, he dealt a little Ecstasy on the side to support his lifestyle. Dawn did what she could to fit into his world—she wore diamond earrings, clipped her hair back, pretended to read the *Wall Street Journal* with him in the breakfast nook of their condo. But the whole thing went sour, and now, maybe as a result of feeling so burned, she spends all her time with skaters and surfers—people with whom she doesn't have to pretend to be anything she's not.

We arrive at the beach around dusk. No one else around, we paddle out to the prime position just off the jetty. It's hard to see in the fading light, and we get rolled by a cleanup set, something that might freak me out if I was by myself, but being out with Dawn makes me feel safe, although she claims that she was possibly the worst lifeguard in history.

We both get some good waves, and though it's almost dark now, we keep paddling back for more. I catch a long ride, hanging on all the way to the shallows. Wading back out in the near-dark, I push my board carelessly in front of me. Just then a swell heaves up and pitches the board back at my face, the thick rail nailing me right in the teeth.

Immediately there is the salty taste of what I hope is seawater, but that I know in truth to be blood.

My teeth are already fucked up; I should've had braces as a kid but didn't—and I can feel with my tongue that getting drilled by my surfboard has knocked my left front tooth another millimeter out of alignment.

Dawn helps me out of the water and onto the beach, where I spit blood and have to resist reaching up to touch my mouth with sandy hands. We make it up to my truck, where, in the rearview mirror, I see matching incisions on the inside and outside of my lower lip. Dawn takes a look but can't tell if my tooth has pierced all the way through the skin.

We luck out and find an ambulance parked next to the boardwalk. Two young EMTs invite me inside, where I swear I smell pot smoke, and where the younger one—a surfer himself—takes a look at my lip.

The verdict is, fortunately, that the tooth didn't go all the way through. I don't need stitches.

The EMT gives me an ice pack. Asks if I need anything for the pain, while making the international sign for smoking a joint. I tell him I'm cool, thanks, and then hold the ice pack to my swollen lips while Dawn drives us back to the city.

HEROIN

A
t a Wednesday-night meeting, my new friend Carlos tells his
story. He grew up in Puerto Rico, in a clapboard shack with
his mother and four siblings. His father was just a man who
came by on Saturdays to sleep with his mom. Hoping for a better
life, his mother moved them all to the South Bronx in the seventies.
Because his family could only afford to buy him Zips sneakers, and
not Keds, Carlos was endlessly taunted and bullied by neighborhood
kids—*Zips have soles that slip.*

As a teenager, Carlos grew his hair out long, started smoking
pot and hanging out with his high school art teacher, who introduced him to abstract expressionism, took him to the Guggenheim
and the Met. One day in Central Park, she leaned over and kissed
him. He ran away from home to live with her in a tiny East Village
studio. It lasted a few months, until she got depressed and kicked
him out. He found work in Manhattan restaurants, where he was
introduced to harder drugs—cocaine and eventually heroin. He developed a taste for both, eventually began mixing the two in a dangerous cocktail known as a speedball. This was the eighties, when
my Brooklyn neighborhood was one of the worst slums in the city:
El Barrio, Sugartown. Carlos spent a lot of time there and in the East
Village, standing in long lines, sometimes wrapping around the entire block, not just homeless junkies but secretaries, men in business
suits, all of them waiting to cop. By then homeless himself, he slept
sitting up on the 6 train.

One night in the subway he got robbed, had his front teeth bashed
out with a lead pipe.

"That was my life for three or four years," Carlos tells us. "When I
finally decided to kick, a doctor prescribed me heavy doses of Prozac,
Wellbutrin, and Valium. I had to take all that plus drink half a gallon
of wine every day. But by the grace of God, I came through. I've been
sober for fifteen years now. I got my teeth fixed and I have a good

job. Every day I'm just grateful to be alive, to help others get through what I did. Right now it feels like I'm walking on this pink cloud."

He goes on to tell us that for him, this group is like graduate school. Because the problem now is that he's hooked on this Russian woman—a person who will sleep with him but won't commit to any kind of emotional relationship, won't let him move in with her, but demands that he help pay her rent.

"It's ridiculous," he tells us. "I'm thirty thousand dollars in debt, but here I am, putting her rent on my credit card, just so I can get laid. I know I need to stop, but I'm confident that my higher power will lift it from me when I'm ready. I'll tell you what—I used to be the biggest junkie in the city, but this love stuff is just as powerful as heroin."

Afterward, we all go out for dinner—"fellowshipping" is what everyone calls it. We eat at an authentic Mexican place I love, where Carlos speaks Spanish with the owners. Then Carlos and I get to talking about how we both did stints in San Diego. It's about the only thing I feel I have in common with him at first, but he's got charisma, a presence that lights up everyone around him. After dinner he hands me a laminated prayer card with the image of a radiant heart, the words *La Luz del Mundo* inscribed beneath.

Carlos and I exchange numbers, and then one afternoon in November we take the subway down to his new apartment in Ditmas Park, where I help him move a heavy dresser.

On the train, he shows me a yoga book he's been reading, with diagrams of the chakra systems.

"Wait, I thought you were Catholic?" I say.

"What made you think that?"

"The prayer card you gave me at dinner. *La Luz del Mundo.*"

"Just something I picked up," he says, then points to the lower chakras on the diagram. "This is the place I lived from as a young person. I was ruled by my animal instinct, my insatiable appetites. In Hindu terms it meant I was unevolved, that I needed to progress upward. That's what recovery's been all about for me, living more from my heart. With this Russian woman, I know I'm still halfway stuck down in the lower chakras, but I have faith. I know I'm moving forward, upward."

I tell him about my *Moby-Dick* obsession, about how the chakra system reminds me of the Nekyia—this idea that all spiritual development begins with a necessary descent to the lower regions.

Carlos likes this idea. "I think the whole world's going through that right now," he says. "Look what's happening over in Afghanistan, Iraq. Or right here in this country. The way we act—the way we treat the planet—we're like a nation of addicts."

THE TAPROOT

The next Wednesday, a middle-aged man named Henry tells his story. He grew up in the South with an alcoholic father and a long-suffering mother. When Henry came out as gay, his father kicked him out of the house. He moved to New York, where, in his twenties, he got heavily into the party scene.

Henry is a tall man, with close-cropped graying hair and a ruggedly handsome but kind face. Unlike some other guys in the group, he doesn't relish telling his "war stories." Just bringing them up seems to cause him pain, and this gives him an air of authenticity, wisdom.

"Suffice it to say," he tells us, "I went down into some really dark places. That's where I spent my time, down in the dungeons."

He leaves it at that, making me wonder if he's talking about real or metaphorical dungeons.

"I was completely unhappy with my life, basically getting nowhere in my career. But, at the time, I didn't see any connection between my extracurricular activities and my work."

He goes on to explain that through recovery, he came to find God, which he envisions not as a supernatural being, but as "Good Orderly Direction."

"And thanks to that direction," he says, "I've finally been able to put down all my preoccupations with romantic intrigue, sex. I've been thinking a lot about this word, *preoccupation*. It's all the things distracting you from your occupation, your true calling. Instead of chasing the next hit, I turned inward, and by doing so attracted more of what I wanted in my life and my career. This past year has been the most prosperous of my life."

I rush up to talk with him afterward, tell him how much I appreciate his share. After we exchange numbers, I give him a hug—in this meeting hugs are like handshakes—but notice it seems to cause him pain, not because he's cold, but because maybe it triggers him a little.

A few nights later I call him. I tell him how much pain I'm in over

Karissa—over this recurring pattern in my life. And how this pattern has seeped into my work life and I can't seem to break away.

"If I've learned anything in this program," he says, "it's to trust pain when it arises. Addiction is all about running from pain, or trying to substitute pain with some other substance or person or behavior. So trust the pain. Pain is the taproot from which all healing arises."

I've never heard this word before, *taproot*. After hanging up I find my dictionary: *a straight tapering root growing vertically downward and forming the center from which subsidiary rootlets spring.*

GOOD FRIDAY

The second or third time I surf Rockaway with Asa, we drive over to the Lower East Side to pick up his friend Maria. There's something exhilarating about rolling with a truck full of surfboards through this storied Manhattan neighborhood, with its narrow streets, brick tenements turned condos, bodegas and upscale ethnic restaurants. Maria has lived here for something like fifteen years, in a rent-controlled apartment with a bathtub in the kitchen. The bathroom used to be out in the hall, until she broke through a brick wall with a sledgehammer, creating a grotto-like passageway from her bedroom to the toilet. She's an artist and a surfer girl, six feet tall with dirty-blond hair and nice skin. Listens to reggae on vinyl, but has long since given up any substances in exchange for a higher power.

Rockaway's flat—no waves at all—so the three of us lounge on the boardwalk and talk. Like Sadie, Maria works as a teacher. She spends half her summer vacation in her family's Vermont cabin, the other half surfing. When I tell her about my history with teaching, she mentions a potential job opening at the private Quaker school where she works, a position she thinks might be good for me.

Maria and I become surf buddies. Weekends we venture out to Long Beach or a spot called Gilgo, and then always get lost on the drive home, wandering around in the dense tangle of highways and overpasses in interurban Long Island.

Months later, Maria emails me with the official job listing for the school's community service director position. Attiq warns me again about trying to change my outer circumstances, but I fantasize that working at a Quaker school, with its focus on inner silence and social action, might restore a sense of meaning to my life.

In other words, it might help me claw my way out of the Pit.

Along with my résumé, I send in a children's book I'd published about community service. Maybe for this reason, my application rises to the top of the two-hundred-résumé-high pile. The first interview goes very well, maybe as a result of the breathing exercises I do beforehand, or my phone call to Henry, who tells me, in his self-possessed voice, that I should *lead with my feelings.*

"Just after they ask you the initial interview question," he says, "take a minute to first tell them how you're feeling about the job, why you're excited about it. Look them all in the eye. Then you can proceed with your regular response."

So I do this—I look all six or seven panelists directly in the eye, tell them all how excited I am by the idea of working at their school, how grateful I am they called me in.

And I totally nail the interview.

Afterward I meet up with Carlos at Veselka, a Ukrainian diner in the East Village, where he buys me a celebratory slice of apple pie.

"You did good," he tells me. "You made some phone calls before the interview, you did some breathing, you took care of yourself. It's all about small steps toward change."

Two days later I receive an email informing me that I've been chosen for a final interview, that they've narrowed it down to me and one other applicant. They ask me to spend an entire day at the school, where I can sit in on classes, meet students and faculty members, and have several more interviews, including a final meeting with the headmaster.

I don't have any spare vacation time, so I have to call in sick the day of the big interview, on Good Friday. On the Thursday beforehand, I schedule a massage and do everything I can to relax. Unfortunately, my bedroom faces a small basement recording studio operated by a shady guy from New Jersey, who brings in a bunch of unpromising indie and punk bands from across the river. One group plays the same shoegazer ballad, over and over, every night for two months. I wear rifle-range mufflers over silicon earplugs, but the repetitive bass lines and formulaic postpunk drumbeats literally shake my bed. I had to pound on their door a bunch of times, ask them to shut it down, until finally I got the owner to agree to a 10:00 p.m. moratorium.

When I walk by the night before my big interview, there's a band playing in the studio, so I poke my head in, explain my situation—that I have an important job interview the next day, and I'd appreciate if they could stop playing a little early, at, say, 9:30. They look to be eighteen or nineteen, tops. One of them, curiously, has a poorly executed tattoo of the Quaker Oats man on his upper bicep. They grudgingly agree to quit early.

But when I go to bed at 9:45, they're still playing. I lie there with my earplugs in and a pillow over my head, praying they'll stop.

I drift into sleep, until a cymbal crash kicks me awake. I look at the clock: 10:45.

The last thing I want is to get dressed, go downstairs, and confront them, because I know then I'll never get back to sleep. But when they're still playing at 11:00, I don't really have a choice.

It takes a solid few minutes of pounding on the metal roll-down door before they hear me, put down their instruments.

The Quaker tattoo kid opens the door.

"What the fuck?" he says. "You just ruined our track."

"I asked you guys nicely," I say. "It's now 11:00 p.m. I have the most important job interview of my life in the morning. I'm sorry I ruined your track, but unless you want to ruin my *entire life,* please quit playing, *right fucking now.*"

They all glance at each other, smirking, still wondering who this square is that crashed their session.

I go back upstairs, get into bed.

The music begins again.

In my head: I put on a pair of jeans but no shirt, storm downstairs, bash down the door, sock the Quaker kid square in the face, kick a hole in the bass drum, crash the cymbals over, swinging and thrashing, taking on all three little fucks at the same time, a feral display of my not-dead-yet punk-rock roots.

I imagine myself at the interview the next morning, trying to explain a black eye and bloody knuckles to a bunch of Quakers.

The other option is to call the police, but I know this will involve several hours of conversations, reports. And my guess is they'll finish playing once they lay down the track I've just interrupted.

The studio finally goes quiet at 12:15. By this point, though, I'm so full of rage I can't sleep.

Around 1:30 a.m., rage morphs into anxiety.

I try breathing exercises, seated meditation, counting backward from five hundred, but nothing works. By 3:30, I feel panicked, drifting around in this hazy sea of nonsleep, wondering how I'll get through a daylong interview without any rest.

At 5:00, garbage trucks circle the neighborhood.

I finally fall asleep at 6:05 a.m.

Ten minutes before my alarm goes off.

An hour later, in the subway, I recall the way so many commuters had ashen crosses smeared on their foreheads two days earlier, on Ash Wednesday. This seems appropriate now—after a sleepless night, I feel like walking death, hot ash blowing through my veins.

I sleepwalk through the Quaker school, which itself is a kind of fantastic maze—all these hidden passageways and stairwells leading to computer labs filled with sparkling white Macs, a huge art room with a skylight, rooftop basketball courts, a private yoga studio, and a library filled with reading nooks, all of it like something from *The Royal Tenenbaums*. Semi-invisible workers in school uniforms cater our interviews with fresh fruit, water crackers and Brie, bottled mineral water.

When Maria and I meet for lunch in the cafeteria, I ask her about this.

"It's not really catering," she tells me. "It's just cafeteria workers bringing food up for meetings."

"That's pretty much the definition of catering," I say, taking a bite of a freshly tossed garden salad. "The cafeteria at my high school served mainly microwave burritos. And the lunch ladies sure as hell didn't *deliver.*"

Maria laughs. "Considering Susan Sarandon's kids go here, I guess it's not such a surprise."

It's good to see her, to have a break in the never-ending onslaught of interview questions. Despite how tired I feel, she tells me I look great.

But things decline steadily from this point. In a fourth-period history class, I feel shredded with exhaustion, as if my bloodstream is coursing with sewing needles and heavy sedatives.

Just before the final interview with the headmaster, I find myself starting to tremble again, like I did the first time I tried to leave my job, so I step out into the park and make an emergency call to my therapist.

"I think I might reschedule," I say. "I'm sure I can come back and meet the headmaster next week."

The phone goes silent while he considers this idea.

"I wouldn't do that," he says. "You've made it this far. You just need to marshal all your resources," he says, this being advice he gives me often, the *marshaling of all my resources,* "and go back in there. I really think you'll do just fine. In fact, I know it."

Taking his advice, I go back in and meet with the headmaster—a smartly dressed, balding man with a patrician southern accent. But despite my most intense efforts, I can't do it, can't *marshal my resources.* Instead, my resources, still enraged about getting no sleep at all, organize a mutiny against me. They hold me captive, lash my powers of locution to the mainmast, so that I can't seem to answer even the most basic questions.

I devolve into a blubbering, stuttering mess.

Hearing that I can hardly form a sentence, the headmaster lobs me a softball inquiry, asks how I found out about the position.

I tell him I know Maria.

"We're surfin' buddies," I say, my old California accent slipping out here, lazily dropping the *g* off *surfing*—a word that should never, ever be mentioned during a job interview anywhere in the borough of Manhattan.

The headmaster looks entirely perplexed. He remains cordial and tries to help me limp through his final questions. But judging by his expression, he's wondering how I made it this far in the interview process, or what the hell I'm even doing in his office. Or maybe this is a practical joke, and I'm just some wily tenth-grader posing as the interviewee.

I drag myself home, collapse into coma-sleep. The next day, thankfully, is a Saturday, so I drive out to Long Island to visit Kyle Grodin.

By myself on the Long Island Expressway, I fly into a rage, slam my fist into the steering wheel, over and over, inadvertently blasting the horn.

The other motorists give me a wide berth.

It feels good to get it all out. To get myself out of the city.

I'm in pretty bad shape by the time I arrive, but Kyle seems to be doing great. He's in unusually good spirits, and when I offer him a sugar-free, natural fruit juice–sweetened cookie that I've brought him from the city, he turns it over and reads the ingredients, something I've never seen him do.

"There's no refined sugar," I tell him. "But they taste great."

"It's not the sugar I'm worried about," he says. "This thing has like three hundred calories."

It takes me a minute to register: I've just witnessed Kyle *fucking* Grodin not only hesitate before eating a baked good, but actually engage in *calorie counting.*

He explains that he and Anka went to the doctor, where they found his blood pressure and cholesterol astronomically high for someone in his midthirties.

"Dude, I could've told you that," I say.

"Yeah, well, they said I need to change my eating habits or I'm headed straight for heart attack city."

He leads me to the refrigerator, shows me the spoils of a recent shopping spree at the health food store—drawers of fresh produce,

low-fat milk, tofu, and tempeh. He opens the cupboards, where all
the boxes of sugared cereal and cookies have been replaced with gra-
nola and rice patties.

I can't believe what I'm seeing.

Kyle stands there grinning.

"Holy shit, Grodin," I say. "This is maybe the most dramatic reversal of character I've ever witnessed."

The next morning, Easter Sunday, Kyle wakes me up early. Another
reversal: usually I'm the one to wake him up, sometimes well past
noon, after I've already gone jogging or surfing or both. But Kyle's
feeling great—a result of his new diet—plus he checked the surf report and the waves look good.

Down at Ditch Plains, mist shrouds the ocean's surface, obscuring the horizon and the surrounding sea cliffs. A handful of locals in
the water, their figures veiled in fog. The night before, Kyle donated
his old four-millimeter wetsuit to my surfing cause. Standing now
on cold sand, I slip into the oversized suit, then follow him down
to the break. Clean, midsize waves, a mild offshore breeze scooping
them out, holding up their spoon-shaped faces. I've never surfed this
early in the spring, and without booties my feet go numb. Ignoring
the pain, I stay out for a solid hour, catching wave after wave as the
sun evaporates the fog, impressing myself, even impressing Kyle—
just *slightly*.

The interview was one of the most demoralizing experiences of
my life. I'd lost an entire night's sleep and the opportunity for a better job, and for a few minutes there in the headmaster's office I'd lost
my dignity, my whole sense of self. But out here in the cold water,
after a good night's rest, I've rolled away the heavy rock of no-sleep
and rematerialized back into my body, and I'm grateful to the ocean
for carrying me back into this bright brisk region of my chiaroscuro
emotions.

SPONSORS AND SPONSEES

One early summer weekend, Asa and I take another trip out to Montauk, where we pitch tents in Grodin's backyard. Andy Kessler invites us over to his current summer rental for a barbecue, along with a couple of his NA sponsees who are out for the weekend. Andy's place is in a quaint old motor motel, built in the fifties, abandoned in the eighties, and boarded up for twenty years. Everything's perfectly preserved—all the Formica countertops, the linoleum floors, the midcentury furniture, even the linens. Andy found a little stack of fifties-era postcards with a photo of his room, containing all the exact same furniture. He gives them out as souvenirs to everyone who visits.

We eat out on the lawn, on a rickety picnic table, where Andy tells us how he came to rent the place. He was out at Montauk during the spring and happened to see workers prying boards off the windows.

"They give me the number for the owner, who I call three or four times before he finally gets back to me. We go back and forth on price, the length of the lease, all that bullshit. I think it was obvious how much I really wanted the place. But right before we're about to seal the deal, he says to me, 'You're not a surfer, are you?' Swear to God, those were his exact words. I'm not going to lie to the guy, so I say *Yes, in fact I am a surfer.* He basically hung up on me."

"You must have been livid," Asa says.

One of Andy's sponsees—this haggard-looking guy with a crew cut—pipes up. "Fucker did that to me, I would've taken a shit in his mailbox."

Andy laughs, puts his hand to his forehead. "You know, there was a point in my life when I would've done just that. But I realized he was basically just this sad old man, you know? I was out here in Montauk when we had that last phone conversation; the whole ride home I felt at peace with it. I figured it just wasn't meant to be. But then two weeks later he calls me back, says he had a change of heart. So here I am, by the grace of God."

DATA. ASSESSMENT. PLAN.

Fridays: 3–11 p.m.
Saturdays: 3–11 p.m.
Sundays: 3–11 p.m.
Mondays: 11 p.m.–11 a.m.

This was my weekly schedule for my first full-time job out of college back in Colorado, where I worked as a counselor in a residential treatment center for adjudicated boys, a place called New Horizons. *Adjudicated* is the technical term for kids who've been through the court system and done jail time; our clients were mostly young gangbangers from Denver, wannabes from the suburbs, criminally minded hicks, and assorted fuckups. It was the most demanding job I ever had and it paid nine dollars an hour.

I was a New Staff and the New Staff always gets the worst shift—in this case the weekend shift—working Friday, Saturday, and Sunday nights plus the Monday overnight. Monday overnights were borderline psychological torture. I had to do administrative work and bed checks all night, and then take part in the Tuesday-morning staff meeting from nine to eleven. What it amounted to was a grueling, twelve-hour graveyard shift that left me pretty well shredded on my two weekdays off. My boss was a conservative hardass named Tammy who eventually joined the military, and who once reprimanded me for not participating during staff meetings, despite my having been awake for thirty straight hours.

Tammy also thought I was too buddy-buddy with the clients. I'd been working with kids my entire life—mostly at summer camps or skateparks, so using a point system and confronting negative behavior was a hard transition. Sunday-night free time was the only part of the job that came naturally. After everyone finished their chores, we pushed the mess hall tables to one side and rocked breakdancing moves on glossy linoleum. A strange reversal: all these black and Latino kids from inner-city Denver, and me, a white guy from a small mountain town, teaching them how to lie back on their elbows, scissor kick their legs wide, then snap into a tight spinning ball—that quintessential old-school move known as the backspin. They picked it up quickly, but no one beat my record of twelve rotations.

After lights out, staff members wrote "DAP" reports on each client. DAP stands for *Data, Assessment, Plan*. First the straight facts about the client's behavior during the shift (Data), then an analysis of these facts for underlying causes (Assessment), followed by proactive plans for dealing with the client in subsequent shifts (Plan). It's a way of communicating with the other staff members and therapists, but also a legal record required by the state.

Despite my ambitions as a writer, I dreaded writing DAPs. I struggled with the act of reducing these kids and their complicated lives to a set of clipped sentences. Tammy pointed out the lack of objectivity in my reports, the overuse of creative language and metaphors.

"DAPs are for therapeutic purposes," she said, "not for poetry readings."

Though Tammy and I rarely saw eye to eye, she was good at her job, especially when it came to making sure the clients were *staying in structure* and *watching their boundaries*. And she had some astute observations about the kids and their personalities.

"There are basically two types of clients: Apples and Onions," she told me during my first day of training. "We mostly get Apples. We call them Apples because there's a deep emotional core at the center of their being. They can be sweet, but when they get angry or fearful they explode—their emotional core causes them to do things they later regret. Onions, on the other hand, basically have no emotions. They have outbursts of feeling like anyone else, but what really motivates them are layers and layers of criminal-minded thought patterns. They're always thinking about how to take advantage of the situation and they're always two steps ahead of you. These are the kids who grow up to be sociopaths, the kind of people who can murder someone and feel no remorse."

Tammy's description of Onions freaked me out. Apples I could

understand, but people with no emotions? They seemed totally im-
plausible, like Vulcans or characters from an Ayn Rand novel.

"Are there any Onions in the house right now?" I asked.

"Oh yeah," she said. "Chris. Biggest kid in the group. Classic alpha
male Onion. Not to mention a total narcissist. You'll meet him tomorrow on your first shift."

Data: During his first shift, New Staff took his shirt off during a basketball game at recreation time. Most of the clients had prison-house tattoos scrawled on their arms—hideous clowns and pot leaves and other
shabby gangster insignias done with homemade tattoo machines. New
Staff wanted to show these kids that he had his own tattoos—real tattoos, *cool* tattoos. Several minutes into the game, Chris fouled New
Staff with an elbow to the ribs. When New Staff called him on it, Chris
staged a tantrum and stormed off the court, then spent the rest of
the shift glaring at New Staff and cursing under his breath. During the
van ride home, New Staff confronted him on his language. "What
the fuck you gonna do about it, tough guy?" Chris snapped back.

By the end of the night, Chris successfully turned every kid in the
house against New Staff.

Assessment: Taking his shirt off was clearly a mistake on the part
of New Staff. It was more an act of vanity than aggression, but Chris
had taken it as the latter, as a direct threat to his alpha dog status.
Chris was a ridiculous white boy wannabe gangster; even so he left
New Staff shaken. Here's a kid whose modus operandi was to gain
control, to humiliate, to win at all costs—a true Onion and a total
asshole. New Staff was hit with the hard realization that his new job
was more prison guard than camp counselor.

Plan: Stand your ground. Learn to throw up some serious personal
boundaries. Rejoice when Chris gets discharged after a month or so.
Glare at him when you see him cruising around town in his father's
convertible sports car. Keep your shirt on.

Data: Maki was a half-Japanese, half-black Crip from Denver. Well before his arrival at our facility, he'd gotten his sixteen-year-old girlfriend

pregnant. Both families supported the pregnancy; they hoped fatherhood might be his ticket out of gang life. But six months later, both the girlfriend and her unborn child were killed in a car accident. Upon receiving the news, Maki went on a weeklong crack binge. Homeboy drove around Denver in a stolen car with a stolen shotgun, raging at the world, looking for someone to fire on, some red-wearing Blood or green-wearing Latino or white-wearing whale upon whom he might unload his towering rage and the tightly packed shell casings of his grief. He was finally arrested for grand theft auto and concealed weapons charges, and after nearly a year in jail, he came to us for "rehabilitation." During his stay, he was treated with extra care by staff and therapists; he was on constant suicide watch and a heavy dose of meds for severe depression. Most of his spare time he spent making dark little sketches of graveyards and tombstones on his notebooks—*RIP, TLF, RIP*.

Assessment: Despite his Crip status, Maki was a charming kid with poetry in his heart, a true Apple. One of my female coworkers commented on his good looks—high cheekbones and green eyes and perfect complexion—and how in another life he might have been a model or a movie star. Maki's was the most profound grief I'd ever witnessed; I wondered if it would keep him out of prison or land him right back there.

Kill or cure, it was hard to say.

Plan: Try not to upset him. Try not to say something ridiculous one day during group therapy about how maybe all his dwelling on death and graveyards is a disservice to his deceased girlfriend, who would want him to move on with his life, to be happy. He doesn't know exactly what *disservice* means, but gets the drift, and doesn't appreciate it one fucking bit, thank you. Leave this heavy shit to the therapists, the people with master's degrees. Shoot hoops, give him his afternoon snack, make jokes, keep him away from sharp objects, and do your best to keep him moving, upright, awake, alive.

It was a relief to leave New Horizons and start graduate school, but I missed interacting with clients and our Sunday-night breakdancing sessions. I worked there for less than a year, but the kids and their stories stuck with me, became the subject of my novice attempts at fiction. And I found myself still thinking in DAP reports, applying the Apple/Onion label to literary characters, especially after I read *Moby-Dick* for the first time.

Data: Client tends to either isolate in his cabin or pace the decks of the *Pequod*. Client has obvious impulse control issues; he's fixated on the idea of exacting revenge against the white whale. Unfortunately, Client's negativity seems to rub off on his men, most of whom blindly follow his lead. Client also uses his disability as an excuse for not participating in recreational activities.

Assessment: Client's elaborate revenge scheme against the perpetrator who took his leg is consistent with symptomatic patterns of post-traumatic stress disorder, as is his loss of spiritual faith and his suicidal ideation. Client wants to lash out against what he perceives as a blank, godless universe that has wrought so much misfortune upon him; Client views the white whale as the incarnate symbol of this universe. Client's lack of empathy for his crew suggests he's an Onion and possibly sociopathic. But Client does display some Apple characteristics in the end, for instance when he says, just before perishing, *"My topmost greatness lies in my topmost grief."*

Plan: Consider reassigning client to a below-deck post such as cook or steward, where he will pose less of a threat to himself and others. Encourage Client to empathize with the crew's plight, to understand that his actions are affecting everyone on board. Place Client on twenty-four-hour suicide watch and discuss an increase in meds with his therapist. Client would also benefit from an increased exercise plan—encourage him to participate in recreational activities such as swimming or breakdancing. If these measures fall short, consider mutiny.

ALL I NEED IS THIS THERMOS

In May of 2006—two and a half years after moving to New York—I fly back home to Colorado for Kyle Grodin's wedding. After arriving in Denver, I pick up a rental at Advantage Rent a Car and drive to my stepsister's new house, which she explains is in a "rough" neighborhood called Five Points, a place that was considered notorious back in the eighties, but that has since started to gentrify. As I pull up to her street, I laugh inwardly at what she considers rough. It looks like a normal urban neighborhood to me—hell, it even has *trees*. And unlike my own Brooklyn street, it has no graffiti tags, rats, broken beer bottles, used condoms, or female junkies shooting smack in broad daylight. I have some trouble finding the house, so I give her a ring on my cell.

"Do you see me?" she says. "I can see you. You're in a silver car. Look behind you."

I turn around and there she is, standing in front of a brick Victorian with a newly planted yard and an unpainted picket fence, a good starter home for my kid sister the lawyer and her firefighter husband. I feel a little stitch of sibling envy—they're probably paying less for a mortgage than I'm paying for rent back in New York. I park and undo my seat belt, anxious to give her a hug, but for some reason I can't get the key out of the ignition. I sit there fiddling with it, until she taps on my window.

"Hey," she mouths. "What's wrong?"

I roll down the window. "The fucking key is stuck in the ignition."

"*That's* weird," she says. She gets in the passenger's side and tries to help me assess the problem. Two years since we've last seen each other, but we've yet to formally greet each other—no *How was your flight?* or *Great to see you!* For some families this would indicate distance, but for us it shows how close we are, the fact that we can forgo pleasantries and team-tackle the problem at hand. If we learned anything from our pastiche family it's this: *Things go wrong, so deal with it*. Our parents actually divorced long ago, so technically we're *ex-stepsiblings*—a complicated label that we mostly ignore.

"So how's New York?" Steph finally asks. She's messing with the gearshift, making sure it's in park.

"Pretty much a disaster," I say, still yanking on the key.

She looks up from the gearshift, scans my profile. "You look tired," she says. "Better let me try." She takes my spot in the driver's seat; I find the owner's manual in the glove box and stand in the street next to her, straining to read in the dim streetlamp glow. I'm baffled by what I discover. *"If a malfunction occurs,"* I read out loud, *"the system may* trap the key *in the ignition cylinder to warn you that this safety feature is inoperable. The engine can be started and stopped but the key cannot be removed until you obtain service."*

"You have to be kidding me," I say. "What *genius* American auto engineer came up with this one?" It's after midnight; I'm tired and just want to go to bed, but now it looks like I'll have to drive the car back to Advantage, or wait an hour or more for a tow truck. The other option is just leaving the keys in the car overnight, which in Five Points doesn't seem like such a hot idea.

Like some excessive punctuation marks to that thought, just then I hear the sound of brakes squealing, tires skidding on asphalt. Suddenly there's an ominous black SUV right behind us.

The back door flies open, apparently kicked from the inside, revealing a kid with a gun pointed right at us.

He has a blue bandanna tied around his face, Wild West style, bandit style.

"Get the fuck out of the car," he tells me. Which is confusing because I'm not actually *in the car.* At first I think it's a joke, some teenagers out pranking people with paintball guns.

But the kid jumps out, puts the gun to my temple, and makes it clear this is no joke. The gun is a revolver—an actual *revolver* with a round cylinder and six bullet chambers. It looks like an old gun, and maybe for this reason—and also the fact that I'm getting a distinct Apple sense from this kid, who doesn't seem like he has it in him to shoot anyone—it doesn't scare me as much as it probably should.

"Give me all your money," he says, that old cinematic chestnut, and now here I am standing in the street, a *revolver* in my face, reaching into my pocket and pulling out *all my money,* which fortunately I have neatly folded into a faux-silver money clip, because it has occurred to me that in Brooklyn a money clip could be an advantage during a mugging, in that you can just slip out *all your money* without surrendering your ID and credit cards, thus avoiding hours of phone calls to all the banks and the DMV—yet now I'm testing out this strategy while I'm on vacation in *Denver,* of all places.

"Now get the fuck down on the ground," he says, stuffing *all my money* into his own pocket—but again none of my credit cards or my ID, which by the way is still a Colorado ID, indicative of my ambivalence about being a New Yorker and my nostalgic attachment to this place where I'm about to be fucking *carjacked.*

Doing what I'm told, I lie down on the pavement near the rear tire.

There is no fear, just a sense of audience-like numbness.

It's like watching everything through one of those wide-angled, handheld cameras in a skateboard film when it gets cold-cocked by an errant skateboard and subsequently tumbles sideways onto the street and despite a cracked lens still captures streetlamp shadows, voices, my own two ghostly white hands, the inflation valve on the rental car tire, the astronomical quantity of pebbles embedded in a foot-wide patch of asphalt.

Then the kid forces open the car door, starts yelling at Stephanie.

"I told you to get out of the car and *get the fuck on the ground.*"

But Stephanie slides across the seat, exits the passenger side, apparently *making a run for it.*

The other carjacker—this one much larger and more menacing—is there to catch her. He drags her by the shirt, forces her to lie down next to me.

"So *this* is weird," she says.

"What the hell were you thinking, trying to run like that?" I whisper.

"I was trying to lie down in the yard," she says. "I have a weird thing about pavement."

The whole thing strikes me as comical—as the exact kind of thing that happens when even just two members of our former family attempt a reunion—absolute par for the course. But then a sinking realization sets in: my laptop computer is in the rental car, with the original, mostly un-backed-up files for the novel I've been working on for two years—a novel that fictionalizes the way my stepsisters and I always seem to find ourselves in just this kind of situation.

The younger kid is in the driver's side, sort of inexplicably taking his time with the carjacking. I cobra myself off the pavement just enough to see that now *he's* trying to get the key out of the ignition—a fairly odd move for someone about to steal a car.

"Look," I say, "you got all my money. Take the car, I don't even care. Just please don't take my laptop."

"Sure man, okay," he says. I can detect the gears in his mind clicking as he catches himself, switches back into carjacking mode and says, "Where the fuck is it?" I explain that it's in the backseat; he jumps out and opens the back door, pitches out my laptop and my backpack, which I hug close to my body.

I look over at Steph, beaming. "This could actually work out well," I say, honestly feeling cheerful. "Now we don't have to call a tow truck!"

But then the other guy, the more menacing one, storms up from behind and rips these items from my hands, chucks them into his ominous black SUV. And after what seems like the slowest carjacking of all time, they finally pull away, drive away with the rental car and all my belongings.

Steph springs up and bolts into the house, but I stay on the ground, trying but failing to make out their license plate number, watching my own taillights fade down the darkened street.

When I was a kid, one of my favorite films was *The Jerk* with Steve Martin, the story of a good-natured imbecile who stumbles into a huge fortune and then loses it all. I must have watched it half a dozen times; even twenty years later I still quote verbatim from classic Steve Martin lines like "I'm gonna buy you a diamond so big it'll make you puke" and "You know, you can tell so much about a person from the way they live. Just looking around here I can tell that you're a genuinely dirty person." In the opening scene of *The Jerk*, we find Steve Martin dressed in rags and living on the streets; he speaks the first lines directly into the camera: "I once had wealth, power, and the love of a beautiful woman. Now I only have two things: my friends, and . . . uh . . . my thermos."

When the larger carjacker ripped my laptop and backpack from my hands, my own thermos fell out of the mesh side pocket and clanked into the gutter. It's a fancy new thermos that my mom bought me for Christmas, the superinsulated kind that keeps a hot drink hot or a cold drink cold for twenty-four hours. From my prone position on the asphalt, I slowly stand up and amble over to the thermos—my sole possession at the moment, along with an owner's manual for a 2006 Chrysler Sebring sedan.

I want to share this hilarity with my sister, so I cradle the thermos and stumble into the house.

"I don't need that car. I don't need my computer, or my clothes, or my toothbrush, or anything. All I need is this," I say, doing my best Steve Martin, still clinging to the thermos.

Stephanie's on the phone with the police, and before I can finish my thermos bit, she puts her finger to her lips and looks at me like I've lost my mind.

With this look all the hilarity bleeds right out of me.

I collapse on the couch and begin shivering. And then from out of nowhere I'm being attacked again, headbutted and clawed and screeched at. Steph cups her hand over the phone long enough to explain that they've just adopted this new cat from New Orleans, that it is in fact a Hurricane Katrina refugee cat, and that it's headbutting me like that because it wants *attention*. I'm allergic to cats, which makes it impossible to either give it attention or fend off its aggressive onslaught. And I recognize him for what he is: a fellow trauma survivor.

The shivers turn to shakes, so hard that something shatters inside me—the fragile sense of inner balance that, like the tiny, delicate vestibular bones of the inner ear, has been keeping me just barely upright for the past year. Steph finally gets off the phone and sits down next to me, at which point I nearly lose it, trying to explain between tremors what a bad year I've been having in New York. Before I can get very far, the cops arrive with their platitudes. One in particular walks in the door and says, "Not good, not good." Which is pretty much the most inane thing anyone could say in this situation. His tone implies that it's our fault for being white people and thinking we can live in places like Five Points or Brooklyn. I want to say *We just got fucking* carjacked, *so we don't need you to tell us it's* not good—*we've got that part pretty much figured out, you dumb bastard.* But somehow I hold my tongue. And notice how strange it is that I'd felt no immediate aggression toward the carjackers—that I actually kind of *liked* the Hispanic kid who robbed us, especially compared to his older accomplice—but now I want to just go completely apeshit on this white, uniformed officer. Fortunately he exits the scene and a somewhat more couth Officer Johnson arrives, asks me some questions, hands me a card that says *Case #2000618224. Offense: Carjacking.* I'm surprised that not even the police have a better word for it.

The kid who robbed us was maybe seventeen, eighteen tops. The whole thing seemed like a gang initiation, like he was just along for the ride, going through the motions to earn his next gangster merit badge. I'd asked him for my laptop and he actually gave it back, confirming my original Apple diagnosis. I'd worked with kids just like him at New Horizons. I can imagine us sharing a joke, shooting some hoops, practicing headspins in the dining room on a Sunday night. His partner on the other hand seemed like a total Onion. Lucky he didn't shoot us in the back of the head, which, as the *not good* cop had explained, was exactly what happened to another couple that got carjacked in Denver the year before.

They say that one of the first stages after a life-threatening trauma is the formulation of revenge fantasies. I stay up most of that night reading the owner's manual, pouring over the syntax, making notations in the margins. My immediate plan is to sue the rental company for giving me a malfunctioning car (and to smear them in the media as *Dis*advantage Rent a Car), or Chrysler for their faulty engineering ideas. A six-figure settlement seems appropriate. My sister's a lawyer, so hell, maybe we can even score seven figures. I imagine exacting revenge on the automobile industry not only for our troubles, our psychological damage, but also for the way they dismantled the public transportation system back in the early twentieth century, buying up all the streetcars and bus systems and rail lines and purposefully running them into the ground, literally paving the way for cars and the ensuing white flight from inner cities—the very thing that created a neighborhood like Five Points in the first place. Not to mention the razing of urban communities by freeways, global warming, oil spills, petro-warfare and the increasing atomization of American society. This isn't just about me, it's about *global justice*. Plus, I'll never have to work again!

Lying there in my sister's spare bedroom in Five Points, the phrase *set for life* occurs to me. I roll it around on my palate all night, savor it like a sip of excellent coffee on a cold day. They say the best revenge is living well, and not only am I about to join the ranks of the idle rich, but I'm going to score a hell of a lot of laughs with the thermos bit.

After a fitful few hours of sleep, I call Advantage Rent a Car. They transfer me to a "risk assessor" named Rochelle. She never once asks if I'm okay or apologizes for what happened—in fact, she clearly suspects that maybe I'm the culprit, that I'd somehow staged the theft and was pulling some kind of insurance scam. When I explain about the keys, she says that the car was brand-new, fresh off the truck, and that Advantage is in no way liable. I'd purchased the midrange insurance plan that covered the value of the car itself, but unfortunately it doesn't cover my belongings. I ask if perhaps as a courtesy to me and what I'd been through they'll at least cover my laptop, but she curtly reiterates that it's not their fault, that the only thing they can do for me is to charge my credit card only for the first two days' rental. I've never wanted to explode so badly in my life—I want to spit every name in the book at her, including the C-word, which I've never called anyone, but I hold back only because calling a risk assessor the C-word won't help during *my big day in court.*

Noticing my distress after the phone call, Steph takes me out for breakfast at this hip vegetarian place called WaterCourse Foods. Both famished, we score a booth by the window and order breakfast burritos.

"I still can't believe you tried to make a run for it," I say, squeezing honey into my tea. "Where did you think you were going?"

"We just landscaped the yard and put down wood chips," she tells me. "I thought they'd be softer than the pavement."

"Let me get this straight: we're getting robbed at gunpoint and you're busy considering the comfort properties of *garden mulch?*"

We can't stop laughing.

We can hardly breathe.

It catches the attention of the other diners, who give us concerned looks, unsure if we're laughing or choking.

Then Steph actually chokes.

"I can't breathe," she croaks, waving one hand in front of her face, clamoring for her water glass with the other.

I have to slide in next to her, pat her on the back, hand her napkins to dry her face.

We get ourselves under control, but after half an hour of waiting for our food, we start to get restless.

Finally we flag down our young indie-rock waiter.

"So sorry," he says, motioning toward some diners who arrived much later than we did, but who are already enjoying two massive breakfast burritos, "but it looks like your orders were *platejacked* on the way from the kitchen."

Later that day my parents drive down from the mountains to give me moral support and help me make some arrangements. They also drive me to the mall to pick up a new sports coat for the wedding. I ride in the back and my mom rides shotgun, where she plays and sings "What a Wonderful World" on her ukulele. I love her for doing this, for the fact that she plays such a sweet instrument, and that she's playing in a moving car, clearly just trying to cheer me up. At the same time, I'm angry that she's singing it, because the world is *not wonderful,* not for me. It's raining now, the sky wrecked with storm clouds, and somewhere between the mall and the Thai place we went for lunch, I break down in the backseat.

"I don't know how much more of this I can take," I say, whispering through salty-damp hands—directing this thought at my parents. At myself. At what feels like an increasingly vacuous universe.

AS WE BEGIN OUR FINAL DESCENT
INTO NEW YORK

> Ahab is a study in the psychology of resentment. His image
> serves as a mirror, showing the true nature of our own
> resentments. Everyone has this problem, a monomaniacal
> inner Ahab.
>
> ～ EDWARD F. EDINGER, *Melville's Moby-Dick:*
> *An American Nekyia*

The waves at Rockaway look good from four thousand feet.

The plane finishes its carve around the tip of Manhattan, over Queens, and down to LaGuardia, and then, the minute I get home from the airport, I load up my truck and head for the beach, listening to NPR coverage of the Iraq conflict and new revelations about the deceptions that led us to war. I arrive at sunset, long after the lifeguards have gone, and just as most other surfers are packing up their gear and heading back to the city. While unloading my board, I notice my heart punching in my chest when a couple thugs blasting 50 Cent in a lowered Nissan circle around the parking lot.

On their second pass, I check behind the backseat to make sure my tire iron is handy.

When the Nissan finally peels out of the lot, I stretch into my wetsuit and paddle out into the lineup, where I catch a few waves in vanishing light, until it's too dark to gauge the swell. Then I turn my board east and paddle way out past the breakers, heading toward the blinking oil tankers on the horizon. The previous summer there was a big *Times* article about a couple local Rockaway project kids who swam out at dusk, right here at Beach 90th, getting sucked into a strong undertow and dragged perilously out to sea. A surfer rescued one, but the other disappeared into the drink.

During its long history as a municipal beach, Rockaway's dangerous currents and riptides have drowned hundreds of New Yorkers.

Floating out in the open ocean now, I turn over on my back to look up at the city-dampened starlight, wondering where I'd end up if I just keep paddling east, if I can reach the oil tankers off in the distance, maybe hitch a ride to Asia or Alaska or Japan. Or maybe I'll drift into the Gulf Stream, let it sweep me northeast across the Atlantic to England, where I might hop another current south along Africa and around Cape Horn, then up toward the Middle East. I wonder if there are soldiers over there feeling the same longing, perhaps staring out at the oil-poisoned Gulf, wishing for the same ocean-bound deliverance home. If I hold fast, I might make it all the way to the South Seas, now tracing Ahab's rage-filled path past the Bashee Islands and into the vast Pacific, the mother ocean that Ishmael describes as having "millions of mixed shades and shadows, drowned dreams, somnambulisms, reveries; all that we call lives and souls, lie dreaming, dreaming, still; tossing like slumberers in their beds, the ever-rolling waves but made so by their restlessness."

My inner Ahab is pacing the decks of my mind now, laid out on the deck of my surfboard, raging at the world, at President Bush and Dick Cheney and Osama bin Laden—Ahabs, all of them—and at the wannabe Ahabs who robbed me in Denver. It rages at a God in whom my trust and hope is flagging. Most of all, it rages at myself for making a series of choices that brought me to this unmanageable point in my life. Out here in the night-roiling sea, I've never felt so connected with this dark, masculine, reckless force that pilots so much of the world's treachery.

Despite the increasing feelings of sinking heaviness, I turn over and start paddling back toward the distant city lights. The hours and hours of surfing, combined with a lack of appetite, have done interesting things to my body. Emotionally I'm in troubled waters, but I've never been in better physical shape. The veins in my forearms are ropy and sea green; my neck has thickened; the lateral muscles below my armpits fan out like a pair of meaty wings. My roommate Natalie says she's never seen someone so emaciated with such a V-shaped torso. It's the unconscious, bodily wisdom in these muscles that eventually gets me back to the deserted Rockaway shore, where it's so late that even the cops have gone home to bed.

Back in Brooklyn I have the first of many insomniac nights, my few hours of sleep disturbed by a recurring dream about captaining a beautiful triple-masted schooner, but watching helplessly as some gangster kids vandalize the ship, leaving nothing but a compacted square box, like an abandoned junkyard car. Waking up hours later in a hot sweat, I skip work and go surfing again, by myself on a Monday afternoon. The summer progresses like this—a blur of insomnia, late nights at Rockaway, crushing feelings of regret and rage, and Iraq War body counts. My productivity at work diminishes, as I can barely muster the concentration to read a few pages, much less the giant stack of manuscripts piling up in my cubicle. My boss calls me in twice to comment on my falling behind and my appearance, the way I've grown my hair down between my shoulder blades, my bangs hanging over my face in a shaggier approximation of the Tony Hawk haircut I'd had in eighth grade.

Part of me hopes he'll go ahead and fire me so I can go live out of my truck in the parking lots at Rockaway and Montauk, where I can wake up before dawn to ride my surfboard instead of the subway.

THE REPORT

Data: After returning home to New York from Denver, Client begins to increasingly isolate. He complains of nightmares and sleeplessness; most mornings he wakes up at four in a state of generalized anxiety. He grows obsessed with revenge against Rochelle and Advantage Rent a Car and General Motors; he spends hours on the phone talking to Colorado lawyers, most of whom explain he has no case, that there's no way to prove any causal relationship between the ignition malfunction and the robbery. Client repeatedly calls his sister to see how "the case" is progressing on her end. He's baffled when she fails to return any of his messages, even when he just calls to see how she's doing, to commiserate, to team-tackle their trauma. It's not just his sister—Client feels an increasing sense that the whole world is screening its calls.

Client experiences life as a series of timed trials—workdays, meetings, subway rides—and he struggles to make it through these minor events. His office phone becomes a source of dread. During important calls, his mind goes completely blank—a harrowing mental blackout that leaves him feeling disoriented and sick.

Everyone explains how lucky Client was to escape the robbery without being shot or killed. But in a mysterious way Client has not entirely escaped the revolver's aim. Through some dark alchemy, the Five Points revolver now lives permanently inside his head, locked and loaded. When Client feels overwhelmed with regret or self-loathing the revolver transmutes itself into the musculature, bone, and sinew of his right hand. Alone in his cubicle, when no one is looking, he repeatedly puts this "hand gun" to his temple, *Lethal Weapon* style, Clint Eastwood style. Carjacker style.

Assessment: Something profound happens to Client that summer. For the better part of two years, he's hated himself for moving to New York, for leaving his girlfriend and his less tangled existence in Colorado, for getting locked into a job he desperately wants to leave.

For having, in his opinion, ruined his own life. Living in Brooklyn brings out the worst in him—he's full of grievances, regret, spite. He is homesick and exhausted by the pace of life in New York, and now the trauma of the carjacking seems to have pushed Client over the edge.

Client's revenge fantasies are consistent with symptomatic patterns of post-traumatic stress disorder, as are his loss of spiritual faith and suicidal ideation. With no recourse against Advantage Rent a Car or Chrysler, Client turns his quest for revenge inward, against himself, whom he perceives as the cause of all his problems, his own white whale.

Plan: Swim every day, hard enough to drown your feelings, if only for a few minutes. On the weekends visit the Atlantic Ocean, immerse yourself in salt water, let the waves scour away your troubles. Stay in motion—you need to be in the best shape of your life to survive this battle, to swim clear of this psychological shipwreck. Take yourself daily to recreation, tell yourself jokes, keep away from sharp objects and large bottles of pills, do what you can to keep yourself moving, upright, awake, alive.

JONAH

In Melville's chapter "Jonah Historically Regarded," he discusses some of the logical inconsistencies engendered by a literal interpretation of the Book of Jonah. According to the author, certain old-fashioned Bibles contained illustrations of a double-spouted whale devouring Jonah. Herein lies the problem: the only whales with two spouts are right whales—a breed also known for their baleen and mouths much too small to swallow anything as large as a man. Melville counters by quoting Bishop Jebb: "It is not necessary, hints the Bishop, that we consider Jonah as tombed in the whale's belly, but as temporarily lodged in some part of his mouth."

While studying an online swell chart, I notice that Long Island is shaped, to quote Polonius, *"very like a whale."* Take a look at a map: the island runs east to west, the twin forks facing east like giant tail flukes. Apropos its reputation, Fire Island resembles a whale's impressive phallus. Brooklyn and Queens constitute a battering ram of a head, very nearly bashing the diminutive island of Manhattan. Jamaica Bay is the gaping maw, and the Rockaway peninsula looks remarkably like the long, thin lower jaw of a sperm whale. So every surf trip to Rockaway is also a cool, collected dive into the very mouth of the beast.

WHALING (2001)

> There is a wisdom that is woe; but there is a woe that is
> madness. And there is a Catskill eagle in some souls that
> can alike dive down into the blackest gorges, and soar out
> of them again and become invisible in the sunny spaces.
>
> ~ Herman Melville, *Moby-Dick*

The situation you find yourself in: late twenties, low-paying job at the local skateshop, six years into a college education, no career prospects, and the only thing you feel you can do with any competence or enthusiasm is roll around on a piece of wood with wheels.

They say you've learned a foreign language when you dream in that language. You dream in skateboarding. In your dreams, you roll through indoor shopping malls and ollie entire escalators.

When you aren't skating you pretend your fingers are two little legs—you fingerskate on everything, you do finger Smith-grinds on the edge of the dinner table at the fancy Italian place your girlfriend likes. You worry that the food's too expensive, although you always seem to scrounge up enough money for new skate shoes every month or two.

On the ride home Nicole wants to discuss the future of your relationship. It's raining as you drive, trees dumping leaves in messy piles. She says the problem is that the two of you see different versions of the future. She wants marriage and kids; she's not sure what it is you want. As she talks you look out the window for skate spots, even though the streets are all washed up with rainwater. You look for banks, slick marble ledges, handrails, old motels that might have empty pools. You notice yourself doing this and it isn't that you don't care about the person sitting next to you. She looks out the window and sees houses, yards, families, stasis. You're seeking something entirely different: the possibility of motion.

You hang out with a seventeen-year-old kid nicknamed Bronco because he used to ride junior rodeo. One day during your skateshop shift he writes the word *scrotum* on the TV screen with black Magic Marker. You put up with these minor annoyances and the fact that he's ten years younger because he's one of the few people you know who's still down to skate at a moment's notice. He ditches high school whenever you call.

You and Bronco skate through the streets at night. You pay particular attention to the different textures of the roads and sidewalks as you roll: the cracks, rows of brick, tile, asphalt, each with its own vibrational frequency. Sometimes if you skate enough, your mind becomes less like a grease fire and more like a candle flame.

One day you and Bronco skate an empty pool nicknamed Satan's Armpit. You take a bone-crunching slam and your hip turns purple and black with yellow marbling, like a murky mud puddle with a gasoline rainbow. You can't afford a visit to the doctor, where you know you'll pay $200 to have some square tell you to ice it. All you can do is buy a pair of used crutches at the thrift store.

While you're hurt you sit around the house reading *Thrasher,* complaining to Nicole, and having imaginary conversations with an amorphous middle-aged businessman, a guy with two kids and a mortgage and a high-paying career in the tech industry.

"You're still skateboarding?" he says, straightening his tie. "You're almost thirty. Why don't you do something with your life?"

"Let me ask you something," you say.

"Shoot," he says.

"Do you own a car?"

"Of course. An Explorer and a BMW."

"If you think about it," you say, "both cars and skateboards have four wheels and two axles. Both roll forward and backward. They're both modes of transportation invented in America. Except that your mode of transportation has a combustion engine that spews thousands of pounds of pollutants, making the whole planet hotter and dirtier and shittier. And the fact that everyone drives your chosen mode of transportation is the reason a bunch of assholes from Texas struck it rich and bought their way into the White House so they can colonize the Middle East and secure our oil interests. So yeah," you say, "I still skateboard."

He looks at you for a moment, clearly unimpressed. "Let me get this straight," he says, "you don't own a car?"

You say no, though it's a bald-faced lie; you've owned plenty of cars, including your current pickup, which gets bad gas mileage and needs $500 in muffler and brake work. And you've actually had this thought while skateboarding on balmy days in the dead of a Colorado winter: *Maybe global warming isn't so bad after all.*

You and Nicole break up. It starts in the furniture store, where she wants to purchase a sofa. After a decade this is what puts you over the edge: a $1,900 neo-Victorian couch. You can't deny that skateboarding has something to do with it. Designer furniture and a wife and kids don't compute in your head; skateboarding is the only equation you've ever been able to decipher.

Nicole packs up and moves out, takes all the silverware but leaves the empty tray. This image sticks in your mind: an empty container, the outlines of knives and spoons and forks. You are the shape of your old self, stripped of all silver. You hang black-and-white skate photos and an old Consolidated deck with Neil Blender graphics on the wall in your bedroom; you do this the very night she leaves. You drape a strand of Christmas lights above the window and this is all you have to keep you going: images of your friends skateboarding and a few tiny points of light.

The friends you used to skateboard with every day now have to make babysitting arrangements a week in advance just to meet you at the skatepark on a Sunday afternoon. You decide to skate by yourself but it starts snowing on the way to the park and it doesn't stop for a week.

You own a T-shirt that says Skateboarding Saved My Life and another that says Skateboarding Ruined My Life. You wear them on different days, depending on your mood.

In the middle of a bleak January, Bronco finds you sleeping on your living room floor. He says a trip down south is what you need. Two days later you're driving through a blizzard, snow swirling on the road like ashes. It warms up by the time you hit New Mexico and you skate a few dinky parks filled with prepubescent kids on Rollerblades who keep asking Bronco, "Are you sponsored? Are you sponsored?" You feel ridiculous, a grown man hanging out with a bunch of kids. You decide not to skate—you sit in the car, trying not to think about how immature it was to let go of a beautiful intelligent woman for this.

When Bronco drives, you read a dog-eared copy of *Moby-Dick,* the story of an old man who held on to something so long that his whole ship sank.

Then: you drive over a mountain pass. On the summit there's a sign that says Elevation 9,000 Feet. Bronco tells you to pull over. He gets out of the car—you're not sure what he's doing. He grabs his skateboard and bombs the hill, like it's the most natural thing in the world. You watch as he leans into a sharp corner and almost gets hit by an oncoming truck. You drive a half mile down and pick him up. His elbows are dripping blood; he is breathing hard and smiling. He gets back in and the whole truck fills up with energy, like invisible steam. You hope that maybe he is alive enough for both of you.

In Phoenix you sleep on your friend Brian's living room floor. Tall oleander bushes, palm trees, and sandstone hills surround his house. The evening sky is bold blue. You sit on the porch drinking your post-breakup cocktails: AriZona Iced Tea Rx Stress mixed with crushed up kava kava supplements. You hope you can drink enough to fall asleep and not wake up in the middle of the night gripped with anxiety, regret.

You speed across white Phoenix freeways listening to Hot Snakes, Minor Threat, Modest Mouse. You zip past twenty-foot saguaro cacti and green glass skyscrapers reflecting hazy sunlight. You hang your arm out the window and feel warmth on your hand; you're almost to a skatepark called Paradise Valley; you have that loose buzzing feeling you only get en route to skate something epic with your friends.

You eat lunch after skating every day at a hole-in-the-wall Mexican joint called Los Betos. You and Bronco like the bean and cheese burritos so much you consider getting *Los Betos* tattooed on the inside of your biceps.

Bronco has no money and when you offer to buy him dinner at a sit-down restaurant he orders fried ice cream. You explain that fried ice cream is not an entree but he eats it anyway.

On your last day in Phoenix you and Bronco sneak down an alley lined with one-story ranch houses, past a couple Mexican kids jumping on a trampoline. At first you think the backyard trees are filled with big golden Christmas lights, until you realize they're real life, honest-to-God lemons. You crawl over a cinder-block wall and find a bone-dry swimming pool behind an abandoned HUD house.

    The pool is the shape of a whale, the shallow end like a tail.

You carve over the pool light, your wheels singing across sea-green plaster. For a while there is nothing in your mind but rolling. You are sweating hard for the first time in months. You decide a frontside air is the thing. You try it four times, feet slapping on the cement as you run out.

    "Bring it home!" Bronco shouts.

    You do.

But you sketch out on the landing and flop like a dead fish into the concrete maw, slamming directly on your bad hip.

Here is your latest situation: you are twenty-nine years old and lying in a dirty hole in the ground, eight feet below the surface of the earth. You cannot move your right leg. Your palms feel like they've been stung by a whole hive of pissed-off wasps, and the Arizona sun feels hot enough to burn a hole through your black T-shirt. You're praying you won't have to go to the hospital because you have fifty bucks to your name and now that you're living alone you have no idea how to pay next month's rent. According to the imaginary bureaucrats in your head, you're way too old to be skateboarding, though you're still thinking maybe you can get up and try the frontside air one more time before the pain really sets in. But your already-arthritic hip hurts so bad that you want to just die right there in the deep end, to be sucked down the drain and swallowed into the sandy ground.

Then Bronco slides down and kneels beside you. "Come on," he says, grinning, "let's get your ass up out of here."

THE POOL

As my boss repeatedly reminds me, being an editor is *not just a nine-to-five job,* meaning that most days I'm expected to arrive early and stay late, making it hard to reach Rockaway before dark. As a substitute for surfing, some evenings I swim laps in a gloomy municipal pool on Bedford, just a block from our apartment. My therapist suggests I try something more social, like racquetball, but racquetball is not and never will be my style. He has a point about the social part, though. The exercise is good for me; I swim so hard that I actually sweat underwater. But swimming is an isolating sport. With earplugs and goggles and my head underwater, the Bedford Pool is akin to a sensory deprivation tank. Instead of getting me out of my head as surfing does, when I'm swimming laps there's nothing to do but ruminate.

In the second half of *Moby-Dick,* a curious thing happens. Though Ishmael is clearly the book's narrator, and has been since page one, we hear less and less of his buoyant voice as the story progresses. We also begin to get glimpses into parts of the ship, including the mad captain's quarters, to which, as a nonofficer, Ishmael would never have been privy. Moreover, the narration turns darker and darker as we get further inside Ahab's splintered mind. According to D. H. Lawrence, "Something glimmers through all this: a glimmer of genuine reality. But it is not a reality of real, open-air experience. It is a reality of what takes place in the musty cellars of a man's soul, what the psychoanalysts call the unconscious. There is the old double set of values; the ostensible Melville, a sort of Emersonian transcendentalist, and the underneath Melville, a sort of strange underworld, under-sea creature looking with curious, lurid vision on the upper world."

In the second half of *Moby-Dick,* it's as if Ahab as a shadow archetype starts to seize control of the book. And my own underworld, undersea self takes over when I swim in the Bedford Pool, where I feel like I'm digesting myself in my own acidic regrets, in the stinging bile of my own self-loathing—for moving to New York, for giving up teaching and stranding myself in the Pit, for leaving Karissa, for not marrying Nicole, for deciding to be a writer in the first place.

This manifests as physical pain in my chest and stomach—a slow chemical burn—and a panicky sense of constriction and loss as my former self slips further and further into the airless belly of the beast. The harder I swim, the more I feel like an emotional depth charge, my crudely soldered seams on the verge of ripping apart, imploding. But then again, the post-swimming exhaustion is the only thing that temporarily soothes the ache.

Maybe this is just something that happens to writers and artists who move to New York: *the White Death; the Melville syndrome.* It's common among those for whom, like Herman Melville, things don't go according to plan, for anyone who loses his own life's narrative. Maybe it's similar to the Jerusalem syndrome, in which Western visitors to the Holy City wrap themselves in their bedsheets, then roam the streets raving, proselytizing, believing themselves to be Jesus or Moses. It's such a common occurrence that medical providers in Jerusalem know exactly what to prescribe: a regimen of light antipsychotics and two days' bed rest. This treatment is so effective that Jerusalem syndrome survivors are usually back on the tour bus within forty-eight hours.

Unlike Jerusalem syndrome, the White Death has no known cure and many victims. David Foster Wallace had more than a touch of it. The poet Hart Crane—who was obsessed with *Moby-Dick,* and who eventually committed suicide by jumping overboard in the Gulf of Mexico—was a definite casualty.

What we need is a treatment center for the White Death and the Melville syndrome; some day I'd like to start one. It'll be housed on a replica whaling ship in the New York harbor, where residents will learn to tie knots and hoist sails. Instead of reading *Moby-Dick* or slaving away on their doomed creative projects, they'll climb in wind-whipped rigging and shout out obstacles from up in the crow's nest. The companionship, fresh air, sunlight, and physical labor alone will do much for their beleaguered constitutions. In the evenings they'll lounge around down in the hold, eating healthy, balanced meals and discussing *Moby-Dick*. Although they will, very gradually, be encouraged to consider other books as well. During art therapy sessions, residents will create likenesses of their inner Ahabs from biodegradable materials—pieces of charred driftwood and crab shells and bull kelp. After embracing their own Ahab-shadows and the death of their idealistic dreams, they'll ceremonially toss them overboard, releasing them to the sea.

JOHNNY GOT HIS GUN

hile my job involves quite a bit of tedium and too many romance novels, I also get to work on some genuinely interesting projects, including a reissue of the famous antiwar novel *Johnny Got His Gun* by Dalton Trumbo—the nightmarish story of a World War I soldier who's rendered limbless, deaf, dumb, and blind by a bomb blast. It's one of many titles on my company's backlist, and this being the height of the Iraq quagmire, we decide on a fast-track rerelease. After weeks of sleuthing I contact the famous antiwar activist Cindy Sheehan and ask her to write a new foreword for *Johnny*. Though she's busy with a major protest at Camp Casey—a tent city in Texas named after the son she lost in the war—she comes through with a very raw, heartfelt introduction.

Two weeks after I finish editing Sheehan's introduction, some old friends from Colorado, Andy and his fiancée, Allison, come for a visit. They stay in our apartment a couple nights, during which I have another bout of serious insomnia. On a Friday, after a sleepless night, I call in sick, even though I'm scheduled to present *Johnny Got His Gun* during an important meeting with our sales department. Though I'd rather be out having fun in the city with old friends, I spend most of the day in bed, trying to catch up on sleep. That evening, before taking the subway to the airport for an overnight flight, Allison pulls me aside, looks me straight in my sunken eyes. She tells me that she's worried about me, that she and Andy talked about it and they'd be happy to have me stay with them.

"We have a nice spare bedroom," she says. "We just want our old Justin back."

I'd like to just pack up and go home. I could probably do some adjunct teaching at the university, see a lot more of my old friends and family. But the other person I'd see is Nicole, and I'm not sure I could handle limping back to Colorado, single and broke, just in time for her wedding.

Plus, though I have a love/hate relationship with New York, the biggest sticking point is this: there's no ocean in Colorado.

THE CASTAWAY

> The sea had jeeringly kept his finite body up, but drowned the infinite of his soul. Not drowned entirely, though. Rather carried down alive to wondrous depths. . . . Pip saw the multitudinous, God-omnipresent, coral insects. . . . He saw God's foot upon the treadle of the loom, and spoke it; and therefore his shipmates called him mad.
>
> ~ HERMAN MELVILLE, *Moby-Dick*

Despite his intense fear of the ocean, in 1996 David Foster Wallace went on assignment for *Harper's* to take a six-day, seven-night Celebrity Cruise through the Caribbean, where he encountered sundry wonders, including a thirteen-year-old boy in a toupee and a woman in a gold lamé dress projectile vomiting in a glass elevator. Reading the piece after Wallace's suicide, you understand that the agoraphobia he alludes to in the essay—a fear of leaving his cabin—was real and not just a literary device. Likewise, if you've ever experienced agoraphobia you understand that this voyage must have caused him serious distress. It's also telling that, in the essay, Wallace mentions a suicide that happened just a couple weeks before his own cruise, when "a sixteen-year-old male did a brody off the upper deck of the Megaship." Wallace then ponders the cause of this suicide in a way that hits very close to home:

There is something about a mass-market Luxury Cruise that's unbearably sad. Like most unbearably sad things, it seems incredibly elusive and complex in its causes and simple in its effect: on board the Nadir—especially at night, when all the ship's structured fun and reassurances and gaiety-noise ceased—I felt despair. The word's overused and banalified now, *despair,* but it's a serious word, and I'm using it seriously. For me it denotes a simple admixture—a weird yearning for death combined with a crushing sense of my

own smallness and futility that presents as a fear of death.
It's maybe close to what people call dread or angst. But it's
not these things, quite. It's more like wanting to die in order
to escape the unbearable feeling of becoming aware that I'm
small and weak and selfish and going without any doubt at all
to die. It's wanting to jump overboard.

Then there are the shark attack statistics—as a kid Wallace kept an
exhaustive mental catalog of history's most gruesome shark attacks,
including "the USS Indianapolis smorgasboard off the Philippines in
1945." To drive home his aquaphobia, Wallace mentions how in college he wrote three different papers about the "Castaway" section of
Moby-Dick, wherein the young cabin boy, Pip, jumps from a whaleboat and is left floating for an hour or more out in the open ocean.
The sheer terror of bobbing in the infinite, inhuman sea cracks his
mind, transforms him into a holy fool.

Based on his experience of despair, Wallace formulates a philosophical theory regarding the cruise ship experience. The Celebrity
Cruise ethos is all about pampering; in his lacerating deconstruction
of the Celebrity promotional brochure, he notes that the word *pamper* is used *fifteen* times. He thinks it's no accident that *pamper* is also
the brand name of a certain type of disposable garment for infants.
His theory, then, is that the cruise ship experience is designed to give
fearful, despairing people a return to the preconscious, prechoice,
and thus pre-adult-regrets womb, where all our needs are met automatically, umbillically.

After reading his essay for the fourth or fifth time, I can't help but
wonder if my obsession with the ocean and surfing is like my own
attempt to crawl back into the womb, to a place where I don't have
any adult responsibilities or choices or regrets. Maybe I'm just trying
to lose myself in another female presence—in this case the feminine
sea, the mother ocean.

But the experience of surfing is often more like the pain of birth
than the solace of the womb. There's a lot of thrashing around, intense physical straining. The ocean holds you under and you come up

gasping for air like a newborn. There's not a lot of *pampering* going on during your typical session at Rockaway; even if you're careful, it's likely that with each paddle out you'll instead get spanked by a wave at least once. And unlike on a cruise ship, you're down sharing the very same water with sharks, a fact that my friend Sadie has confirmed for us all.

THE ATHEIST

A word concerning the 1945 shark massacre. This is the same massacre that the old, Ahab-like captain details in the film *Jaws*. This fictional captain was in the Navy; he witnessed the whole bloody, horrific scene—he tells Roy Scheider all about it just hours before Jaws swallows him whole.

My stepfather volunteers as a hospice chaplin, ministering to the sick and dying during the last few weeks of their life. If the patients are Jewish, he'll read from the Torah; if they're Christian, he'll read from the Bible; if they're atheist, he'll read from whatever secular book they request, avoiding any talk of God. One of his most memorable patients fell squarely in the latter category. He'd grown up Catholic but was in the Navy and witnessed firsthand the 1945 USS *Indianapolis* tragedy. The *Indianapolis* was a naval cruiser that delivered parts for the Little Boy atomic bomb—which was eventually dropped on Hiroshima—to Guam. On the covert return journey through the Philippine Sea, the *Indianapolis* was attacked and sunk by a Japanese submarine. Of the nearly nine hundred men who went into the drink without lifeboats, only three hundred survived. Most died from dehydration and exposure, but many were killed by sharks—in fact, it's known as one of the worst shark attacks in human history.

After witnessing this, my stepfather's patient lost his faith in a benevolent God.

THE CITY SWELL

Forecast for Long Beach: East swell, 2–3 foot waves at 10 seconds. Winds from the south at 7 mph. Water temp 59, air temp 67. Surf: knee to waist high and fair conditions.

In May of 2005, Asa and I check out the Jean-Michel Basquiat retrospective at the Brooklyn Museum. Back in the late nineties I'd seen the biopic *Basquiat;* in one scene another painter tells Basquiat that his audience hasn't even been born yet. Looking at three entire museum floors filled with his paintings, I get the sense of how prescient his work was back in the 1980s, how much it influenced the street art scene that's so much in vogue in 2005, with other self-taught artists like Mark Gonzales, Swoon, and Banksy as direct descendants of Basquiat. Basquiat was just as much a DJ as an artist; he sampled and repeated words, phrases, and motifs to create something entirely new and visionary. My favorite pieces were executed on found materials—wooden fence planks, cabinets, dressers, and doors, all nailed together like scrappy altars to Grandmaster Flash, Malcolm X, Miles Davis, and Joe Louis. And as a writer, I dig the textuality of his work, the way many of his paintings read like jumbled essays or inspired, furious poems.

A few months earlier, at a Chelsea gallery show called "In Word Alone," I'd seen another of his pieces in which he'd simply copied the table of contents of *Moby-Dick* across nine sheets of white paper—the titles of all 135 chapters written in black crayon. The center page on the bottom row reads "threadbare in coat, heart, body, brain," followed by one of Basquiat's © symbols. There's also a trademark sign after the phrase "Call me Ishmael." I like this idea, that Basquiat was taking a classic work and reclaiming the copyright, making it his own. He was poking fun at Melville as a member of the mostly white literary canon, but also acknowledging his kinship—they were both highly political, anticolonialist, anti-imperialist artists. Both experienced poverty in their young adulthood; many of Basquiat's paintings are haunted with spike-headed ghosts of slavery and destitution, or grimacing figures crowned with Byzantine halos. There's a pervading darkness in Basquiat's work, coupled with a grasping toward the sacred—a kind of street-smart chiaroscuro that's reminiscent of Melville's own nightshade vision of America.

You don't really get a true sense of Basquiat's paintings until you're surrounded by them, and then both the darkness and the halo shine seep into your bloodstream, exciting and provoking you the way some jazz and hip-hop does—and for me these alternating currents hum with the noise and chaos and electric allure of New York City life. Maybe it's for that reason, paired with the fact that it's sunny out as we leave the museum, that Asa and I make the spontaneous decision to escape to the coast. It's just like I imagined the first time I witnessed a surfer emerge from a West Village subway station: in New York it's possible to see great works of art and go surfing, all in the same afternoon.

We pack up my truck and drive to Asa's favorite surf spot at Long Beach. The water's still wetsuit temperature, but the swells are small and clean and fun, and we're the only ones out, trading wave after wave.

"You think you'll ever move back to the West Coast?" I ask Asa between sets.

"Hard to say. I like New York; I like how real people are here. And where else can you take the subway to the beach? I think this is one of the best-kept secrets in the surf world. The waves are better in California, but the breaks are packed."

"That's part of the reason I never surfed much in San Diego," I say. "And it's why I still think about moving to Oregon all the time." I'm always bringing up Oregon with Asa, telling him how much I'd like to relocate, reminiscing about our old times there.

"I lived in Portland for three years; I had a great time. But I can't really see myself there now. That's the thing: I try to be present with whatever place I'm in," he says, then catches a nice left-hand peeler, working every section of it, cross-stepping up to the nose—making it all look so natural and effortless.

Forecast for North Shore Oahu: North swell 12 feet at 15 seconds. Winds from the south at 12 mph. Water temp 72, air temp 85. Surf: solid overhead and hollow; excellent conditions.

Early in the film *Basquiat,* the eponymous young artist has a kind of ecstatic visual hallucination in which he envisions a giant surfer superimposed above a New York City skyline, trimming backside down the face of a sun-shimmering, double-overhead wave. At the time, Basquiat is living in a cardboard box, writing "Samo" graffiti and selling street art for a couple dollars a pop. But the surfing vision indicates awareness of his imminent ascent—it's a fairly obvious but nonetheless bitchin' metaphor for his real-life slash across an overblown swell of 1980s art-world fame and fortune. Acccording to the film's creator, Julian Schnabel, the Manhattan skyline surfer was "a barometer of his [Basquiat's] emotional state—in the beginning, optimistic, sparkling, exuberant. As things get more problematic, the sea becomes more ominous." In the end they get severely problematic: the skyline surfer takes a harrowing wipeout just as Basquiat begins his own terminal plunge into heroin addiction.

Basquiat the man wasn't necessarily a surfing devotee, but he visited Hawaii a handful of times, and like so many mainlanders he fantasized about moving to Oahu or Maui. Just before his fatal overdose in 1988, he chose the remote, idyllic town of Hana on Maui as a clean, quiet spot to kick heroin. Rumor has it that while in Hana he slept in a fruit stand and spent his days painting on a friend's kitchen cabinets.* It's unlikely that Basquiat ever actually rode a surfboard, especially while going through the DTs. In fact, there wouldn't be any surfing in *Basquiat* if it wasn't for Schnabel, himself a painter

---

* This friend eventually dismantled the signature Basquiat cabinets and sold them for hundreds of thousands of dollars. He made a lucrative, set-for-life, never-work-again career out of them—his *kitchen cabinets.*

and lifelong surfer.* The story goes that a fledgling filmmaker came to interview Schnabel about his friendship with Basquiat, in hope of making a feature film about the deceased artist. Sensing that the filmmaker was a tourist who'd turn the nuanced story into one big art-world cliché, Schnabel snaked the cinematic wave and directed the picture himself, effectively launching a second career in film. More than a few critics complained that *Basquiat* the movie has a little too much Schnabel in it, that the story was remade in the artist's own notoriously outsized image (Schnabel was once quoted as saying, "I'm the closest thing to Picasso that you'll see in this fucking life.") But any of Schnabel's artistic indulgences† are mostly made up for by his painterly sense of scene and by understated performances from one of the best casts ever: Gary Oldman,‡ David Bowie,§ Jeffrey Wright, Dennis Hopper, Willem Dafoe, Parker Posey, Christopher Walken, Benecio del Toro,** and the luminous Claire Forlani.

Critics also griped that the New York City skyline surfing imagery was at once lowbrow and heavy-handed. To his credit, Schnabel

---

* In his memoir Schnabel writes, "Being in the water alone, surfing, sharpens a particular kind of concentration, an ability to agree with the ocean, to react with a force that is larger than you are."

† For instance, casting his actual parents to play the part of his character's parents in the film. Schnabel also put heavy emphasis on his own obscenely successful career and his cozy family life—one scene depicts him waltzing around his Versailles-sized studio with his lovely young daughter—which, contrasted with Basquiat's downward spiral and lack of real human connectedness, seems sort of, well, *cruel.*

‡ Schnabel is famous for wearing silk pajamas pretty much everywhere, from his outdoor painting studio to televised interviews with Charlie Rose, and word on the street is that Oldman's wardrobe consisted of pajamas straight from Schnabel's armoire.

§ Schnabel apparently pulled his weight at the Warhol museum and scored the deceased painter's wig and glasses for use during filming. It's hard to imagine a more hip and/or creepy tableau anywhere in cinematic history: David *fucking* Bowie wearing Andy Warhol's wig.

** Coincidentally, when del Toro originally moved to California, he was much more interested in becoming a surfer than an actor.

made the film on a relatively tiny budget, using the surfing footage in lieu of shooting on location in Hawaii to capture some of Basquiat's important final days.* And though I first saw the film circa 1997, it was the surfing imagery more than any other aspect that stayed with me over the years—in fact, I'd had my own versions of Basquiat's surfing vision when I stepped off a few of my first subway rides into the churning center of a city that was now home. Mostly in spite of myself I imagined the surfer up there above Union Square; the idea of it gave me a sparkling sense of exhilaration and, for lack of a better word—stoke. For anyone who grew up in the West or the Midwest or anywhere small and pastoral, or even a city like San Diego, your first few days as an actual New York City resident feel a lot like the awkward, euphoric self-consciousness you get the first time you ride a wave: *I'm in New York City! I'm doing this! I'm* totally *doing it!* In the beginning I was able to focus on that ride, on the excitement of living in the big city with its infinite cultural amenities and beautiful women and subway-accessible coastline, and kept the memory of the skyline surfer and Basquiat's inevitable wipeout deep down in my subconscious. But it doesn't take long to realize how hard and heavy a city like New York can come crashing down on you. And so it's strange and oddly synchronistic when, a few years later, during a weekend surf trip to Montauk—and just before pretty much the biggest symbolic bail of my own lifetime—I wind up at Julian Schnabel's beach house in Montauk.

Forecast for Montauk: Northeast swell 5–7 feet at 13 seconds. Winds from the south at 10 mph. Water temp 64, air temp 66. Surf: clean, head-high waves from the north with offshore winds; good to excellent conditions.

On a Friday afternoon in early September 2006, just a month after my thirty-third birthday, I receive an important phone call. It's from a nonprofit literary organization in Portland, Oregon, a place

---

* The filmwork is vintage footage by Herbie Fletcher, at what looks like Sunset Beach on Oahu.

called the Independent Publishing Resource Center, and after several rounds of phone interviews, they offer me the executive director position. I tell them I need the weekend to think it over, but I'm already celebrating on the inside—Portland's my dream city, where my stepbrother and my best friend live with their families—a place I always hoped I'd end up. I'll be taking a serious pay cut, but it's a rare noncorporate job in the field of writing and publishing, and the cost of living in Portland is a fraction of what it is in New York. I'd taken the call on my cell phone in Paley Park; after hanging up I consider going back in and quitting my publishing job on the spot—forgoing the whole two-weeks-notice thing and instead taking those two weeks to surf out at Montauk before heading back west. I fire off a text to Dawn—*Holy shit, I think I'm moving to Portland*—then call my dad and tell him the good news.

I curb my *Generation X* meets *Endless Summer* quitting fantasy, but later that evening I do drive out to Montauk to spend the weekend at Grodin's. A crisp fall night, a few dim stars, light traffic on the Long Island Expressway. I listen to the Rolling Stones, hammering out euphoric air-drum solos and fantasizing about my upcoming cross-country road trip.

The house is dark when I arrive—it's past eleven and everyone's out at the bars or already asleep. I spread my sleeping bag on the couch and switch off the lamp. As I lie there in the dark and contemplate the move, powerful waves of anxiety start roiling around in my stomach. Small at first, but soon they're jacking up way overhead, scaring the hell out of me, threatening to swell into another tidal wave of generalized anxiety, the kind that nearly drowned me the first time I tried to leave my job. What the hell am I getting myself into? I'm in a precarious emotional state just a few months after the robbery; getting out of bed every morning is a challenge, and here I am faced with moving three thousand miles across the country, finding a place to live, surfing in a new ocean—completely reinventing my life in a notoriously rainy city. I finally have an escape route out of the Pit, but it's cluttered with so many uncertainties. My biggest fear is that I'll move to Portland and have some sort of meltdown, the kind requiring ambulances and those weird foamy hospital slippers and heavy rounds of pharmaceuticals. This is the beginning of a crippling cycle of regret and indecision, and my celebratory mood is quickly erased and reprogrammed with a kind of relentless binary code, my mind infected by an endless, almost computational shifting between zero and one, New York and Portland.

After a shaky night of sleep I wake to dark skies, intermittent rain, rolling thunderstorms. There's an objective correlative–style storm brewing off the coast, very conveniently accentuating this new wave of anxiety and gloom. I text Dawn and Kessler; we agree to meet at a diner in Montauk, just up the street from the Memory Motel—the namesake of the Rolling Stones song about Annie Leibovitz.

The place is packed with weekenders, windows all fogged up, obscuring the view—not that there's anything to see but clouds and rain.

"So what's up with Portland?" Dawn asks, sipping her coffee.

"I don't know," I say. "I told them I'd take the weekend to think it over."

"That's a big decision for a weekend."

"Tell me about it." I think about my room in Brooklyn, all my stuff, the three thousand miles of red states between here and Portland. As much as I'm sick of New York, I also feel oddly insulated by it, protected and enabled in my isolation and anonymity, where none of my friends back home can see how hard I'm struggling.

Dawn brought along friends from the city, tall blond women in their late twenties with successful careers in the fashion world. Their names are Sarah and Tia; they both work for some big-deal fashion photographer and are in Montauk to celebrate her birthday.

"How long have you been in New York?" one of them asks.

"Three years, almost to the day."

"Have you accomplished what you wanted here?"

I shrug, take a sip of coffee.

Outside, water pours off the eaves, the rain gutters failing.

And I'm embarrassed to say it. Three years in the city, only one accomplishment: learning to surf. The best thing that's happened to me. The worst way to get ahead in New York.

After breakfast we drive out to a secret spot on the beach cliffs south of the Montauk lighthouse. Pulling up our hoods, we follow Kessler through an opening in the dense bramble and into a cavernous, dripping path toward the sea.

"If you move to Portland," Dawn says, following just behind me, "I'll probably come out and join you in a couple years. You can settle down there, buy a house. And they have actual *trees* there. A shitload of them."

We emerge from the brush onto a knoll covered in thick, wet grass overlooking the Atlantic. The rain has tapered off, the sky quilted with a hundred hues of charcoal and gray. Some seriously formidable waves are rolling in a hundred feet below, creasing in off the horizon, then rearing up sharply to reveal cobalt faces—swelling with silver—before collapsing into white, exploding around rocky crags, fizzing and clambering toward shore. Dawn and I look out into the vastness, comment on the *fucking amazingness* of it. We put our arms around each other, pose for photographs, hold on even after the cameras are put back in purses. It's already starting to feel like a going-away party.

By evening the storm blows over, just in time for the photographer's catered fortieth birthday party out on the beach. Wooden tables and chairs set right out on the sand, flickering storm lanterns and a beach bonfire, dogs and children running around, all the fresh lobster and corn on the cob and homemade bread you can eat. I have a couple cold beers, then sneak off to my truck, where, feeling both festive and anxious, I do something I haven't done in over a year—I dial Karissa's number. According to program language, what I'm doing is *acting out,* or *breaking my bottom line.*

She picks up on the third ring.

"Karissa Vasquez?" I say. "Is that you?" It's an old inside joke, one that we'd borrowed from her dad, who'd pretend to be terribly sick even if he just had a little head cold, mostly to garner sympathy and favors from Karissa. From his sickbed on the couch he'd reach out and grasp for her, ostensibly blinded with illness, and say *Karissa, is that you? If it's you, could you bring me some ice cream?*

"Oh my God, is this *Justin Hocking?*" she says. "I thought maybe you were dead or something."

It turns out she's at work at her new job as a hair stylist and only has a couple of minutes to talk. But that's all it takes for us to fall back into our old, easy way of relating—our buddy-buddy intimacy and all our inside jokes. I tell her about the job offer in Oregon and that I'm thinking seriously about taking it, and ask what *she* thinks about the idea.

"Will you be making a million dollars a year?" she asks.

"No, I'll pretty much be making the opposite of a million dollars a year. I've always been better at making friends than money."

"Well, that's debatable."

"I have lots of friends. It's girlfriends I have problems with."

"Yeah. Tell me about it. Hey man," she says, "I kind of need to finish coloring this person's hair. I'll have to call you back."

The sand chills my feet as I walk back to the bonfire where Dawn's still sitting, drinking a beer. Embers spark from the fire, flare brilliant orange, then fade into tangled coils of ash.

"Did you tell her about the job?" Dawn asks.

"Yeah, definitely."

"Her response?"

"Hard to say. She said she'll call me back."

"You think she still has a boyfriend?"

"I really hope not. Because if I move out there and she's still with someone, I'm not sure I can deal."

Dawn takes a sip of beer and stares into the fire, then looks over at me. "You know what? Don't worry too much about Karissa. Do what's best for you and the rest will work itself out."

The next morning we arise to find that a clean swell has rolled in on the storm's wake. I drive from Grodin's out to Montauk Point, blasting the Rolling Stones again and savoring one short section where pines canopy the entire highway. Trees surround the Oregon coast roads for hundreds of miles, but here you only get a few hundred feet of forest.

I meet up with Dawn and Kessler in the parking lot near the lighthouse, just above a spot called North End that breaks only once or twice a summer during a rare north swell. And a rare north swell's exactly what we have: line after line of five-to-seven-foot waves merge around the point and peel horizontally across the bay. The water's a kind of charcoal blue, the dark color of clouds before they dump rain, but with an aquamarine hue—a residual effect from the tropical storm.

Dawn and Kessler and I suit up and walk barefoot down an overgrown dirt trail, then hobble across the stony beach to the water. The waves aren't breaking close to shore, so getting out is fairly simple. After paddling ten minutes or more out into the lineup, I feel apprehensive—we're way off shore, at a spot where technically surfing is illegal. It's a major thoroughfare for commercial fishing boats; for this reason the shark danger is high. And Montauk was the setting for the original *Jaws* film—a commemorative sign reminds you of this every time you drive into town.

I'm actually comfortable in the water, though. The main thing causing me anxiety is this impending life decision. It's now Sunday and I have less than twenty-four hours to chart the course of the rest of my life. Being out here in these beautiful waves, just south of the lighthouse, and all my closest city friends out with me—it makes the idea of leaving New York seem painful. I watch Kessler get a couple good rides; he blasts past me with his laid-back stance, knees bent slightly, back arched—the epitome of style, earned only after a lifetime of surfing in one form or another.

There's something that happens between people who surf together, an alchemical bonding that comes from partaking in intense physical activity, from looking after one another out in the sea, and watching Kessler float by on a plunging wave I feel such warmth for him—the same guy who'd told me to *get out of his town* the first time I met him. More than any of his outer abrasiveness, he has what can only be described as *soul*—a word that derives from the ancient Germanic, meaning "coming from or belonging to the sea." It's in his surfing and his skating for sure; it's in the way he cruises casually through life; it's especially in the way he treats other people, looks after his friends, takes care of so many recovering addicts with all their endless needs, cravings, complaints. He's the kind of person you always want to be around; if he shows up for a session you know it's going to be good. But *good* isn't a strong enough word—surfing and skating with Kessler are *transcendent,* because, yes, you're in the presence of physical greatness—of one of the most stylish skateboarders ever, a true originator of the rolling art form—but more than that, beyond the whole *East Coast living legend* thing, you're also in the presence of an authentic heart. In my experience with yoga I've heard that devotees who meet certain enlightened masters never want to leave them; they'll follow the teacher all across India just for a glimpse, just to experience the teacher's gaze. There's a living Indian saint named Amma who sometimes visits New York; people line up around the block, wait for hours just for a single, life-changing embrace from her. It would be a major stretch to ascribe this kind of guru status to Kessler—he definitely wouldn't want it. And there are times when he comes right up to you on the street, usually in the East Village with a couple of recovering junkies in tow, and straight up heckles you for talking on your cell phone, or for wearing your square-looking work clothes and not having a skateboard, so that you want nothing more than to get the hell away from him, to shut him the fuck up—*Kandy Hassler.* But then again there are times like these, north of the lighthouse on a rare swell, when his presence makes you feel grateful, safe, fully inspired. In the face of all the shit I've been through in the past three years, these surf sessions with Kessler and Dawn are some of the best times of my life, and I never want them to end.

It takes a while to get in the proper position, but I finally score a wave, a long right-hander that I surf parallel with the shore for thirty or more yards, my first true point break ride. After the long paddle back toward the lighthouse, I spot Grodin making his way out toward us.

"So you moving to Portland or what?" he asks.

"I don't fucking know."

"Dude, your face looks really pale. You look like you saw a ghost. Actually, *you* look like a ghost."

"It's my sunscreen," I say. After he paddles off toward an outside takeoff point, I wipe my finger across my face. It comes up clean. It occurs to me that actually, I'd forgotten sunscreen. What's making me pale is the way I'm floating around between two worlds—the past and my unimaginable future, New York and Portland. A ghost indeed.

After we're all surfed out, Kessler invites Dawn and me up to visit his friend Daniel, an assistant to Julian Schnabel who's staying at the artist's house for the summer, taking care of Schnabel's pit bulls and working on paintings. The closest I'd been to Schnabel's place was his caretaker's quarters, where Casual Chuck lives and keeps his impressive quiver of vintage surfboards. I'd only caught a glimpse of Schnabel's house from Casual Chuck's, so I jump at the chance to check it out.

Following Kessler's directions, we take a private lane through a tangled thicket of brush and ivy; around each bend spray-painted signs read Beware of Dogs and Keep Out: Private Property. We pull up outside an expansive wooden structure, which Kessler explains is Schnabel's "surf shack." It looks like an oversize log cabin, one of those multimillion-dollar affairs that movie stars build in Aspen and then inhabit for only two or three weeks a year. Daniel appears on the front porch. He's a diminutive Irish guy, a chain smoker with curly, dishwater-blond hair that he keeps out of his face with a red bandanna. We follow him through massive double doors into the foyer, where the ceilings soar overhead, tall enough for Schnabel's enormous canvases. One's a line portrait painted on a large Kabuki theater backdrop that I faintly recognize from the *Basquiat* film. Then he leads us back outside through another giant door into an open-air painting studio. It's the size of a large racquetball court, with wood-plank flooring surrounded by tennis court–green walls on three sides. There are a few colorful, weathered paintings in progress, executed on big canvas tarps—mostly Daniel's work. Just off the studio's open wall is a garden trellis with an arched entranceway leading to a diving platform. The large rectangular pool below has a small, overgrown island at the end with a twisted Asian tree growing up from the center, like something from a Japanese landscape painting or a Dr. Seuss book. The emerald water looks a little murky, but given the go-ahead I'm ready to dive right in.

The lawn around the pool is well cared for but shaggy; it's slowly overtaking a set of antique chartreuse lawn furniture—two ornate, rusted-out chairs and a curlicue Victorian love seat. Old beach cruisers and a blue tandem with weathered whitewall tires are strewn all over the grass, along with isolated patches of dog shit. The whole place has the aura of John Cheever's story "The Swimmer,"* but unlike the Swimmer's world, Schnabel's place speaks of a kind of casual, healthy idleness. Whereas you feel pity for the Swimmer and relief when you close the book on him, you never want to leave a place like Schnabel's— you find yourself hoping for an invitation to come spend the weekend or the summer or, like Casual Chuck, the rest of your life.

After smoking a cigarette and making idle talk with Kessler, Daniel invites us back inside to tour the rest of the "shack." On the north

---

* The story of a Connecticut suburbanite who tries to swim his way home from a cocktail party by linking up a series of his neighbors' backyard pools. In the beginning he seems good-natured, robust, adventurous, but slowly the reader begins to understand that he's despised or pitied by most of his neighbors, that he's embroiled in at least one extramarital dalliance, and that he's actually been kicked out of the home he's swimming toward, so that in the end he finds himself naked and lost and cast out of his suburban Eden.

wall of the main room there's a gigantic painting of a blond girl in a sailor blouse, a thick black stripe obscuring her eyes, an image that I recognize from the cover of a Schnabel retrospective art book. Above a long dining room table hangs an ornate red-and-green Venetian blown-glass chandelier. There's a cavernous fireplace, so big that Dawn can enter without bumping her head. An electric guitar and a little amp sit in one corner; most of the furniture is rustic and obviously handcrafted. There are photos of Schnabel and friends surfing in Hawaii; up in the rafters hangs a stunning black big-wave surfboard, shaped by Schnabel's pal Herbie Fletcher and painted by Schnabel with the words *Blind Girl Surf Club*. Surfboards, guitars, a massive fireplace: the place is essentially an enormous, tastefully decorated man cave.

Daniel's cell phone rings; he excuses himself and takes the call in the kitchen. While he's out, Kessler explains what's going on: earlier that day at Ditch Plains one of Schnabel's RCA-style pit bulls got away from Daniel and bit some guy right in the crotch. News of it is all over Montauk; even I had heard about it from Grodin but didn't make the connection until now. The guy had to be carted off in an ambulance; animal control whisked the dog away, and now there's a possibility it might have to be put down. Of course, Daniel's worried he'll be cast out of Schnabel's bohemian garden of Eden. I feel sorry for him—I'd want to live there forever too. And given what he's going through, he's incredibly cordial to us; if I was in the same predicament, the last thing I'd want would be a bunch of strangers milling around.

While Daniel handles the dog situation, Kessler walks us up the road to the main house. It's one of the most beautiful homes I've ever seen—a cross between a Cape Cod and a gabled Victorian, the second story done in shingles and covered with red-fingered ivy, the lower level painted dark green. Two towering chimneys, big cathedral-style leaded-glass windows, an elongated front porch. Kessler points out Schnabel's expansive quiver—custom-built surfboards of every shape and size, stacked three or four high.

As I later learn, the house was designed by famous Gilded Age architect Stanford White, who contributed designs to Penn Station, Columbia University, the stunning Boston Public Library, and the iconic arch in Washington Park near NYU. He was considered a major force in the Renaissance Revival period. The Renaissance aesthetic, with its emphasis on ambidexterity and mastery across genres, seems appropriate for Schnabel, who along with painting dabbles in architecture, interior design, and film. As Kessler explains, at the present he's off in France shooting a movie called *The Diving Bell and the Butterfly.**

Though the house looks massive to me, White considered it a "fishing cottage"; it was modest in size compared to those he designed on the wealthier north side of Long Island. It was part of a colony of cottages, all designed by White and his firm. Andy Warhol was the first artist to buy one back in the 1970s, when he paid something in the ballpark of $500,000. Just adjacent to Schnabel's, Warhol's place is now worth $50 million—making it one of the most expensive pieces of real estate in the country. I wonder how much of that price is just for the history: it was a famous hangout for the whole Factory crew; the Stones recorded *Black and Blue* down in the basement. Legend has it you could hear them rocking all the way down to the trailer park at Ditch Plains—our go-to surf spot when the North End isn't breaking.

Something about this visit seems auspicious for me and my imminent life choice. On one hand, I feel assaulted by the level of Schnabel's success. In a scene from the film, the fictional Basquiat pisses in the fictional Schnabel's stairwell, maybe as a result of feeling similarly assaulted, as a minor insurrection against Schnabel's magisterial presence. Or then again, maybe Basquiat was just an asshole; maybe the drugs made him that way.

And on the other hand, I want a little piece of what Schnabel has.

---

* After I watch it a year and half later, *The Diving Bell and the Butterfly* becomes one of my all-time favorite films, further warming me toward Schnabel as a director.

I don't need a giant beach house or a swimming pool with an island or my own four-thousand-square-foot man cave, but I do need some creative autonomy. To surf when I want, write when I want, answering to no one but myself—this is the wealth I'm after. Something needs to change in my life, and visiting Schnabel's place crystallizes the feeling.

Forecast for the Manhattan Skyline: Small craft advisory. North swell 13 feet at 9 seconds. Winds from the south at 30 mph. Water temp 60, air temp 55. Surf: fair to poor conditions, with strong winds, dangerous rips, and sneaker waves.

Back in the city, I'm paralyzed with indecision. My hope is to hear back from Karissa, that her romantic status will help me decide one way or another, but Sunday and Monday come and go with no word back from her. Finally, on Wednesday, I get an email from the Portland people saying they need to know right away, that if I don't want the job they'll have to go with their second choice.

I have a long phone call with my best friend, Gabriel, who lives in Portland and originally sent me the job listing.

"Just call them and tell them you want it," he says.

"I'm in a bad way after the whole robbery thing," I say. "I'm worried I might get out there and completely lose it."

"I'm more worried about what might happen if you stay in New York," he says.

"Karissa's another issue."

"Portland's not that small. You'll probably never even see her."

"But we run in a lot of the same circles. I'm sure I'll bump into her."

"Then you'll bump into her. Worse things have happened. Now call them up and accept the job."

"But what if—"

"Call them up and take the goddamned job."

I haven't heard Gabriel raise his voice with anyone for years. He's possibly the least authoritarian person I know, but since I can't supply one myself, he gives me this final voice of authority. So I call. And accept. And try to do so with the most enthusiasm I can muster. And then fall asleep feeling relieved that I've made a choice; that is, until I wake up in the middle of the night, in the throes of an even deeper, more dislocating anxiety attack than the one I'd experienced out at Grodin's.

A few days later, after a series of sleepless nights, I stumble into work and open my email, and there it is, finally, a note from Karissa. She apologizes for taking so long to get back to me, and explains that she'd been on vacation up in Massachusetts with her *boyfriend*, and that during the trip her *boyfriend* asked her to be *his wife*.

Forecast for the Manhattan Skyline: New LARGE groundswell that should show strongest over the afternoon/evening. Look for 15–20 feet+ faces at many spots. Select outer reefs hold occasional bigger sets 25 feet+ late in the day. These are conditions for expert and very experienced surfers only. Anyone else should NOT paddle out as conditions are life-threatening.

Near the end of the film *Basquiat,* the eponymous artist has lunch with his estranged girlfriend, played by Claire Forlani. It's an awkward, tragic scene; Basquiat is strung out on drugs, drowning in his own fame, and this is all exacerbated by seeing how well his ex-girlfriend is doing for herself and learning that she's romantically involved with a mutual friend. He excuses himself to go to the wash room, where he scrutinizes and picks at his blemished face in the mirror, while the lugubrious Tom Waits song "Who Are You" plays in the background. At this very moment, the film cuts to the skyline surfer, who takes an epic, potentially fatal bail and then gets hammered by the falls, a not-so-subtle metaphor for Basquiat's own fall from grace and his impending heroin overdose.

As I'm sitting at my desk, staring at Karissa's email, something like a wave crashes over my own head, a neurochemical storm surge that holds me down for a long, long time. When I finally surface, I call Gabriel.

"The fact that you loved her so much shows that she's a really good catch," he says. "So it's not all that surprising that someone else asked her to marry him."

For the first time in my life, I hang up on my best friend.

My therapist agrees that I should go to Portland, but he strongly suggests that, after everything I've been through, I need to start taking some medication first.

When I object, he recaps my past two years: How he's watched me grow increasingly despondent at my job. How exhausted I am by the city, by my long daily commute from Brooklyn to Midtown. And how having a gun pointed at my face has brought me right to the breaking point.

"Why should you suffer any longer?" he asks.

It seems risky to me, beginning a heavy psychotropic and then moving across the country a couple weeks later, but if it means relief from the kind of pain and anxiety I've been feeling, then I'm all for it. And doubly so if it can help me deal with this new blast of depression over Karissa's engagement.

I book an appointment with a psychiatrist up near the Columbia University campus. He's a youngish doctor, personable, and in a few minutes I feel more comfortable talking to him than I ever have with my therapist. After listening to my story, he agrees that I need some meds. He prescribes a low dose of something called Celexa, an older version of Lexapro that apparently has fewer side effects.

"I think this will definitely help you with your transition to Portland," he says. "But more than that, it might change your life."

Nothing much changes at first, but after a few days I feel a new kind of edginess, like the way I imagine an alcoholic or a chronic smoker must feel after going cold turkey. The shrink warned me that the transition onto an antidepressant is often accompanied by some anxiety, so he'd also prescribed a tranquilizer called Ativan that I was to take "as needed." I'm in some serious need, so I start taking an Ativan every night to help me sleep. I'm amazed at how a tiny white pill can make me feel so much better, a wave of automatic serenity that puts me fast asleep, until I wake up at three or four craving another.

The first weekend in October breaks sunny and crisp and warm; under any other circumstances I would've gone surfing, but now all I want to do is sit at home, watch TV, and take Ativan. Things progress like this for a few more days, until I start to worry I might end up like a pill-junkie version of Basquiat.

I visit the psychiatrist and tell him what's been happening. He looks concerned when I explain I've been taking the Ativan in the afternoons and every night to help me sleep. He suggests that if I'm having trouble sleeping, then what I really need is a sleeping pill.

He writes a prescription.

On the way home, I pick up the grenade-sized bottle of Ambien.

I've never done hallucinogens, but what happens to me that night is comparable to a really bad trip. I have a terrible reaction to the Ambien, and combined with slight withdrawal from the Ativan and my difficult adjustment to Celexa, I nearly lose my mind. I can't sleep; all I can do is lie in a fetal position, my whole body trembling, held under by a heavy pharmacological crush, probably looking and feeling a lot like Martin Sheen having a nervous breakdown in a Saigon hotel room at the beginning of *Apocalypse Now.** When I close my eyes, I see dark, endlessly transmogrifying shapes behind my eyelids, like an evil game of Tetris that you can never slow down or shut off, a kind of hideous phantasm that no amount of conscious will can terminate. The Ambien also causes an awful chemical taste in my mouth, as if I'd polished the Pfizer laboratory floor with my tongue.

I feel like the human version of Newtown Creek, flooded with bad chemicals.

On top of the shadow shapes and tastes, I have severe anxiety and self-destructive urges—*three years in New York and only one*

---

* The scene was apparently culled from footage of Martin Sheen having an actual nervous breakdown.

accomplishment. At the very height of it, the dark, shifting shapes morph into obsessive visual hallucinations.

Vision: the Manhattan skyline surfer.

Vision: an epic bail, washed over the falls.

Vision: a plunge off the Williamsburg Bridge.

And Melville's in the room with me now; I can hear his ragged breathing, can sense his bitterness and gloom emanating up from under my bed, his body directly beneath mine, like a shadow print burned into the floorboards. This time he's accompanied by his son Malcolm, who, at the age of eighteen, climbed the stairs of the Melville family home, locked his bedroom door, and shot himself with a pistol, perhaps the result of growing up in the thick fog of such failure.

I somehow endure until dawn and call in sick for the third time this month. After my roommates leave for work, it's all I can do to get myself from my bed to the couch. I flip through the channels until I find *The Gods Must Be Crazy* playing on AMC. I'm still shaking, feeling sicker than I've ever felt, but somehow I'm able to laugh at the movie—the less-than-PC story of a misguided little Kalahari tribesman who ventures from his homeland to the big city just to return an empty Coke bottle. In one scene, he gets locked in prison for poaching a goat; he finds himself trapped in a tiny, dark cell, having no idea how or why he ended up there.

"Poor little bugger," one of the main characters says, "if we don't get him out of there, he's gonna die for sure."

BELLEVUE

In the wake of the commercial failure of *Moby-Dick*, Melville wrote the novel *Pierre*, the story of a young writer whose creative ambitions are crushed by New York City. While railing against Christian taboos and toying with bisexuality and an incestuous relationship with his sister, he becomes increasingly unhinged. According to Melville biographer Laurie Roberston-Lorant, the book reads "like a narrative nervous breakdown."

The bizarre story concludes with the main character's Hamlet-style suicide, followed by this nihilistic passage:

> Deep, deep, and still deep and deeper must we go, if we would find out the heart of a man; descending into which is as descending a spiral stair in a shaft, without any end, and where that endlessness is only concealed by the spiralness of the stair, and the blackness of the shaft.

Whereas *Moby Dick* earned the author only a few hundred dollars, Melville ended up actually owing his publishers close to that amount after the publication of *Pierre*, mainly because, while *Moby-Dick* received somewhat mixed reviews, *Pierre* and its author were positively crucified by the press—one New York journal ran a review beneath the headline "Herman Melville Crazy." The sentiment was often shared by Melville's family and friends. A neighbor, Sarah Morewood, wrote, "the recluse life he was leading made his city friends think he was slightly insane." His wife, Elizabeth, grew increasingly alarmed by his "ugly attacks." In response to a fellow artist's suicide, Melville himself remarked that "This going mad of a friend or acquaintance comes straight home to every man who feels his soul in him . . . For in all of us lodges the same fuel to light the same fire."

The Melvilles' Manhattan residence was just uptown from the

original Bellevue Hospital—one of New York's longest-running psy-chiatric institutions, having housed a number of the city's troubled literary minds, William Burroughs, Allen Ginsberg, and Eugene O'Neill among them. Given that Melville's in-laws once conspired to effectively kidnap Elizabeth from his abusive household during this post-*Pierre* darkness, it's not a stretch to imagine that they might also have considered having him committed.

The evening after my Ambien reaction, I call my mother and tell her what happened. Clearly distressed, she asks if I've considered hurting myself.

I tell her the truth.

Early the next morning she calls my therapist and the psychiatrist who prescribed the medication. My therapist is unequivocal: if I pose a danger to myself, I need to be hospitalized. When my mother relays this information, I picture Bellevue looming there on the banks of the East River. Part of me wants it: to give up, check in, change into pajamas. But I also worry that it might make things worse, fuck up my life beyond repair.

My psychiatrist takes the more practical, pharmaceutical approach, although his blunt statement—"For God's sake, don't take any more Ambien"—brings his overall competence into question. But while I'm still clenched in the jaws of deep depression and anxiety, dump-ing the bottle of sleeping pills down the toilet does help me finally get some rest.

DECISION/INDECISION

Though I've verbally accepted the job in Portland, I'm far from making up my mind whether or not to actually leave New York. Since the nonprofit job in Oregon doesn't provide health insurance, I apply for a personal health coverage plan through Blue Cross Blue Shield in Oregon. But because I'm now taking medication for depression, they deny me coverage based on a preexisting-condition clause.

This makes the decision even more agonizing. I want to get out of New York, but it seems almost irresponsible to give up a job with full benefits, especially at this point in my life when I need serious medical care. On the other hand, part of the reason I need this care is the fact that I live in New York.

I call Blue Cross in Oregon to explain the situation—that I've been through a traumatic event and the meds are helping me recover. But there's nothing anyone can do for me.

So along with my laptop and rental car, the Denver gangsters also jacked my insurability.

And then, like a final kick to the gut, in late October thieves break into the Independent Publishing Resource Center in Portland. They steal the new staff computer and three expensive Mac monitors—and I know it's because the organization is a captainless ship, in chaos without me.

THE SCRIVENER

> But he answered not a word; like the last column of some
> ruined temple, he remained standing mute and solitary in
> the middle of the otherwise deserted room.
>
> ~ HERMAN MELVILLE, *Bartleby the Scrivener*

After mixed critical reception for *Moby-Dick* and outright hostility toward *Pierre,* Melville descended into a period of hopelessness. From the wreckage of his career as a novelist, he escaped to short-form fiction like *Bartleby the Scrivener,* written for *Putnam's* in 1853. *Bartleby* is a tale of the eponymous young scrivener, hired by a Wall Street lawyer to copy out legal forms in triplicate and quadruplicate, like a human photocopier. He's a fastidious and productive employee, at least at first.

But as the story progresses, Bartleby begins refusing to carry out simple tasks. Eventually he gives up copying altogether.

I prefer not to, he says, over and over, a kind of haunting refrain.

Being a Christian man, the employer can't find it in his heart to fire him, especially once he learns that Bartleby has been spending nights in the viewless office chambers—that he has no home or family—"he seemed alone, absolutely alone in the universe. A bit of wreck in the mid Atlantic."

Though Bartleby does nothing but stare out the window at an opposing brick wall, the lawyer allows him to linger for weeks. His spectral presence disturbs clients and the other scriveners, casting a dark pall over the office and tarnishing the good lawyer's reputation. After begging him to leave and receiving the same response—*I prefer not to*—the bewildered employer sees no other option than to relocate his offices to a new building, abandoning Bartleby in his gloom.

In one unforgettable final scene, the lawyer returns to his old building, only to find Bartleby "haunting the building generally, sitting upon the banisters of the stairs by day, and sleeping in the entry by night."

While toiling in the windowless Pit, I can't help but think of the melancholy plotline in *Bartleby*. And though I don't say it out loud, the refrain *I prefer not to* plays over and over in my head, especially when asked to edit yet another romance novel. But I'm never so Bartleby-like as when, after trying but failing to leave my job for a solid year, and then finally winning and accepting a new job on the opposite coast, I can't find the resolve to actually give notice, to pack up my things and send out the obligatory farewell emails.

A few weeks pass like this.

Then a full month.

Then another.

But still I remain, a shadow presence in the Pit, a hazy apparition of my former self, haunting my cubicle.

THE WHITE DEAD

~ *Philip Weiss,* contributing writer for the *New York Times* and confirmed Melvillian, who, in his 1996 *Times* article, describes how after reading Melville's exalted letters to Hawthorne, he found himself in a sort of *Melvillian dream;* who, in the same article, states *I had lost my own mind to Melville.*

~ *Laurie Anderson,* who claims that *Moby-Dick* is the strangest book she ever read; who hails Melville as a *master of the jump cut;* who spent the 1990s creating a two-hour performance art opera entitled *Songs and Stories from* Moby-Dick.

~ *Elizabeth Schultz,* who admits to being obsessed with the novel; who wrote the meticulously researched *Unpainted to the Last:* Moby-Dick *and Twentieth-Century American Art,* a work that documents the hundreds of American visual artists who have attempted to paint what Melville believed could not be painted.

~ *Junot Díaz,* who quotes liberally from *Moby-Dick* in *The Brief Wondrous Life of Oscar Wao;* whose own literary voice mixes an ecstatic, *wild style* vernacular with highbrow sensibilities that can be described as *Melvillian;* who in a 2012 interview with Bill Moyers said, *I had grown up in a place called Lemon Terrace, New Jersey, where the guy down the street was Uruguayan, the woman across the street was Korean, the person around the corner was Egyptian. There were Dominicans. There were African Americans. There were white folks. And I felt like we were growing up in this tiny little* Pequod. . . . *And when I was reading* Moby-Dick, *I was like, "Man, this guy really has his finger on the pulse of the America that I came up in."*

~ *David Foster Wallace,* whose father read him *Moby-Dick* as a bedtime story; who counted *Moby-Dick* as one of his favorite works;

who, while struggling with his own mental illness in college, wrote three essays about the "Castaway" section.

— *Jocko Weyland,* who spent years writing his memoir *The Answer Is Never: A Skateboarder's History of the World;* who struggled with piecing together so many disparate personal memories, history, interviews, sketches; who was then directed to *Moby-Dick,* where he found the answer.

— *Jackson Pollock,* who, according to Elizabeth Schultz, spent years in Jungian analysis, where *its emphasis upon primitive archetype, myth, and symbol, prompted his interest in Moby-Dick;* who executed several paintings based on the novel; who, according to Ellen Landau, *may have been able to associate Ahab's search for the great white whale with what Jung called the Nekyia, or night sea journey.*

— *Sena Jeter Naslund,* who grew fascinated with the book at age thirteen; who, decades later, spent more than five years researching, writing, and revising the stunning 666-page novel *Ahab's Wife.*

— *Damion Searls,* who, after learning of Orion Press's recent abridgment of *Moby-Dick* into a compact edition for the overly busy or impatient reader, decided to trace every item excised by Orion's anonymous editor, down to the last semicolon, and publish this four-hundred-page demi-book called *; or the Whale* in a special edition of the *Review of Contemporary Fiction;* who did this to preserve and celebrate the original novel's *digression, texture, and weirdness.*

— *Tony Kushner,* who became obsessed with *Moby-Dick* in graduate school; who claims the novel is the single most important influence on his work, including the second act of *Angels in America;* who is quoted in the *New York Times* as saying *One falls in love with him, and I certainly have, completely, as most of the other Melville freaks have;* who learned from Melville that *it's better to risk total catastrophe than to play it safe as an artist.*

— *Frank Stella,* who spent twelve years creating more than fifteen hundred abstract sculptures, collages, murals, paintings, engravings, and prints, each titled after *Moby-Dick* chapters; who claims that this obsession nearly destroyed him; who felt that abstraction was the most effective way of re-presenting the novel, that it mirrors Melville's drive to express the raw, ineffable powers of nature.

— *Salman Rushdie,* who claims Melville as a literary parent in his *polyglot family tree;* whose novel *The Enchantress of Florence* features a seafaring main character and a maximalist narrative style reminiscent of *Moby-Dick.*

— *Orson Welles,* who played Father Mapple in John Huston's black-and-white film version of *Moby-Dick;* who wrote and directed a play called *Moby-Dick Rehearsed* that was performed in London in 1955; who apparently made a film version of the play that is now lost; who later made another twenty-two-minute film in which he enacts scenes from the production, playing the parts himself—Ishmael and Ahab—while footage of rippling water projects on his face and the wall behind him.

— *Andrew Delbanco,* who wrote the definitive biography *Melville: His World and Work;* who claims that *Moby-Dick was not a book for a particular moment. It is a book for the ages;* that *Melville experienced the great city as every true New Yorker has always experienced it—with a combustible combination of love and hate;* that *Moby-Dick* is the *story of a young man's rebirth.*

— *Gilbert Wilson,* who, during the mid-twentieth century created more than three hundred paintings and drawings related to *Moby-Dick;* who became obsessed with the idea that the white whale was a potent symbol for the destructive power of the nuclear bomb; who tried and failed to stage an opera called *The White Whale,* which he hoped would promote world peace.

— *Barry Lopez,* who read the book three times before college, while living in New York City; who cites *Moby-Dick* as one of the main inspirations in his drive to render in writing both the light and dark aspects of the natural world.

— *Richard Serra,* who grew up near the shipyards in San Francisco's Ocean Beach neighborhood; whose monolithic steel sculptures are influenced by the process of shipbuilding; who made a famous piece entitled *Call Me Ishmael;* who said *Moby-Dick has become America's central epic poem. We are all influenced by it.*

— *Dan Beachy-Quick,* who created *A Whaler's Dictionary,* a collection of essays about *Moby-Dick,* where he writes, *What follows is the result of the mad task I found within myself after more than a decade spent reading the same novel. I meant not to exhaust* Moby-Dick *of meaning, but to exhaust myself of the meaning I found in it.*

— *John Updike,* who was a lifelong admirer of Melville's novels and stories; who, in a 1982 *New Yorker* article, explained that despite Melville's failure as a novelist and a life filled with personal tragedy, he never quit writing, not until his death.

— *Hershel Parker,* who apparently wakes up in the middle of the night to pore over Melville's personal letters; who wrote the seminal two-volume work *Herman Melville: A Biography,* each volume weighing in at 941 pages.

— *Elizabeth Renker,* who cried as she read from *Moby-Dick* at her wedding; who loves Melville's work but not necessarily Melville the man; who writes openly of his alleged misogyny, alcoholism, and abuse of his wife.

— *Adrian Villar Rojas,* who created a life-size, impaled white whale from unfired clay at a *Moby-Dick*–themed art show at the Wattis Institute for Contemporary Arts in San Francisco.

— David Dowling, who documents his participation in a twenty-four-hour marathon *Moby-Dick* reading in his book *Chasing the White Whale;* who writes, *If we are up to the challenge of endurance that the novel poses, especially as it is read in the marathon format, great rewards not only of survival but also of exultation are in order.*

— Nathaniel Philbrick, who in his book *Why Read Moby-Dick?* states that *This redemptive mixture of skepticism and hope, this genial stoicism in the face of a short, ridiculous, and irrational life, is why I read* Moby-Dick; that it's *the one book that deserves to be called our American bible.*

— David Shields, who in *Reality Hunger* writes *The novel is dead. Long live the antinovel, built from scraps;* who prizes *Moby-Dick* as a prototypical antinovel; who, in *How Literature Saved My Life,* lists *Moby-Dick* as one of fifty works he swears by.

— *Matt Kish,* who on August 5, 2009, began making one drawing a day, every day, for all 552 pages of his edition of *Moby-Dick;* whose work was later published in a book entitled *Moby-Dick in Pictures.*

— *Margaret Guroff,* who created a copiously annotated online version called *Power Moby-Dick.*

— Nick Flynn, who loosely based the structure of his memoir *Another Bullshit Night in Suck City* on *Moby-Dick;* who writes in the final chapter, *We know [Ahab] lost his leg, and that that loss became a story, and the story became the obsession that in the end defined, and ended, his life. We have to be careful of the stories we tell about ourselves.*

— *Hart Crane,* who wrote the poem "At Melville's Tomb"; who ended this poem with the line *This fabulous shadow only the sea keeps;* who later drowned himself in the Gulf of Mexico.

RUBIN MUSEUM

In late October I head for a twelve-step meeting for artists, hoping to talk out my decision, even if it's with strangers. It's located downtown, in a LGBTQ advocacy center. I walk in and the place is mostly empty, except for a volunteer who points me toward the third floor. Walking upstairs, I pass a gorgeous Latina woman with thick black hair, pouty lips, a masculine jawline. Something happens when we pass—we both turn around, take each other in.

I make it to the third floor, but the place is a labyrinth. I wander around, looking for the right room, until I see the woman coming back up the stairwell, apparently looking for me. I turn and walk the other way, heart racing. I duck into the men's room, thinking I might lose her there, close myself in a stall.

Attiq doesn't answer his phone when I call; wanting to avoid detection, I don't leave a message.

Then the bathroom door opens.

High heels click across the tiled floor.

She opens the stall next to mine, enters.

Her feet look like women's feet— women's feet here in the men's room.

I'm sweating now, feeling simultaneously aroused and sick. I'm still making the difficult transition onto Celexa. Still wracked with indecision and at what amounts to the all-time low point in my life, when I've never wanted a moment of connection so badly—I imagine how it will feel, like swallowing an Ativan, how all my problems will evaporate for a few minutes of bliss. This cold collision in my head— between Portland and New York, man and woman, wanting to live and wanting to die, hope and no hope, God and no god, Ishmael and Ahab—comes to some kind of violent, jackknifing apex, and I want so badly to make contact, to crack through the thick ice of my paralysis with just one moment of blowtorch heat.

Then someone else enters the room.

In response, the woman in heels clicks back out the door.

This new visitor wears a pair of nineteenth-century fisherman's boots, the aged leather creased with brine, soles worn thin by hard, remorseless service and his world-weary gait.

He too takes the stall next to mine, but remains standing and impenetrably silent. And I sit there beside him, missing the entire meeting, the whole room bleary beneath a saltwater tide that keeps rising and rising and rising, the force so strong I fear it might drown me completely.

I finally get myself collected, stumble out of the building and onto the street, where my phone rings. I tell Attiq what happened, that I can't make up my mind about anything. That I'm afraid I might be completely losing it. He says he'll have to call me back.

I buy some tea and sit in the park, still feeling dizzy, nauseous. He calls back, says there's something he wants to do for me, that I should meet him in an hour at a museum on the west side.

I take the train to Seventeenth and Seventh, to the Rubin Museum, an unassuming building that houses a large collection of Buddhist and Himalayan art. Attiq doesn't arrive for another twenty minutes, so I sit and listen to a group playing Indian music beneath a spiral staircase—one man on sitar and another on tabla, streaming out rich, soothing melodies and rhythms. There's a trickling fountain in the lobby, the smell of frankincense and chai tea. *Breathe*, I tell myself.

Attiq arrives and takes a seat at the table I've saved in the museum café. He asks me what's happening, so I tell him what I've already told him, six or seven times—that I'm paralyzed with indecision, that I can't figure out whether to stay or go, that I don't think New York is healthy for me, but I also don't want to take what they call in twelve steps a "geographical cure." That I've always wanted to live in Portland, but I'm scared to move there for a low-paying job with no health insurance and Karissa's impending marriage. He listens quietly, as usual, trying not to appear alarmed as my mind continues to split itself down the middle.

Until he stops me.

"Listen," he says. "We can sit here and have this conversation, and you'll just talk yourself in circles all night, like you've been talking your-self in circles for the past month. So I want to try something different."

He takes me up to the café counter, where he buys us both large bowls of asparagus and shrimp soup with French bread on the side. And two steaming cups of tea.

"I'd like this to be a silent meal," he says. He tells me to pay atten-tion to every bite of my food, every sip of tea. And to feel gratitude for it all, for the sun that grew the asparagus, for the soil and rain that fed it, for the clouds that created the rain and the ocean that created the clouds. For the people who prepared the food and the families who raised them. He tells me to feel gratitude for the fact that we have homes as winter approaches, that we have so much abundance right here in front of us. And he instructs me to listen for my inner voice, to hear what it tells me.

"We'll take our time," he says, "and then we'll go upstairs."

I follow his instructions. Savor every spoonful of what tastes like the best soup I've ever eaten. I take deep breaths in between sips, and feel, maybe for the first time in weeks, a sense of calm, silence. And from that silence comes a small voice, the same one from my bath-room back in Colorado.

The message is clear now: *It's time for you to go.*

After eating, we walk silently up the spiral staircase to a sunken al-cove with red meditation cushions and walls covered with paintings of deities—gold deities, red deities, black deities, deities with many heads stacked on one another like a totem pole, deities with multiple arms. A crimson demigod drinking blood from a cup. Teachers and saints floating on stylized clouds above mist-ribboned mountains.

Attiq asks me to sit down. He instructs me to close my eyes, take deep breaths.

"Listen to what they have to tell you," he says. "If you ask, they'll answer."

I'm well beyond irony now, willing to try anything, even begging assistance from a bunch of old paintings.

The response is different than it was downstairs; instead of one voice I now experience a convocation of voices, but it's not crowded or chaotic—they're all saying the same thing, that it's time for me to go.

What if I get to Portland and have a total breakdown? I ask.

The answer is clear: *Your breakdowns have always been break-throughs.*

What about Karissa? I ask. At this there is laughter; a voice explains that I'm not to worry, that I'll meet a girl who does yoga and surfs. This strikes me as fucking ridiculous, but I remind myself that this is just me talking to myself—that yes, maybe I'm channeling some kind of disembodied spirits here, but mostly this is just me—my own inner wisdom—leading me back west.

It's okay, the voices say. *It's really time for you to go.*

Attiq walks me outside, where I explain what happened and thank him for this kind thing he's done for me. In my months of agonizing over this decision, he's the first to not give me direct advice, to instead create a situation in which I could guide myself.

"It seems like you manifested this job," he says. "And you'll get into recovery out there. It's not just in New York. Recovery is everywhere."

He instructs me not to talk about what just transpired, not to process it too much or get back in my old ratiocerebral Ping-Pong game. He tells me to buy some incense, listen to some calming music. Sleep on it.

We hug good-bye and I watch him cross the street toward the West Village, walking with his slight limp, dressed in his orange cap and his fleece vest, until finally I lose sight of him in the crowd.

THE NEKYIA

In *The Odyssey*'s eleventh book, Odysseus descends into the underworld, where he consults with the soul of the prophet Teiresias, in order that he might find out how to get back to Ithaca—that after such a long battle, he may finally reach home.

Teiresias asks for a blood sacrifice, and once he is appeased, he and a host of spirits tell Odysseus what he must do.

THE JOURNEY

The next day, I tell my therapist what happened at the Rubin Museum, that I think I've made up my mind.

He looks at me like I'm crazy. He doesn't like the idea of me hearing voices, even though I've explained that they were inner voices, a form of channeling, maybe, and nothing like aural hallucinations. But still he launches in with a line of questioning I know is designed to determine if I'm bipolar. *Do I have bursts of energy? Have I ever gone more than three nights without sleep? Do I ever have racing thoughts, grandiose ideas?*

"I know where you're going with this," I say, "and I'm not bipolar. I've never had anything close to a manic episode. The problem here is that you're totally unwilling to accept the validity of mystical experience. You and me sitting here, this whole conversation is like a microcosm of the shortcomings of Western medicine. I tell you I just had this subtle transformative experience that finally helped me make up my mind, and you start trying to *diagnose* me. But it's a moot point," I say, "because I'm leaving New York."

Though I tell my therapist I'm going, I don't truthfully find the inner resolve to leave until Thanksgiving—more than two and a half months after accepting the Portland job—when my father and stepmother come to visit me in New York. Having family around buoys my courage, especially when my father offers to make the cross-country drive with me.

He helps me pack up my truck, strap my surfboard on top, and together we begin the three-thousand-mile trip back west, driving through the aftermath of a Midwestern ice storm that transformed all the tree limbs and fence posts into sharpened, sun-glinting harpoons, and where I'm surprised to find myself unnerved by so many miles of barren, unoccupied space.

THE TRY-WORKS

I drop my father off in Colorado and pick up my stepfather, Jerry, who makes the second half of the drive with me. Somewhere in Wyoming we begin hearing unsettling news reports about a California family that went missing deep in the wilderness of southern Oregon.

As night falls in western Wyoming, Jerry and I pass a string of oil refineries, like some dark vision of Hades, fire spouting out smokestacks, feeding on the night air, releasing a dull chemical stench. In the "Try-Works" section of *Moby-Dick,* Melville describes the American whale ship as a kind of floating factory, complete with a furnace—a "try-works"—for rendering whale blubber into oil. During a night watch, Ishmael finds himself mesmerized by the hellish scene of the "savage" harpooners tending the try works. It occurs to him that "the rushing Pequod . . . laden with fire, and burning a corpse, and plunging into that blackness of darkness, seemed the material counterpart of her monomaniac commander's soul." As it occurs to me, nearly two centuries later, that this monolithic Wyoming refinery is the material counterpart of Dick Cheney's soul, George Bush's soul, the light and dark soul of America. Of my own soul as I drive in a gas-powered vehicle toward an uncertain future. But as Ishmael warns, "Give not thyself up, then, to fire, lest it invert thee, deaden thee; as for the time it did me."

LOST

Jerry and I roll into Portland around noon on a gray day in early December. We drive down Hawthorne Boulevard, toward my new rented room, not far from my stepbrother and his family's home. My friends have all assured me that Portland is not that small, that the likelihood of bumping into Karissa is slim. But I haven't been in the city for more than five minutes when she sends me a text.

I just saw your truck drive by! Welcome to town:)

As it turns out, the hair salon where she works is located five blocks from my new house.

I'm tempted to flip a U-turn, drive myself and all my shit straight back to Brooklyn.

Jerry takes me out to lunch, orders some tea to help calm me down. It's pouring outside now, and the cover of the *Oregonian* shows a surfer riding a thirty-foot storm swell down at Lincoln City. Below that is a follow-up to the headline news about the lost California family. They've finally been located—it turns out they got their car stuck in the snow on a remote back road, and the wife and children lived in this vehicle for days, burning the tires for warmth, rationing out energy bars and bottled water.

All except for the husband, who made the choice to leave his family, wander out in the snowy woods in nothing but tennis shoes, jeans, and a rain jacket, searching for help.

It wasn't the right decision.

SRI LANKA

After four years in Bequia, my uncle John and aunt Ann moved to Seattle to raise their children. By the mideighties, though, they craved more adventure, so they took my cousins out of school for a humanitarian mission to Sri Lanka. Their plan was to spend a year or more building a water system for a small village. But soon after their arrival, civil war broke out between the Tamil Tigers and government forces. The U.S. Embassy advised my uncle to leave, but after the Red Cross gave him a special sticker for the family's van—allowing them access to remote villages where they could deliver much-needed food and supplies to refugees—he decided to stay on.

They witnessed suffering and atrocities, but they survived the civil strife and helped hundreds of people. Things were going along okay—that is, until my uncle's ocean obsession got the best of him. Down at the local harbor, he discovered a deal on a sailboat he couldn't resist. His plan was to fix it up and eventually take his family cruising in the South Seas. Not long after he finished rebuilding the derelict craft, though, armed forces came aboard and located two handguns hidden up in the hold, likely left there by the former owner.

My uncle was thrown into a cramped prison cell with concrete floors and a bucket for a toilet, which he had to share with five other inmates. Within a week of his incarceration, infectious conjunctivitis rendered him practically blind; he developed a terrible case of dysentery and lost more than thirty pounds. He was so sick that he found himself wishing for death, but another prisoner was kind to him, helped nurse him back to health. Once my uncle regained his vision, this man drew all the Hindu deities on slips of paper for him. He taught John their names: Shiva the lord of destruction, Kali the Destroyer, Vishnu the Preserver, Ganesh the elephant god, Hanuman the monkey god.

But closest to this man's heart were Ram and his lover Sita. He explained to my uncle how, with help from Hanuman, Ram rescued Sita from imprisonment by the demon Ravana, whose prison lair was located on the very island of Sri Lanka.

THIRTY-THREE

The poet Hart Crane was almost thirty-three when he committed suicide. He was on a U.S.–bound ship from Mexico, where he made a sexual overture toward a male crew member; in response the sailor beat Crane to within an inch of his life. Crane then finished the job for him by casting himself overboard.

David Foster Wallace was thirty-three when he voyaged aboard the cruise ship *Zenith*, which he rechristened the *Nadir*. Midnight chocolate buffets, skeet shooting, five-star dining, conga lines—these entertainments only intensified the despair he felt at night, on board the *Nadir*. "I am now 33 years old," he writes in *A Supposedly Fun Thing I'll Never Do Again*. "And I'm starting to see how as time gains momentum my choices will narrow and their foreclosures multiply exponentially until I arrive at some point on some branch of all life's sumptuous branching complexity at which I am finally locked in and stuck on one path and time speeds me through stages of stasis and atrophy and decay until I go down for the third time, all struggle for naught, drowned by time. It is dreadful."

Herman Melville was thirty-two when *Moby-Dick* was published. At thirty-three, and partly in reaction to the commercial failure of *Moby-Dick,* he wrote *Pierre*—a semiautobiographical novel in which the author passive-aggressively rages against the literary establishment, antebellum American culture, Christianity, his own family, and himself. It's one of the most bizarre, nihilistic books ever written. The main character's suicide in the end symbolizes Melville's own career suicide. It would take seven decades to resuscitate his dormant, shrouded reputation.

When he was thirty-three, William Faulkner wished to marry a young woman named Estelle, a family friend who'd been like a sister to him when they were growing up. Since he'd embarked on what they feared would be a nonlucrative writing career, both his family and Estelle's parents forbade him from proposing. When Estelle became engaged to another man, Faulkner poured his rage and heartache into *The Sound and the Fury*—a narrative that spins furiously around a sister character, Caddy Compson, like electrons around a nucleus. Three of the book's four sections follow the Compson brothers in the wake of Caddy's elopement. Benjy Compson, the "idiot" brother, wails by the golf course whenever a player calls for his *caddy*. Quentin, the suicidal, intellectual older brother is tortured by his incestuous love for Caddy, so much so that he eventually drowns himself. Jason, the oldest, rage-filled brother, tries in vain to keep Caddy's illegitimate daughter (also named Caddy) from ending up like her mother.

This kind of authorial-biographical analysis isn't much in vogue these days, but to me the novel reads like Faulkner's heartsick howl for Estelle. Though formally challenging even by contemporary standards, *The Sound and the Fury* helped earn Faulkner his epic literary ascension; on the heels of his success he and Estelle eventually married.

In the first Canto of *The Inferno*, Dante writes, *"Midway along the journey of our life / I woke to find myself in a dark wood."* Since the life expectancy for men of his era was about sixty, we can guess that Dante was around thirty-three when he made his symbolic voyage down into hell, out through purgatory, and, eventually, up to paradise.

In 1992, famous pro surfer Mark Occhilupo had a mental breakdown during a surf trip to France. Though he'd been on his way toward a world championship and was nearly thirty, he moved back home with his parents in Australia. For several seasons he did nothing but lie on the couch, watch TV, and drink beer. Having reached obese proportions, and diagnosed with bipolar mood disorder, he disappeared completely from the world of surfing.

He was the opposite of *lost at sea*.

Then, at age thirty-three, he rejoined the pro surfing circuit and made one of the most miraculous comebacks in the history of sports. According to Australian surf writer/photographer Sarge, "The highlight of the life of Jesus Christ was his rising from the dead, after dying nailed to a cross. He was thirty-three; so is Occy. [Mark] has already come back from the 'dead' and he is currently doing the nailing."

THE EMERGENCY

> Now then, thought I, unconsciously rolling up the sleeves
> of my frock, here goes for a cool, collected dive at death and
> destruction, and the devil fetch the hindmost.
>
> ~ HERMAN MELVILLE, *Moby-Dick*

Whereas I'd been lucky to get a few hours' rest in *the city that never sleeps,* the ever-present overcast makes Portland my *city that always sleeps.* During the dark month of December I often sleep until noon or later, making up for the countless hours I'd missed in New York. My first weeks are spent struggling to adjust to the demands of a new job, avoiding parts of town where I think I might see Karissa, and missing Dawn, Asa, my roommates, and all my other friends back in the city.

During my first staff meeting at my new job, I have another mental blackout, similar to those I'd suffered back in New York. But in this case, rather than sitting alone in my cubicle, I'm now surrounded by volunteers and fellow employees—people I barely know, people who've been waiting three months for me to show up.

Someone asks me a question about a problem with our database— a problem that has arisen as a result of the theft of our old staff computer—and while I'm trying to explain what little I know about the situation, the circuitry of my mind abruptly powers down. It's not like having a word escape you for a moment—this feels more like I've been robbed of words, like my capacity for language has been ripped from my body, pitched into the back of a black SUV, and driven off into the night.

Somehow I recover and finish the meeting, and, fortunately, this being just a few days before Christmas, the next morning I fly back to Colorado to stay with my parents over the holidays. It's a good trip, and I get some much-needed rest, and by the time I head back, I'm feeling a little better about everything.

Until the flight home, when, just after takeoff, I feel the plane start to descend, and I know immediately that something's wrong.

As confirmation, the captain's voice echoes over the loudspeaker. "Folks, it looks like we have a little problem," he says.

It's amazing how one short sentence can conjure so many images of major disaster. Right away my mind is full of 9/11 and Lockerbie, Scotland—two hundred suitcases and seats scattered through a pasture. And also scenes from the comedy *Airplane,* where the panic erupts into full-blown chaos, and an actual wrestling match—turnbuckles and singlets and all—breaks out in the aisles.

"The flaps on our left wing aren't working properly," the captain explains. "Flight control is advising that we swing back around Denver. We may have a bit of a hard touchdown, so I've asked the flight attendants to prepare you for an emergency landing. Emergency crews will be on the ground waiting for us."

The attendants seem overly chipper and happy, as if they're thrilled about this hard landing we're about to make.

"What's that mean, anyway—*a bit of a hard touchdown?*" I wonder out loud.

It turns out the guy sitting next to me is an amateur pilot. He explains that a hard landing could mean anything. An extra little bump, the kind that causes overhead bins to spill open, a thing I'd witnessed when I flew with my family to Cancun in the fifth grade. Or a hard landing could mean the kind whose aftermath you see on the nightly news: a fuselage in flames, the nose cone crunched up like a recycled Pepsi can. Emergency crews? That means fire trucks, rescue crews, ambulances equipped with special burn victim units.

"And if you ask me," he says, "the thing about the flaps is bullshit. They never tell you what's really going on."

The flight attendants take to the aisles, still masked with strained smiles as they guide us through emergency landing procedures. Instead of putting your head between your legs, contemporary protocol calls for placing your hands up on the seat in front of you and resting your face against your forearms, as if this will mitigate the force of a 500-ton aircraft smashing into the earth.

Whereas I was once scared to even set foot on a plane, now I'm surprised to find that I'm not the least bit anxious—something for which I have the New York City subway to thank. In fact, I find myself not really caring what happens either way, a *bit of a hard landing* or a full-on, flaming disaster—something for which, again, I have New York to thank.

Fuck it, I keep thinking, *let's do this.*

In Dan Beachy-Quick's *A Whaler's Dictionary,* he writes, "The book to come is as much the story of Ishmael's not killing himself as it is the story of the death of Ahab and his crew. Ishmael had to survive himself before he could survive the destruction of the Pequod."

I love this idea, and I'd take it a step further: my theory is that the *Pequod*'s destruction was itself the result of suicide. It's not a new hypothesis; in 1963 Edwin S. Sheridan wrote a "psychological autopsy" on Ahab, concluding that his was a case of "victim-precipitated homicide," that Ahab "permitted suicide." It fits with the Jungian interpretation of *Moby-Dick*—the idea that the book can be read as the night sea journey of a single soul, that Ahab is basically Ishmael's own dark side. This explains why Ahab takes over narration at the end, why Ishmael as narrator has access to Ahab's inner thoughts. Any modern practitioner would most likely diagnose Ahab as having PTSD and severe depression as a result of his being dismasted. And I know from experience that a common symptom of both is suicidal ideation.

For Ahab, a shipwreck would make it all look like an accident.

When I was in college, a young Air Force fighter pilot broke formation, not far from my plane's current airspace. He intentionally crashed a $10 million jet into a mountain just twenty miles from my parents' house.

Maybe this was Ahab's plan all along.

Red ambulance lights strobe the runway as we begin our descent back into Denver. The guy next to me is sweating, white-knuckling both armrests. Everyone on board seems gripped with fear.

Everyone except me.

I don't really feel anything but numb.

We hover for a moment over the runway, then touch down with nothing more than a slight skid.

The cabin erupts with applause.

We spend an hour at the gate while they repair the flaps. But when we take off again, the same thing happens. The captain comes on and says, "Folks, it looks like the flaps *still* aren't coming up."

The death drive in me—what Jung called *thanatos*—kicks up again. *Let's fucking crash this thing,* I think.

But immediately I'm aware of all the other passengers on board, people with kids at home, husbands, wives, families. These are people whose lives are working out, and what I want more than anything is to be one of them. And then the captain comes back on, explains that since he has full control of the aircraft, air control has suggested that we continue on to our destination.

So we fly back to Portland, broken wing and all.

THE RIP

In January I purchase a thick, hooded Body Glove wetsuit and a pair of Quiksilver booties. Homesick for Rockaway and anxious to get back in the ocean, I arrange a surf trip with an old friend from snowboard camp, Becky, along with her friends Dana and Cedar and their newborn baby, William.

We make the two-hour drive through miles of bucolic farmland, trout streams and pine trees, orchards and dairy farms and red barns. Waves of mist envelop the car as we summit the Coast Range, giving us the sensation of floating through a liminal, phantom forest, our destination obsured by a thick wall of whiteness.

Cedar takes us to a deserted beach north of Pacific City—a beautiful spot, but rarely surfed due to its lack of a protective headwall. The day turns balmy, sixty degrees and sunny, but the wintry ocean is breaking heavy, with ten-to-twelve-foot swells out at its angriest point. Given that the sea is a chaotic mess of foam and battling currents, it's decided that Becky and Dana will stay on shore and I'll go out with Cedar, a seasoned Oregon surfer who shapes his own boards from balsa and salvaged redwood. For William's sake, he promises not to go in deeper than his neck. Sitting on the bumper of his Volvo station wagon while we stretch into our wetsuits, Cedar produces a large pair of binoculars from the bottom of his wetsuit duffel.

I ask if he and Dana are bird-watchers.

"No, not really," he says.

"Then why the binoculars?"

He points with his chin at the turbulent, foamy sea. "In case one of us gets lost out there," he says. "The girls will need some way to spot us."

Shrugging off what seems like a preposterous notion, I finish pulling the hood over my head and pose for Becky's digital camera. Cedar and I lug our surfboards down to the water; the minute I step in, a strong undercurrent yanks at my feet. The waves themselves come in a relentless, short-period progression, breaking every few seconds and from all directions. From water level I can see that on the outside, they're cresting way overhead, some as high as thirteen feet.

These are by far the most chaotic conditions I've ever braved, and yet, because of my reckless Rockaway habit, my obsessiveness, I paddle right out past Cedar, hoping to catch one of the midsized lefts I'd spotted from the shore. A few pounding breakers try to send me sprawling back to the shore, but I persist, paddling hard though I haven't been in the ocean or even a swimming pool for months.

Spotting a clean face, I stroke hard to the left, hoping for a good frontside ride. But the wave walls up quicker and steeper than I expected. Dropping down the face, I arch my back hard to keep my nose from pearling, then try to stand up, only to find myself crushed from behind. An ice-water torrent pummels me down to the depths, rolling me through a series of twisting somersaults until I no longer know which way is up and my lungs shriek for air.

I finally surface, only to find another saltwater avalanche about to break directly on me. I take a quick gasping breath and dive beneath it, feeling it wrench on my leash like some malevolent creature hellbent on dragging me down. Sputtering and coughing, I reel in my board and paddle hard for the beach, my arms and shoulders already cramped.

The small windows in which I can see to the shore reveal an alarming sight.

Cedar has exited the water.

He's standing with Dana and Becky on the beach, watching me through the binoculars—the same pair I'd laughed at earlier—from what seems an impossible distance.

I'm too petrified to look behind me, but I can hear the thundering of the huge breakers on the outside, the ones I'd gauged to be upward of thirteen feet—waves for which I am far from ready. I've ended up much farther out than I'd meant to, and now I'm getting chewed up—soon to be swallowed whole if I don't act fast.

I know my only chance is to catch a swell, hold fast, and ride it in on my stomach. I attempt this a few times only to find that, despite the thrashing each breaker gives me, I'm going nowhere.

Worse than nowhere: the current's pushing me farther from shore.

I realize now I'm stuck in a rip current—and that like a reverse river of water, it's carrying me out into the open, sledgehammering seas.

I look up at Dana and Cedar and wave my arms in distress, but I'm too far out, buried behind wavebreak. The only soul in the water, the water getting deeper, the depth growing wider. Something in me cracks open, this tremendous dread—*the deeper midnight of the insatiate maw.*

Describing Pip's harrowing experience in the "Castaway" section, Melville writes, "But the awful lonesomeness is intolerable. The intense concentration of self in the middle of such a heartless immensity, my God! who can tell it?" And though thousands of pieces of artwork have been made in the wake of *Moby-Dick,* one of the most memorable, for me, is at a *Moby-Dick*–themed art show in San Francisco; it consists of a single period—a period that the artist Kris Martin cut from the last line of *Moby-Dick*—pasted onto a blank white page:

Caught up in a raging force so far beyond my control—a tiny dark speck in this vast white maw, a bit of wreck in the mid-Pacific— I'm further from any benevolent universal force—from God—than I've ever felt.

I know from reading the warning signs at Rockaway that to escape a rip, you have to paddle parallel with the shore. But when I try this, the waves dump me sideways off my board, rolling me back under. Salt water floods my sinuses, burns my throat, triggers my autonomic drowning response—a second rip current of panic flowing backward through blood vessels, across tattered synaptic channels, inundating all the pulsing chambers of my chest.

At the climax of *Moby-Dick,* Ahab has his final confrontation with the white whale after a three-day chase, the final chance for the retribution that he's risked life and limb and an entire crew to wreak. Completely possessed now, he wrenches harpoons from the hands of his crew, spouting Bible verses and drawing down thunder and lightning from the heavens. In a line that, with the benefit of hindsight, Colin Powell might have used on President Bush on the eve of the Iraq invasion, Starbuck cries to his captain, "Oh! Ahab, not too late is it, even now, the third day, to desist. See! Moby Dick seeks thee not. It is thou, thou, that madly seekest him!"

After a bloody battle, Moby-Dick rams the *Pequod,* sending the ship and a hundred or more souls to the deathcold depths. Ahab meets the worst fate of all; tethered around the neck to the great whale the way "Turkish mutes bowstring their victim," he's dragged under by his ancient foe. Only Ishmael survives, borne up from the sea in a buoyant coffin, a spiritual pilgrim reborn out of death to renewed life.

Numb with cold and pain, laden by soaked neoprene, my arms are close to losing the battle against the current. The events of the past year are ballast, weighing me down in what may be a final culmination of my inability to *marshal my resources.*

Exhausted, I lay my head down on my surfboard and pray like I've never prayed, begging for help. Still not fully believing—*Where are You in all of this?* But more uncomfortable than ever in my disbelief.

I try a more acute angle toward shore, point my nose directly at the tiny figures of my friends—*safety, comfort, hearthstone*—back on the beach.

One dead-arm stroke after another.

Until my arms will no longer move under the weight of the wetsuit and sodden gloves.

I try swimming beside the board, kicking with my legs. Which feels even more precarious, nothing between me and the yawning depths.

Back on the board, I force my dead arms. Stroke after stroke.

Until I reach the rip's ragged edge, a thin shoulder of a wave propelling me a few feet forward. Where I windmill my arms, expending my last shred of energy for another ride on the edge.

Which delivers me closer to the white-water scrum, the impact zone.

Another wave explodes behind me, rocketing me forward across the shallows, back to land.

KOOKS

D ivine intervention and literary allusions aside, what I did was a total kook move, and in the end I simply got lucky. Two months later, in March, a surfer from California makes the same mistake I did, fatally misjudging the power of the Oregon coast in winter. His friends watch from the shore, pleading for help from the 911 dispatcher. But before the Coast Guard helicopters arrive, and though he's tethered to a seven-foot flotation device, the ocean over-powers him.

The dark Ahab force I'd been flirting with at Rockaway finally goes under that day in Pacific City, lashed to the white whale of my own hubris, my self-destructive tendencies, my anger and helplessness at what had happened to me at gunpoint that night in Denver. My true rebirth, I learn, had only begun that day in Rockaway when I rode my first hurricane swell. My inner Ahab was basically just a kook—a true, red-blooded American kook who shows up without permission on foreign shores and, ignoring warnings from the locals, dives into a dangerous situation, thinking he can avenge his own and the world's resentments with his big guns and his go-it-alone attitude. Life is much better now that he's been formally impeached by that most powerful of legislative bodies known as the Pacific.

At the end of the film *Waking Life,* Richard Linklater posits the no-tion that we're all living the same story. It's an idea echoed by mysti-cal writers like Philip K. Dick, Raymond Carver, Hafiz and Rumi, the exuberantly populist Walt Whitman, and, in his re-creation of Bible stories and sea yarns, Melville himself. The story is that through struggling with the vicissitudes of life and the threat of death, we move beyond ourselves, beyond the treachery and selfishness of our egos, and connect with something larger. We come to see that we are not separate, isolated individuals or even nations, but rather we're inextricably connected to every living being, regardless of form or creed or religion, all of us like molecules of water pumping through the tide-beating heart of the singular sea. We eventually get over ourselves, learn from our mistakes, turn the other cheek, pull out the troops, forgive our enemies, embrace our shadow. We move from self-consciousness to earth-consciousness, sea-consciousness. That's how we're saved in the end; it's how we escape to tell the tale and live the rest of our lives in relative peace and forever free from the tyranny of kooks, all of us.

THE PASSAGE

After my uncle John was thrown in prison, my aunt Ann worked night and day to secure his release. One hundred typewritten letters, one hundred phone calls to consulates and embassies, members of Congress and ambassadors.

One hundred nights in a cell, then one hundred more.

Until Ann's work paid off.

Upon his release, my uncle was surprised to find the sailboat in its slip, his name still on the title. He renamed her *Sadhu*, the Hindu word for a wandering holy person, and then quickly assembled a crew and charted a course through the Indian Ocean. They sailed through the Strait of Malacca and the South China Sea, where the crew was on high alert for pirates, so much so that they often motored at night, without running lights, to avoid detection. But a less-experienced crew member ran the boat aground off the Philippines. The propeller was destroyed; John spent two days underwater, trying to pry it off. Fortunately, a ship came and towed them to a remote harbor, where a logging company helped John repair the prop.

As the *Sadhu* motored out of the bay, armed men in a dugout canoe with a 150-horsepower outboard engine overtook their ship. This was the piracy my uncle feared; he could see from their scrappy uniforms that some were actually underpaid police officers. They demanded money in their broken English; they threatened to impound the ship if he didn't comply. No one on board had much currency, so my uncle finally appeased them by handing over a pair of binoculars and all their foodstuffs, cans of soup and Spam.

Free once more, he sailed on up the Philippine chain, to Taiwan, where he survived the first typhoon of the season. He battled another typhoon in Masaki Harbor, near Tokyo, sustaining enough damage that he had to lay over several weeks for additional repairs. Eventually he made a great circle route over the crest of the Pacific:

they skirted the Aleutian Islands—islands that Rachel Carson names as the stormiest in the world—and crossed the Gulf of Alaska, finally threading through the Strait of Juan de Fuca and Puget Sound, to Seattle, where, on the day of his arrival, his family was there on the docks, waving, welcoming him home.

PORTLAND

B y early spring I start to settle into my new position at the Independent Publishing Resource Center. With help from my friendly, heavily tattooed coworker Georgia, we create a new outreach program, designed to teach teenagers about media literacy, critical thinking, and creative writing, including a viewing of *Tough Guise*—a film that deconstructs the way our culture and popular media encourage men and boys to mask their vulnerabilities with toughness and violence. I also find that I have a modest talent for grant writing; I'm able to raise enough money to implement this new initiative, which Georgia names the Media Action Project, in six or seven public schools and youth treatment centers.

On a warm evening in March, Kelly Peach, an IPRC volunteer, and I sit in the conference room and chat while she works on a zine containing her drawings of sea creatures—macro views of diatoms and plankton and rare, deep-sea jellyfish. She tells me she went to school in Santa Cruz, where she spent every spare moment at the beach, gazing into tide pools, conducting research, even learning to surf. She also explains that she's just been offered a full ride for graduate school in marine biology back down in Santa Cruz.

"I'm really excited about it," she says, "but I've only been in Portland for less than a year, and I'm really not ready to leave. I mean, I still can't get over how ridiculously *fun* it is here." Back on the East Coast, most conversations involved some sort of complaining about the subway, about hectic work schedules or the terrible weather or the hunt for a decent therapist—all the colossal inconveniences of living in a place like New York.

But in Portland, all anyone talks about it is how awesome Portland is.

The self-congratulatory talk can get old—and my first few weeks in Portland have been anything but *fun*.

But there's something to it. Compared to New York, Portland feels like a quiet ecotopia, where even the cabdrivers never honk; where, within a one-block radius, there are outdoor food carts selling Korean barbecue, Thai noodles, vegan bratwurst, and authentic Mexican food. And where I can hike into Forest Park—the largest urban park in the world, so large that people can and do get lost there for days at a time—and eat my Japanese bento lunch under the shade of redwoods and Douglas firs.

In New York, despite my close friendships and all the progress I made at surfing and in recovery, I still never felt at home, not really, even after three full years.

In Portland it takes about three months.

The paradox, though, is that it was New York, not Portland, that transformed me into an ocean-obsessed surfer and environmentalist.

Kelly tells me that after graduate school, she plans to move back up to Portland, maybe start a nonprofit geared toward teaching inner-city kids about the ocean. Sitting with her, listening to her plans for things that I want to be a part of, I realize that for the first time in a very long time, I actually feel *lighthearted.* Although I'm making a fraction of what I made back in New York, I'm also saving about $900 a month on rent. Granted, the kitchen of the house I'm living in has been completely ripped out during a remodel, but I'm saving enough that I can eat out every night. I also save on transportation costs by riding my father's hand-me-down 1973 Schwinn Super Le Tour—given to me as a gift since my old bike was stolen just before I left Brooklyn. I consider getting rid of my truck, but Portland's one downside is the hour-and-a-half drive to the beach—although it's a beautiful drive through forests and farmlands and vineyards, all these rolling green vistas like you'd imagine seeing in New Zealand.

Along with Kelly, I spend time with Gabriel and his family, and my old friend Dan, the tattoo artist, and my stepbrother Tim and his family, who live just a few blocks away. And I meet people like Moe Bowstern, who works summers on an Alaskan salmon boat, then spends winters in Portland working on her writing and artwork, and who leads the crowd in singing sea shanties at IPRC benefits. And Dan Hack, who turns out to be my very distant cousin, both of us descendants of Hockings in Land's End, Cornwall, both of us having fulfilled some genetic imperative to migrate west across the continent, to finally settle down in a lush, forested place near the sea.

SHIPMATES

My new workplace is located directly above a bookstore called Reading Frenzy, in many ways the epicenter of Portland's vibrant indie lit scene. I spend my lunch breaks there, perusing zines and comics, or across the street at Powell's City of Books. One of the largest physical bookstores in the world, Powell's spans an entire city block, and, unlike most retailers, stocks both new and used titles on the same shelves. For this reason their Melville section is uncommonly robust. It's the first place I gravitate during daily visits, where I search for rare *Moby-Dick* editions or obscure Melville criticism. I haunt the section so often that I start to think of myself as kind of freelance *Moby-Dick* salesperson, offering unsolicited advice on the cheapest, most portable version (Signet Classics); the most pedantic version, with poorly laid out text and some stuffy critical essays, but an impressive illustrated section on whaling and whalecraft (Norton Critical Edition); or my all-time favorite version, with artful typesetting and abundant illustrations by Rockwell Kent that give it the feel of a prototypical graphic novel (Modern Library Classics).

Beyond having such an expansive Melville section, Powell's Books was literally built on a foundation of *Moby-Dick*. A sandstone pillar shaped like a stack of classic books supports the store's northwest entrance: *The Mahabharata, Hamlet, War and Peace, Psalms, The Odyssey,* and *The Whale. The Whale* was the title of the English first edition of *Moby-Dick;* according to the founder's legend, a leather-bound version of *The Whale* was one of owner Michael Powell's first great finds as a rare-book dealer. Copies of the first American edition now sell for upward of $40,000, so it's not a stretch to assume that *The Whale* provided some of the seed money that established what many consider to be America's finest independent bookstore.

It's fitting, then, that some fellow Melville freaks and I persuade Powell's to host the first part of a twenty-four-hour marathon reading of *Moby-Dick.*

The lead crew members on this epic, semilunatic undertaking—
which we name "Take to the Ship"—include my new friend Amy, an
environmental activist who happens to have been a close high school
friend of Asa Ellis's; a writer/researcher named Tom; and the writer
Kevin Sampsell, who moonlights as the manager of Powell's impressive small press section.

The first five hours take place in the third-floor Powell's reading
room, where we enlist sixteen local artists and writers to bring the
book breathing to life. After I welcome on board the audience—whom
I call *shipmates*—I read the first chapter, "Loomings," which contains some of my favorite lines—*Why is almost every robust healthy
boy with a robust healthy soul in him, at some time or other crazy to
go to sea?* The entire section reckons with this particular madness;
it's a sorting out of Ishmael's cracked motives for signing on to "this
shabby part of a whaling voyage," just as, a few paragraphs into our
eight-hundred-page undertaking, I wonder just what the hell I'm getting myself into here—a question I'm sure many audience members
share, as do the intrepid runners of actual, 26.2-mile, foot-pounding
marathons.

By chapter's end, we have the answer: *Chief among these motives
was the overwhelming idea of the great whale himself. Such a portentous and mysterious monster roused all my curiosity.* At the heart of
the book—and in the hearts of us marathoners—lies an obsessive
quest for even a glimmer of knowledge of the deep mystery within
ourselves and within nature. Here at the start, the room feels electrified by a powerful sense that we've put in motion something large
and important and a little frightening—*twenty-four straight hours*—
but this is also what draws us shipmates together: like Queequeg and
Ishmael, we sit shoulder to shoulder, pulling oars together on an insane task—*I felt a melting in me. No more my splintered heart and
maddened hand were turned against the wolfish world. This soothing
savage had redeemed it.*

And I can't help but feel that somewhere, from whatever inscrutable vantage point, Melville might appreciate what we're doing here—
that we're part of a vibrant ongoing revival that in so many ways re-

deems his literary spirit, his decades of toiling in relative obscurity. If *Moby-Dick* was far too postmodern for Melville's contemporaries (one hundred years before the term *postmodern* even existed), those of us living in the internet age are perhaps more comfortable channeling its polyphonic host of voices, its endlessly digressive, hyperlink-like associative riffs.

Two chapters later, actor Mykle Hansen performs "The Spouter-Inn." His animated, irreverent delivery of lines like "a boggy, soggy, squitchy picture truly"—and his description of the tattooed harpooner Queequeg inadvertently crawling into bed with Ishmael—elicit waves of laughter. I hadn't anticipated the way that, in the right hands, live reading can so enhance the book's bizarre humor, its radical weirdness.

Of course, transcendent moments abound. We enlist the musician Laura Gibson to perform an angelic, a cappella version of a hymn from "The Sermon":

> *In black distress, I called my God,*
> > *When I could scarce believe him mine,*
> *He bowed his ear to my complaints—*
> > *No more the whale did me confine.*

The writer and filmmaker Arthur Bradford gives an impassioned version of Father Mapple's sermon, gesticulating like a preacher, his powerful voice hitting all the heavy registers—*But oh! shipmates! on the starboard hand of every woe, there is a sure delight; and higher the top of that delight, than the bottom of the woe is deep.*

By chapter five the house is packed, though there's an expected ebb and flow within the crowd. Most people drop in for a few chapters. One tall, bearded young gentleman shows up at Powell's to purchase his first copy of *Moby-Dick* and happens to hear a loud-speaker announcement about the reading. He stays for the entire event, as does a sweet, soft-spoken woman in her fifties, who wears a contented expression of authentic awe for the better part of twenty-four hours.

Amy refers to them both as *our new converts.*

After the sixteenth chapter, we move the reading to Amy's candle-lit living room, where she's draped a quilted harpoon over a podium, creating an oddly cozy, wake-like atmosphere.

Throughout the night and well into the next afternoon, one hundred people read the remaining 119 chapters.

In the dead hours of a February night, the sense of questing transforms into something more akin to a vigil, a midnight mass. As my energy dwindles, I'm continually astonished by Melville's colossal creative vigor—his endless currents of Shakespearean prose; his stunning ear for sound, song, and syntax; his encyclopedic knowledge of everything from whaling to coconuts to metaphysics—and the staggering fact that he channeled and scribed and collaged such an immortal masterpiece in just two years.

There are also moments of deep, unshakable boredom, as when Melville conducts a long-winded taxonomy of whales in the "Cetology" section—a chapter that, in the light of day, I love for its genre-defying digressiveness but by one in the morning find tedious. And thus for me, though I fight it, there is a period of sleep.

Amy's a hardier breed of Melville fan, someone I often describe as simply *badass.* A veteran antilogging activist, she's spent many all-nighters one hundred feet up in old-growth Douglas firs, where nodding off might mean falling to your death, just as Ishmael warns during his reverie from high in the crow's nest during the "Mast-Head" chapter. She stays awake the entire time, recording every minute on her laptop and posting frequent updates on the Take to the Ship website, even reading a few extra chapters for late-night no-shows.

After a few hours' rest, I spontaneously agree to read "A Squeeze of the Hand" for another no-show. It's an infamous chapter in which Ishmael describes rendering spermaceti oil by hand—*squeezing sperm*—with his shipmates, and how they sometimes mistake each other's hands for sperm—*let us squeeze ourselves into each other.* Reading the chapter—*a sweet and unctuous duty!*—I find myself going a little unglued, maybe from the lack of sleep or as a result of immersion in Melville's manic creation.

Like Ishmael squeezing spermaceti, I am overcome by *a strange sort of insanity* while reading the chapter—a few paragraphs in I begin bouncing from foot to foot, doing a crazy little jig.

While I read, Amy posts the following on the website:

Justin Hocking is getting a little excited with chapter 94—A SQUEEZE OF THE HAND.

Then, awaking from my brief Melvillian trance-dance, it hits me: I'm standing in front of a room full of people, getting intensely *worked up* while describing what amounts to a kind of cosmic circle jerk. Reading the line "I squeezed that sperm till I myself almost melted into it," I'm overcome by what I dimly recognize as shame. You can only imagine how most prudish nineteenth-century readers might have reacted to this chapter during an era when, in many circles, it was taboo to mention the *leg* of a chair. On both aesthetic and emotional levels, writing *Moby-Dick* was a profound act of exposure and courage. With chapters like "A Squeeze of the Hand," Melville invokes a classic dockyard bawdiness, but beyond the sailor's antics there's a sense of him jettisoning conventional decorum, defiantly jettisoning shame—*Oh! my dear fellow beings, why should we longer cherish any social acerbities, or know the slightest ill-humor or envy!* Melville's brazenness buoys my own courage to write about things that will always carry a mild current of shame: the codependency issues and twelve-step program, the romance novels and the dark emotional periods. Whether or not Melville embodied this fact during his lifetime, he often grasped it within his writing: only by risking exposure and vulnerability do we find deep connection—*such an abounding, affectionate, friendly, loving feeling.* And now, spotting my best friend, Gabriel, in the audience, making quick sketches of me and all the other readers, I find the resolve to continue reading, knowing full well that like anyone else worth having in my life, Gabriel has witnessed all of my most shameful falls from grace and has never so much as blinked—*let us squeeze hands all round.*

By nightfall, having traversed a literary Atlantic and Pacific, we arrive at the end.

The final full chapter—"The Chase—Third Day"—goes without question to Fred Nemo, a performance artist and dancer in his early sixties. Back in the nineties, Nemo performed unhinged improv dance pieces with the seminal Portland indie rock band Hazel—he'd often strip naked, shimmy into an evening gown, then break into animated lip synchs on an old-fashioned telephone, coiling himself in the phone cord and bouncing around the band members like a straitjacketed maniac.

With his unpredictable energy and his long, grizzled gray beard, he's pure Ahab.

There's a palpable shift in the room's energy when Nemo steps up to the pulpit, clasping a five-foot-long, splintered oar in his left hand: the mad old captain is at the helm now, about to bring down the ship—*the voyage is up.* During his reading, he employs the oar to strong effect as harpoon, crutch, wizard's staff, and wooden leg. Halfway through the chapter, Ahab lowers with the harpooners Daggoo and Queequeg; Moby-Dick charges and narrowly misses their boat, but turns flank, revealing the gruesome sight of Ahab's mercenary agent, the Parsee, his corpse ripped to shreds and lashed by frayed harpoon lines to the white whale's scarred underbelly.

Unnerved by this ghastly sight, Ahab drops his harpoon. At this moment, Nemo slams the oar down on the hardwood floor, the thunder of this dramatic action booming through the floorboards, startling us into military attention.

In the final showdown, a full fourteen pages into the chapter, Nemo's voice begins to falter, from the vocal burn of speaking aloud Melville's incandescent prose, and also the pathos of Ahab's struggle—*Am I cut off from the last fond pride of meanest shipwrecked captains? Oh, lonely death on lonely life!* At the grand culmination of our twenty-four-hour journey—filled with so much light and dark, so many dives and breaches—the collapse of Fred's voice feels entirely appropriate, imbuing the novel and Ahab with a shattered grace, especially as he lifts the oar above his head and howls the mad captain's last line—*Thus, I give up the spear!*

His incarnation of Ahab is not so much a kook as a heroically flawed, fully human being, wounded to the core.

Amy—the true mastermind behind this event—delivers the Epilogue: *one did survive the wreck.* Among us crew members is the momentous sense of having *endured,* a feeling I carry for days after the reading—the lived experience of *Moby-Dick* as a survival story.

Amy finishes the final lines and then we break into exalted applause, all of us embracing our shipmates, and most of all Fred, the man who went down with his vessel, who so poignantly draped *the great shroud of the sea* across the day's dark finale.

THE EVENING OF MY LAST NIGHT
ON EARTH

Just a few blocks from my house, there's a business with a large red sign that reads Disaster Restoration.

And just beyond this is a yoga studio, where I meet a woman named Lisa Mae. She's an instructor there, and totally beautiful—and as it turns out, also from New York City. We have a slow, healthy courtship, beginning with a trip to Portland's new aerial tram, which we ride three times in a row, chatting about our families and gazing out on the blurry-bright city lights. She tells me about a recent yoga retreat she led down in Costa Rica, where she rekindled her interest in surfing. She originally learned to surf during school in San Diego; in fact, we're surprised to learn we went to rival high schools at exactly the same time, although being something of a brainiac, she graduated early and went off at age seventeen to NYU, where she double-majored in religious studies and philosophy.

Our parallel trajectories across the country, from Southern California to New York City and back across to the Pacific Northwest, and the way we hit it off so well—and also the way her smile lights up her whole face—are all very intriguing. But after going for a drink at a pub, I drive her back home, giving her a hug and a gentlemanly goodnight kiss on the cheek. This is something I learned in recovery—how to actually date someone, without too much intensity, especially in the beginning.

In early March, a month or so after we first meet, Lisa Mae and I go cross-country skiing. We take her Subaru up to Trillium Lake, near my old snowboard camp on Mount Hood. There's a book of Rumi poems on her dashboard; while she drives, I read one out loud.

"I've never had a guy read Rumi to me," she says.

"I've never met a girl with a copy of Rumi on her dashboard."

I choose Trillium Lake as a flat, easy trail for Lisa Mae, who's never cross-countried before. What I didn't anticipate, though, was that the main access road to Trillium would be closed in winter, so we have to ski down a steep hill to reach the lake trail. Lisa Mae ends up falling on her ass every hundred feet or so; she mostly laughs it off, but it's apparent that she wonders if maybe I'm trying to kill her. And this being only our third or so date, I'm afraid I might have indeed killed my chances.

But she's a good sport, especially once we reach the mellow lake trail, where she gets the hang of gliding along in the snow.

She does great until I pick up the pace, moving a couple meters ahead of her. As we bend south around the frozen lake, Mount Hood appears, a brilliant castle of frost. But then something catches my attention, a small dark shape on the snow, directly in Lisa Mae's track. Moving in closer, I realize it's some kind of *lizard*, lying right there in the snow.

I stop and poke at it with my pole, but it doesn't move.

"Hey, Lisa Mae," I shout back. "Watch out. There's some kind of *snow gecko* in your path."

But this doesn't register, and by the time she spots the lizard thing she lets out a little shriek and tries to stop but instead sort of spazzes out and falls right on her ass again. I take my skis off to help her up.

"What *is* that thing?" she asks, laughing again.

"I guess it's some sort of amphibian. I've never seen anything like it."

Back on our skis, we move in closer to investigate. The snow gecko is brown on the top, with a reddish underbelly. About the size of my palm. It remains totally motionless—half-frozen, it seems—even after I pick it up. Turning it upside down, I can see that it's actually still breathing. After examining it closely, wondering how the hell it got here, I move it off the trail, out of harm's way.

On the way home, Lisa Mae and I visit the Kennedy School—an old grade school in North Portland that's been converted into a hotel with several restaurants, taverns, a movie theater, and a public soaking pool. The pool's located in a hidden courtyard, surrounded by palm trees; it's like a large hot tub, the entire underwater surface finished in terra cotta and dark blue mosaic tiles.

We sit there soaking our tired muscles—especially Lisa Mae, who has a very sore ass—and laughing about our odd encounter with the snow gecko. There are a few other soakers in the pool, including a fortyish guy in steamed-up glasses, sitting just across from us. He apologizes for eavesdropping and explains that he's a wildlife biologist, that he's curious to hear more about this *snow gecko*. Still curious myself, I describe it for him.

"What you saw was a rough-skinned newt," he says. "They're not uncommon in Oregon, although it's rare to see one so early in the spring—probably a result of climate change. The interesting thing about rough-skinned newts is that they're one of the most poisonous animals on the planet."

"Come on," Lisa Mae says, a little of her New York accent revealing itself. "You're totally shitting us."

He explains that one one-thousandth of the poison contained in the skin of these newts is enough to kill a grown man.

"Seriously," Lisa Mae says. "You're *serious?*"

"They don't bite or anything. You'd have to actually swallow an entire newt for the poison to kick in. Either that or lick its skin."

This freaks me out a little bit, as I recall handling the thing with my bare hands.

"It shouldn't be a problem," the biologist says, "as long as you washed your hands afterward."

But I didn't wash my hands, and then, just twenty minutes later, Lisa Mae and I had sat in her car eating a lunch consisting mostly of finger foods: baby carrots and celery with peanut butter and salad wraps.

We drive back to Lisa Mae's house, where a quick internet search confirms the biologist's identification and his claim about the rough-skinned newt. She reads me an online account of some yahoos down in Coos Bay, Oregon. During a drunken camping trip, they dared one of their buddies to swallow an entire newt.

So he did.

And died within ten minutes.

"Holy shit," Lisa Mae says.

"Holy shit is right," I say. "I totally handled that thing."

"So I guess this is it for you?" she says, leading me over to the couch.

"I don't know. Maybe," I say, playing along.

"This might be your last night on earth," she says, smiling. "So what would you like to do?"

"Well . . ." I say, coyly, reaching over for her, tucking a dark ringlet of hair behind her ear.

"It's okay," she says, smiling, "I'm game."

So I lean over and kiss her—my final request.

And although it might be my last night alive, we end up taking our time, because in reality there is no urgency between us, no sense of dire need—both of us having emerged whole from respective periods of darkness. Instead of raw lust there is a kind of playful attraction; in place of intensity there is an easy intimacy, made possible in part by our offbeat senses of humor, our shared bicoastal sensibilities, our synched-up spirituality.

More than anything, it feels like we have all the time in the world.

THE SPILL

I n May of 2010, while a hundred thousand gallons of oil bleed daily from an offshore well into the Gulf of Mexico, I spend a two-week writing residency at an art and ecology center off the central coast of Oregon. Surfers in particular have a gut-level reaction to offshore oil spills and beach contaminations. I feel sick about the news from the Gulf Coast, more so after hearing radio interviews with fishermen and tour guides, people whose entire lives and livelihoods are threatened by the spill. But at the same time, being here in Oregon, where the sea is clean and cold, and there are no offshore oil derricks, I feel somewhat removed from events unfolding in the south.

One evening after writing, I paddle my surfboard across the mouth of the Salmon River to a sandy spit that marks the confluence of river and sea. On the lee side of the grassy but formidable Cascade Head, and without an access road from the south, the beach is accessible only by river, and therefore deserted, nearly untouched.

It's cloudy on the coast, the ocean like brushed cement. But on the edges, over the mountains, the sky's gleaming.

After surfing the chaotic river-mouth break, I comb the beach, finding charred driftwood, barnacle-studded limpet shells, exquisitely preserved crab carapaces, sea felt, and a rare, twisted length of bull kelp. And also, tucked behind some rocks, two weatherworn plastic water bottles and the remnants of a Styrofoam drift net float. It's not enough to make the beach feel egregiously polluted, but here they are, on what had seemed like the most pristine beach I've ever seen. It occurs to me here, seemingly for the first time, that plastic is a petroleum-based substance.

A fellow resident and sculptor points me toward the center's library, to which the Surfrider Foundation donated a copy of a documentary called *Synthetic Seas*. The film shows an ocean map of areas seriously affected by plastic contamination—an expanse the size of the contiguous United States, Canada, and Alaska combined. Within the boundaries of this area are two concentrated garbage patches, or "gyres."* There's some dispute over their dimensions—some say they're only the size of Delaware; others claim they're larger than Texas. Regardless of their actual magnitude, it's just like Sadie told me: giant atolls of trash poisoning the sea.

Unlike crude oil, the plastic in these gyres and elsewhere doesn't eventually absorb into the sea. Plastic never really goes away; according to the film, every piece of plastic ever made still exists somewhere on the earth or in our seas. And while they don't fully reabsorb, ocean-bound plastics do slowly leach micron-sized particles into the water; these particles are then ingested by fish and birds, which are in turn ingested by larger mammals. To make matters worse, floating plastic waste absorbs and concentrates other harmful toxins like PCBs at 100,000 times the normal levels. These chemicals—most of which bind to estrogen receptors—move up the food chain, eventually reaching the humans who created them, where they can cause cancer and may harm female reproductive processes.

It's a kind of semi-invisible "oil spill" taking place every day, in every ocean and on every beach in the world.

---

* The term *gyre* reminds me of a William Butler Yeats poem, "The Second Coming," that I'd seen in the New York City subway: *"Turning and turning in the widening gyre / The falcon cannot hear the falconer; / Things fall apart; the centre cannot hold; / Mere anarchy is loosed upon the world, / The blood-dimmed tide is loosed, and everywhere / The ceremony of innocence is drowned."*

THE WHALEBOAT

> The decimation of whale life that commerce initiated, seen
> through the scaling lens of history, does not destroy the
> dignity of ordinary men in the fishery, their effort to work,
> to survive, to provide. It only instructs us in the infernal
> paradoxes of life.
>
> ~ BARRY LOPEZ, *About This Life*, "THE WHALEBOAT"

After moving back west, I rediscover the writing of another Melville-obsessed Oregonian who used to live in New York. Barry Lopez was born in California, but after his mother remarried, his family relocated to Manhattan. Though he disliked New York at first, he ultimately benefited from his literary education in the city. He attended private school, where he was challenged academically, well beyond what he'd ever experienced back in California. He ended up reading *Moby-Dick* three times before college—a book that, as an eventual environmental writer, he found most akin to his own desire to "describe what happened, what I saw, when I went outside." And while *Moby-Dick* is undeniably dark, Lopez also credits it as a major influence in his desire to contribute to what he calls the literature of hope.

His essay "The Whaleboat" orbits around his contemplation of a handcrafted model whaleboat on display in the study of his Oregon home—"it bore so well an elaborate and arcane history of human encounter with the wild." He writes equally exquisite descriptions of the myriad woods and trees he can spy directly from his writing desk—red cedar, pine, spruce, his hardwood floor made from "ship-lapped Douglas fir."

It's hard to pinpoint exactly what this richly complex essay is about—his work defies easy explanation or pigeonholing—but beyond wood and light, one continuous theme is a meditation on the difference between contemplation and action. He uses Melville's Ishmael as a symbol of contemplation, and Ahab as one of action. What brought

the *Pequod* down, according to Lopez, was Ahab's ceaseless productivity, his relentless action and motion lust, combined with a total
lack of contemplation. Lopez has some fairly pointed opinions about
American culture's general lack of contemplation:

> In the modern era, launched from a pelagic vessel manned by
> men often unknown to one another at the start of a two-year
> voyage, [the *Pequod*'s] employment marked a shift from a
> community-based to a corporate-based technology designed
> to exploit nature. Its advent marked the beginning of the late
> Holocene die-off of nonhuman life. Ishmael, with his modern
> ironies about the "all-grasping Western world" and man "the
> money-making animal" worked here, pulling second oar in
> Starbuck's boat.

But again, Lopez doesn't come to any facile conclusions. He be-
lieves that both contemplation and action are necessary for a balanced world. He sympathizes with men in the historical whaling
industry—ordinary men who, like Ishmael, were just trying to survive, provide for their families. Therein lies the paradox: the whaling industry, like so many modern corporations, was full of good,
decent people just trying to make a living. I love the subtle wisdom of
Lopez's work, the acknowledgment of beauty and darkness in nature;
reading him, I realize how dogmatic I've been in my revisionist cri-
tique of the whaling industry, in my attack on the contemporary oil
industry. The truth is that the very keys I'm typing on now are made
from petroleum; petroleum fueled all those trips from Brooklyn to
Rockaway in my Toyota pickup, as it fuels ambulances, Meals on
Wheels, the Buick that allows my elderly neighbor to drive herself
to church every Sunday.

And my obsession with movement mirrors the larger culture's
obsession with action, frenetic commerce, relentless productivity—
which are the reasons we need oil in the first place.

I'm not changing my mind about anything, or apologizing for my
arguments. What I am doing is longing for balance, for wisdom, for

the ability to fill a canvas with both light and dark. For the equanimity to write like Melville or Barry Lopez—who, at the end of his "Whaleboat" essay, ultimately transcends the political, concluding on a more mysterious note: "When I look at Mr. McCreery's boat, when I imagine the oar blades plunged in the green transparency of a storm-raked sea, the boat cranking off a wave crest, six men straining in drenched motley wool and oilskins, their mouths agape, I know that life is wild, dangerous, beautiful."

EKKOLI; OR, THE WHALE

By the winter of 1805, members of the Lewis and Clark expedition had reached their westernmost destination: the Oregon coast. They established a winter camp, Fort Clatsop, near the Columbia River, where they hoped abundant elk and wildlife would sustain them through the Northwest's damp dark months.

Finding little game for hunting, however, the unhappy party subsisted mainly on dog meat.

That is, until some Clatsop Indians offered them a gift of fresh blubber, stripped from a beached whale. Hungry for more—for anything besides dog—William Clark, Sacagawea, and other explorers set off in search of the whale. After the treacherous ascent of Tillamook Head, they descended southward, crossing Ecola Creek, which Clark named after the Chinook word for whale—*ekkoli.*

Emerging from a dense thicket onto the sandy beach, Clark and the others discovered, instead of an abundant supply of meat, a completely stripped, 105-foot-long whale carcass—an empty white corridor of bones. The local Tillamook villagers had harvested the entire creature, utilizing every part of its body, the way they'd been doing for eons. They were now busy tending beach bonfires, rendering blubber into rich oil.

When approached by Clark and his men, the villagers were understandably reluctant to part with their spoils.

Just over two hundred years later, Lisa Mae and I venture west from Portland, to Ecola

State Park. The road up from Cannon Beach winds through a dense rain forest, home to moss-covered spruce, western hemlock, Douglas fir, western red cedar. The forest floor is carpeted in moss and ferns and dappled with sunlight, giving the place a kind of mystical charm, so much so that Lisa Mae and I name it "fairyland."

We park in a lot just above Indian Beach, the exact spot where Clark found the whale carcass. Like Clark and his Corps of Discovery, Lisa Mae and I are on our own quest.

In our case, the sustenance we need is surf.

And in Oregon, there's always plenty to be found.

From the parking lot, we watch waves scroll in off the horizon, spilling white across the cove, like snowdrifts that soon dissolve on the sand's sun-fired glaze. To the south, two tree-lined spits of land reach out, slowly surrendering haystack rocks to the Pacific.

We unload surfboards and wetsuits and take a wooden footbridge across Canyon Creek. Above the water's surface, cliff swallows make tight circular turns, banking and planing and diving for insects, sunlight sparking their iridescent blue tail feathers. Much higher, over Tillamook Head, seagulls prowl for scraps, and above them, way up in the troposphere, a pair of bald eagles carve ever-widening spirals.

This is what rings my bell: walking barefoot down a wooded trail, surfboard under my arm, side by side with Lisa Mae.

But it also stirs up some fear. I never completely get over my experience at Pacific City. But maybe this is a good thing: the same forces that give this coastline such unbounded beauty make it a relatively dangerous place to surf, requiring strong paddling skills and a healthy respect for the sea.

There's a riptide by the rocky cliffs on the north side of the beach, and although it makes me uncomfortable, the waves are small and manageable today, so after suiting up and wading in, I let it pull me outside, and then paddle safely to the south, away from the rip, where the good waves roll in. And I notice how surrendering myself to the current, letting it ferry me outside, helps conserve my arm strength for the hard part—the actual catching of waves.

I've handed down my old board to Lisa Mae and graduated to a shorter model, a six-foot-eight-inch swallowtail—a board that performs much better than my huge beginner model, which Lisa Mae nicknames "the garage door." It's a kind of revelation: dropping in on a wave, banking a big bottom turn and carving back up the face, over and over, pumping for speed, staying close to the curl, my fingertips communing with the water. I've even figured out how to turn up the face just as the wave closes out, snapping off the lip and then floating on top, riding it down like a foamy escalator. I'll probably never be a great surfer, but I have my moments, times when I feel almost as comfortable surfing as I do on a skateboard.

For me—a person who used to be scared of the ocean, and who still has a very healthy fear—this is more than enough. And whereas in New York I needed surfing to stay sane, here in Oregon it's just something I do when time permits, when the conditions are right.

I still love it, maybe more than ever, but the obsession has unclenched its jaws, released me from its dark, twisting interior.

Although she avoids the rip, Lisa Mae eventually makes it outside. Sitting on our boards, we joke around, making sideways fists and milking the surface of the sea, splashing each other, until we spot a good wave and ride it in together, working every section all the way to shore, where we turn back around, hungry for more.

After surfing, we hike up the Clatsop Trail, following Indian Creek upward through dense salal shrubs, salmonberry, oxalis, maidenhair ferns. Farther up the trail, giant Sitka spruce stand with lower limbs stretched horizontally from their trunks, like great mossy arms welcoming us into the wild, like candelabras lighting our way.

An Oregon State Parks guidepost explains that this wind-battered forest is in constant flux. As trees age, they're likely to get toppled by howling ocean winds. But seedlings grow in patches of sunlight created by windthrown trees, the same way that shadowy parts of ourselves finally collapse, making room for new growth. And like Whitman's idea of grass as "hair of graves," spruce saplings often grow directly on the great trunks of fallen trees. Sometimes the dead host tree rots away, and new trees, called "clothespin spruce," are left with hollow archways in their trunks—like tiny, negative-space cathedrals in which is written the universal story of life arising from death. It reminds me of the way that Melville—whose life was nothing if not windthrown—left behind such a monolithic body of work, the fertile ground for a thousand offshoots—for modernists writers like Joyce and Woolf and everyone who followed, for so many visual artists and even improvisational jazz musicians, for filmmakers and scientists, for environmentalists like Barry Lopez; his legacy and corpus like the negative but light-filled core of the great, grizzled tree that is American culture.

And after my own long descent—my Brooklyn-based Nekyia and my severe humbling by the Pacific—I can't help but sympathize with Melville's most legendary human character. During Shakespearean soliloquies at the end of *Moby-Dick,* in "The Symphony," Ahab reveals his human side; he laments his young wife—"I widowed that poor girl when I married her"; he has a moment of connection with his beleaguered first mate—"Close! stand close to me, Starbuck; let me look into a human eye." In Starbuck's eyes he sees the capacity for warmth, for love of family and hearth and home, and although he can't experience it himself, he orders Starbuck not to lower during the final whale hunt, that he may preserve the good mate's life.

"Oh, my Captain! my Captain!" Starbuck cries in response, "noble soul! grand old heart, after all!" I feel some of the same reverence for my own obsessive shadow side, for the dark, watery soul work it forced on me in New York, combined with compassion for the part of me that wanted to die—the part that did drown that day at Pacific City. Jung never advocated that we sublimate or destroy our shadows—just as Ahab is the driving narrative force behind *Moby-Dick,* so is our darkness an important source of power. What Jung called for instead was that we bring the shadow up into the light, so that it doesn't pilot us from down below. Up into the light, where we can embrace it—the way we all embraced Fred Nemo after his embodiment of Ahab—where we might revere the paradoxical strength it gives us, the complexity and depth: *grand old heart, after all.*

But my still-young heart is always with the survivor. My favorite *Moby-Dick* passages belong to Ishmael—his ecstatic rhapsodies about the ocean and whales; his longing for universality, for union with nature, with the divine. Lisa Mae and I live together now, in a little Craftsman bungalow with a big front porch, and directly below our attic bedroom is the temple room, where she keeps a rambling altar populated by half the Hindu pantheon—Sita and Ram, Hanuman, Lakshmi, and Krishna, but also the Virgin Mary, Jesus, and Buddha, all of them surrounded by flowers, fruit, votives, and beads. At night, before we fall asleep, she reads me poems by Hafiz, perhaps the same verses that Melville read two centuries ago, verses about whales and the sea, verses about the transcendent God beyond God.

Though the Tillamook villagers were hesitant to trade away their precious whale oil, Captain Clark and his men eventually bartered for three hundred pounds of blubber and a few gallons of oil. On January 8, 1806, Clark wrote in his journal: "Small as this stock is I prise it highly; and thank providence for directing the whale to us; and think him much more kind to us than he was to Jonah, having sent this monster to be *swallowed by us* in sted of *swallowing of us* as Jonah's did."

I love this part of the story, the way the Indians made the white men do something they're otherwise reluctant to do: actually *share* in a very small portion. And also that Clark contents himself with this modest portion, that he gives effusive thanks for it. If only all Americans who followed in Clark's wake had the same economy in their use of oil, the same reverence and gratitude for nature, the same respect for the natives. Perhaps then we might not have been *swallowed,* as Clark says, into the proverbial belly of the whale, into this ocean-killing belly of oil in which we now find ourselves.

Reaching the top of Tillamook Head, Lisa Mae and I discover a hiker's camp, a circle of small wooden bunkhouses, picnic tables, and a central fire pit. We follow the trail west, past the ruins of a World War II radar station, through a dripping copse of Sitka spruce, descending to the Tillamook Rock Lighthouse viewpoint. A series of steep muddy steps leads us down to a cordoned-off ledge, perched on the edge of a cliff, the same spot that Clark described as "the grandest and most pleasing prospects which my eyes ever surveyed, in my front a boundless Ocean."

The sun was out all morning at the south-facing Indian Beach, but here at the summit a thick fog bank veils the sea, giving us the mysterious feeling of standing on the edge of the known world. We can't see the ocean through the haze, but we can hear its susurrations on the shore below, feel its misty presence on our skin, imagine the way it fills up the horizon and how it, like fog, shrouds the earth's body, reflecting light on the surface but remaining impenetrably dark beneath, down in the deep soul of the world.

EPILOGUE

As promised, Dawn moves out to Portland after leaving Brooklyn and doing a stint in L.A. Though she's perhaps the most employable of all my New York surfing friends, she has trouble landing a job in Portland, where the market is saturated with young creatives, never more so than during a recession. She takes this in stride, puts herself on what she calls her *month-long yoga retreat,* sometimes practicing with us at Lisa Mae's studio. We surf on the weekends, and as always her cheery fearlessness emboldens me to try new things, to surf new spots, to paddle farther outside than I would alone.

Toward the end of the summer of 2009, I take a personal writing retreat at a friend's cabin up in Washington's Olympic Peninsula. For several days my work circles around Andy Kessler and memories of our Montauk surf trips. Three years since I've seen him, and after spending so many days writing about him, I realize how much I miss his company. Once I'm back in cell-phone range on the drive back to Portland, I give him a ring. It's good to hear his voice, even on his voicemail. I leave a long message, tell him what I've been up to, ask him to call me back when he has a chance.

Two days later, Dawn calls.

"I've got some hard news," she says.

My first thought is that she's been offered a position back in New York or L.A., that she'll be leaving Portland after only a month. But this turns out not to be the case; just a few days later she lands a good job back in the fashion industry.

Her news is about Andy Kessler.

"I don't know how to say this," Dawn whispers. "Apparently what happened is that he got stung by a wasp out at Montauk and went into anaphylactic shock. They tried to get him to the hospital but it was already too late."

It takes a few seconds for this to register.

What the fuck? is my first—and best—and most Kessler-like response to such an absurd series of events, leading to the death of someone who'd already conquered such formidable demons, a person whose life was oriented around helping other people, encouraging kids to skate, taking it easy out in the ocean.

It happened on a Monday, so Dawn and I wait most of the week for word of funeral arrangements. I get in touch with Sadie's fiancé, who sounds totally stunned, especially since he happened to be on his way out to visit Andy that same day. Sadie's on a surf trip in Mexico at the time, but she cuts the trip short and flies home to help organize the memorial. She takes it especially hard; Andy was a kind of father figure to her—a healthy version of the biological father she lost. Having lost his own family and looking up to Andy as a kind of wily uncle figure, Kyle Grodin takes it equally hard.

We get the final word on Wednesday or Thursday: there's a paddle-out memorial planned at Montauk on Friday and a memorial party at the Autumn Bowl on Saturday night. But this late in the week, I can't find plane tickets for much less than a grand. Lisa Mae and I are just about to buy tickets for a surf trip to Costa Rica, and on my non-profit director's salary, I really can't afford both. I feel guilty about this, and concerned that I need to go pay my proper respects. But while skating Burnside with my friend Bryce—another of Andy's longtime skate compatriots—I try to listen for Andy's opinion on the matter.

"Are you kidding me?" I can hear him saying. *"Go to Costa Rica, man, that's what I'd do. Forget a funeral—go surfing."*

Having just started a new job, Dawn can't fly back either, so we decide to organize our own memorial service down at her favorite surf spot, Pacific City.

A paddle-out is a traditional Hawaiian ceremony, a way to pay tribute to the deceased, to release the person's spirit to the eternal sea. It usually involves five or more people, who paddle out well beyond the break, join hands in a floating circle, and say a prayer before casting leis into the ocean.

Since it's just Dawn and me, we paddle out and sit parallel on our boards, facing the sea. We say our good-byes here, and I recall out loud how the first time I met him, Andy said, "Welcome to town. *Now get out of my town.*"

Back on the beach, Dawn and I fly Andy's minikite, the one he'd given me back when I visited him on the sailboat. At Pacific City, you can pull your car right up to the sand, so we make a bed in the back of my truck, and when Lisa Mae and some friends show up to meet us, we hang out back there, strumming ukuleles and telling stories about Andy, like the time he said I needed to learn more than three chords.

"So have you learned more chords?" Dawn asks.

"Oh, definitely. Now I know at least four."

On the way home, we stop by the Lincoln City Skatepark—in my opinion the hands-down best skatepark in the world. The writer Jocko Weyland claims Lincoln City and other similar Oregon parks as masterpieces that rival any sculpture by Richard Serra or James Turrell, even surpassing sculpture, "because they combine aestheticism with athletic functionality."

I roll around in my favorite bowl, named the Cradle for its insane central feature: a seventeen-foot-high full-pipe capsule, like a cereal bowl turned up on its edge, allowing competent skaters to roll completely upside down. Dawn snaps some photos while I hurl myself into the Cradle, getting partially inverted. But mostly I just cruise around and have fun, feeling like somehow Andy has a hand in the session, because, like him, I don't care so much about doing tricks anymore. I just want to go fast, stay loose and low, taking long flowing runs, pretending I'm on a surfboard, the same way I pretend I'm on a skateboard when I surf.

In the smaller section next to the Cradle a young redheaded kid takes runs while his grandmother watches. I roll over and take a few turns with him, and because I'm feeling outgoing, sentimental—and because I know it's what Andy would do—I introduce myself to him and his grandmother.

He tells me his name's Wolf. He's all excited because the previous weekend he took seventh place at an amateur contest right here at Lincoln City.

"I won this shirt, and this hat!" he says, showing off his new items, clearly stoked.

I drop in and do a backside Bertelmann slide on a steep concrete bank. I do this because it's my favorite move of all time—an explosive, arched-back slash that was originated in the ocean by Hawaiian surfer Larry Bertelmann—and also because I'd seen Wolf attempting it earlier.

Seeing that I've got it down pretty well, he asks my advice and then tries again, but slides out and barrel-rolls down the bank. Sprawled out on the flatbottom, he breaks out laughing. I fetch his board for him, and with my encouragement he attempts it again and again, five or six times, until he finally nails it, and Dawn and I and his grandmother all cheer for him.

Back at home, alone on the internet, I check out photos from the big paddle-out in Montauk. More than two hundred people showed up. Sadie and Kyle both tell me how huge the circle was, so big that you could barely see across to the mourners on the opposite side. Kessler's friend, Harry Jumanji, paddled into the center, where he told everyone how he was only seven days sober off heroin, and how he'd been there when it all happened, that Andy brought him out for the weekend to get him away from the city, to help him kick. In a *New York Times* article about Andy's death, Jumanji is quoted as saying, "He saved my life. I wish I could've saved his."

In another *Times* piece, my friend Bret Johnston writes, "Kessler's great and lasting contribution to skateboarding was recognizing its transformative and transcendent qualities, the myriad ways in which a highly individualized endeavor invited, not precluded, community."

Even more showed up for the Autumn Bowl party the following night, everyone from the New York City skate community, all Andy's surf buddies, his recovery community, and his immediate family. From what I hear, everyone took runs on Andy's skateboard; someone posts online that she'd never seen so many grown men cry. Later that night, our friends Buddy and Rick showed their documentary *Deathbowl to Downtown*—a film that traces the history of skateboarding in New York City, with Kessler as a prominent figure, the undisputed godfather of East Coast skateboarding. In one scene, the forty-five-year-old Andy bombs a steep hill in Riverside Park that, as kids back in the seventies, they called Suicide Hill. Wearing nothing but shorts and a dirty T-shirt, he screams past the camera, weaves in between a jogger and a woman with a stroller, then slides out and takes a nasty slam. Resilient as ever, he gets right back up with a devious grin and does it again, rides it all the way out this time, hanging on—speed wobbles and all—to the very end.

After the feature, Buddy and Rick showed an extra fifteen minutes of unedited Kessler footage, during which everyone chanted *Kessler! Kessler!,* the whole warehouse echoing with his name, with his all-embracing influence, with his radical, ineffable energy.

It's the first time in three years that I wish I was back in Brooklyn—that I'd been there to witness this, to pay tribute at Montauk and take a spin on Andy's old deck—and I realize maybe for the first time what I had back in New York, that however much it took from me in terms of money and sanity, what it gave me in friendship and experience is irreplaceable, and I feel an overpowering sense of gratitude for the city that both ruined and saved my life—and for Andy, who was always there on the saving end, the surfing end.

The feeling resurfaces in 2012, when Hurricane Sandy batters Rockaway—the entire boardwalk stripped to its bones, houses flooded or destroyed by fire, several lives lost. During the fifteen-foot storm surge, a surfer named Dylan Smith rescued six people using his surfboard and an improvised rope bridge. In the terrible aftermath, a grassroots organization called Shore Soup formed to serve over fifty thousand hot meals to those left stranded by the storm, to neighbors helping each other sweep raw sewage from their living room floors and rip out ruined sheetrock, to volunteers who drove in from every borough to lend a hand.

Rockaway: a neighborhood that, like Andy Kessler, is tough as nails on the outside, pure aloha on the inside.

At the end of *Moby-Dick,* Ishmael, the sole survivor of Ahab's madness, is rescued by another whaling boat, the *Rachel.* The epic eight-hundred-page novel ends with the following line: *"It was the devious-cruising Rachel, that in her retracing search after her missing children, only found another orphan."* After Andy passes away, I learn something that I hadn't known: that he, like Kyle Grodin, was adopted. That he was, in some sense, an orphan himself. So once again I'm struck by the image of Ishmael the orphan, floating on his coffin life buoy, having survived the darkest work imaginable—having been reborn from death to new life in the wake of catastrophe.

It's the central image that first sparked my obsession with *Moby-Dick.*

And now, as ever, it both haunts and sustains me.

ACKNOWLEDGMENTS

The author wishes to thank the following:

Sitka Center for Art and Ecology, and Signal Fire, for writing residencies that helped make this book possible.

My teachers: John Calderazzo, Steven Schwartz, Leslie Becker, Deanna Ludwin, Rosemary Whitaker, Bruce Rhonda, and Barry Lopez.

My family, for their stories, memories, and support: Roger and Nat Hocking, Harrel Lawrence, Jerry McMahan, John and Ann Lawrence, Sara and Lindsay Lawrence, Stephanie Zehren-Thomas, Kristen and Taylor Zehren, and the entire McMahan clan.

For their friendship and encouragement: Krista Miller, Mark and Kasia Roth, Gabriel Liston, Danielle Donohue, L.A. Zar, Nicole Georges, Beth Burns, A.M. O'Malley, John Scognamiglio, Michael and Katherine Burnett, Chloe Eudaly and everyone at Reading Frenzy, Dan and Bean Gilsdorf, David Heatley, Danny O'Connell, Raphael Maestra, the Sharzer family, Erica Simpson, Dan Hack, Dawn Andreas, Jeff Knutson, Jered Bogli, MaryKay West, Pollyanne Birge, and the entire IPRC Board of Directors and volunteer crew, Kevin Sampsell, Heidi Mager and the entire staff of Powell's Books, B. Frayn Masters, Cheryl Strayed, Steve Church, Sophie Beck, Matt Roberts and everyone at the *Normal School*, Lisa Dusenberry and everyone at the *Rumpus*, Hannah Fries at *Orion*, Trevor Spangle, Vendela Vida, Jocko Weyland, Chris Coyle, Suzie House, Tony Farmer, Paul Jacobson, Natalie Kaire, Andreas Trolf, Lori D, Patrick Devine, Candi Sari, Amy Harwood, Andy and Allison Weiss, John and Jess Skibo, Joseph Robertson, Michael Heald, Remy Jewell, Lisa Pate, Marianne Tanner, Arthur Bradford, Jon Raymond, the Liston family, Richard Nash, Vanessa Veselka, Rachel Bennett, Sharon Donat, Chris Johanson, and Lucy Bellwood.

For early reads and feedback: Matt McGowan, David Shields, Junot Díaz, Bret Anthony Johnston, Barry Sanders, Molly Padulo, Michael D'Alessandro, A.M. O'Malley, Polly Bresnick, Joseph Ahearne, Ron Nugent, Ben Moorad, Anne Rasmussen, Courtenay Haymeister, Ishai Goldstein, Liz Moyer, Gabriel Liston, and Jason Glover.

For believing in this book: Matt McGowan, Steve Woodward, Fiona McCrae, Marisa Atkinson, Katie Dublinski, Michael Taeckens, and everyone at Graywolf.

Special thanks to Ishai Goldstein and Steve Woodward.

Finally, and most of all, to my partner in surfing and in life, Lisa Mae Osborn.

A portion of the author's proceeds from this book will be donated to the Surfrider Foundation.

JUSTIN HOCKING was raised in Colorado and California and has been avidly involved in surfing and skateboarding for over twenty years. He created and contributed to the anthology *Life and Limb: Skateboarders Write from the Deep End;* his work has also appeared in the *Rumpus, Open City, Thrasher, Orion,* the *Normal School,* the *Portland Review,* and *Portland Noir.* He is a cofounder, with A.M. O'Malley, of the yearlong Certificate Program in Creative Writing at the Independent Publishing Resource Center (IPRC), and also teaches in the Wilderness Writing MFA program at Eastern Oregon University. He lives in Portland, Oregon.

The text of *The Great Floodgates of the Wonderworld* is set in Minion Pro, an original typeface designed by Robert Slimbach in 1990. Book design by Ann Sudmeier. Composition by BookMobile Design & Digital Publisher Services, Minneapolis, Minnesota. Manufactured by Versa Press on acid-free, 30 percent postconsumer wastepaper.